LEON TROTSKY
and the Struggle for Socialism in the Twenty-First Century

David North

Mehring Books
Oak Park, Michigan

Published by Mehring Books
P. O. Box 48377
Oak Park, MI 48237
Printed in the United States of America
© 2023 Mehring Books

All rights reserved.

Library of Congress Cataloging-in-Publication Data
Names: North, David, 1950- author.
Title: Leon Trotsky and the struggle for socialism in the twenty-first century / David North.
Other titles: Leon Trotsky and the struggle for socialism in the 21st century
Description: Oak Park, Michigan : Mehring Books, 2023. | Includes bibliographical references and index. | Summary: "Leon Trotsky remains the towering figure in the history of revolutionary socialism in the twentieth century. Trotsky's greatest achievement was the founding of the Fourth International (FI) in 1938, after the Third International under Stalin facilitated the coming to power of Hitler in Germany. Written over a forty-year period, the essays in this book are devoted to bringing rich historical lessons to a new generation in order to resolve the "historical crisis of mankind." David North discusses Trotsky's Theory of Permanent Revolution, the dialectical materialist method, Stalin's Great Terror, the struggles of the Left Opposition, and their relevance for today"-- Provided by publisher.
Identifiers: LCCN 2023021099 | ISBN 9781959124016 (paperback) | ISBN 9781959124023 (ebook)
Subjects: LCSH: Trotsky, Leon, 1879-1940. | Fourth International. | Permanent revolution theory. | Communism--Soviet Union--History. | Socialism--Soviet Union--History.
Classification: LCC HX313.8.T76 N68 2023 | DDC 335.43/3--dc23/eng/20230616
LC record available at https://lccn.loc.gov/2023021099

Book and cover design by Kevin Reed.
Cover photo of mass demonstration in Paris:
© World Socialist Web Site

Contents

Preface vii

1. Leon Trotsky & the Development of Marxism 1
2. An Intellectual Pygmy Denounces Trotsky 59
3. The Classical Marxism of Leon Trotsky 67
4. Trotsky's Victory over Stalinism:
   Seventy-five Years of the Fourth International 1938–2013 81
5. Why the GPU Assassinated Trotsky 95
6. Lenin, Trotsky, and the Marxism of the October Revolution 107
7. Trotsky and Trotskyism in the Contemporary World 125
8. Eighty Years of the Fourth International:
   The Lessons of History and the Struggle for Socialism Today............... 131
9. Leon Trotsky's Four Fateful Years in Prinkipo: 1929–1933 151
10. Trotsky's Last Year: 1939–1940 161
11. Trotsky and the Self-Determination of Ukraine 239

12. Leon Trotsky and Revolutionary Strategy
    in the Twentieth and Twenty-First Centuries.................................... 245

13. Greetings to the Fifth Anniversary Meeting
    of the Young Guard of Bolshevik-Leninists.. 251

14. Forward to May Day 2023! Build a Mass Movement of Workers
    and Youth against War and for Socialism!.. 259

15. Index.. 271

Preface

The material compiled in this volume was written over a period of forty years. The first essay, *Leon Trotsky and the Development of Marxism,* was initially published in the late autumn of 1982. The last items—a letter to a youth organization founded by Trotskyists in Russia, Ukraine, and other countries of the former USSR, and a call for the celebration of May Day—were written in the opening months of 2023.

Despite the many years that separate the first and last document, they are connected by a central argument: that Leon Trotsky was the most significant figure in the history of socialism during the first four decades of the twentieth century, and that his legacy remains the critical and indispensable theoretical and political foundation of the ongoing contemporary struggle for the victory of world socialism. The events of the last forty years have powerfully substantiated this appraisal of Trotsky's place in history and his enduring political significance.

Let us begin with the fact that Trotsky's condemnation of Stalinism as a counterrevolutionary force has been vindicated by history. But when the first essay was written, the Soviet Union and the associated Stalinist regimes in Eastern Europe still existed. Stalinist political parties affiliated with the Kremlin bureaucracy boasted of millions of members. Trotsky's prediction that the Stalinist bureaucracy would restore capitalism, and that the rotten structure of the regime would collapse beneath the weight of national economic autarchy, incompetence, and lies was dismissed as "Trotskyite sectarianism" and even "anti-Soviet propaganda" by the petty-bourgeois academic apologists for "real existing socialism."

Leon Trotsky and the Development of Marxism was written precisely during the months when the long-time and increasingly senile Soviet leader Leonid Brezhnev passed from his sickbed to the Kremlin Wall Necropolis in Red Square. The Stalinist bureaucracy transferred its allegiance first to Yuri Andropov and then to Konstantin Chernenko—both of whom, within little more than two years, joined their predecessor alongside the Kremlin Wall—and, finally, in March 1985, to Mikhail Gorbachev.

For all the latter's promises of a new "openness" [*glasnost*] in the study of Soviet history, the Kremlin continued to denounce the struggle waged by Trotsky against the Stalinist regime and its betrayal of the October Revolution.

As late as November 1987, as the Stalinist regime was careening toward collapse, Gorbachev included in his address on the seventieth anniversary of the October Revolution a defense of Stalin and a venomous denunciation of Trotsky. But, as Trotsky had once noted, the laws of history proved to be more powerful than even the most powerful general secretary.

The only political tendency that foresaw and warned that Gorbachev's policies were directed toward the dissolution of the Soviet Union and the restoration of capitalism was the International Committee of the Fourth International (ICFI). As early as March 1987, amidst the global adulation, known as "Gorbymania," of the new Soviet leader, the International Committee warned:

> For both the working class in the Soviet Union and the workers and oppressed masses internationally, the so-called reform policy of Gorbachev represents a sinister threat. It jeopardizes the historic conquests of the October Revolution and is bound up with a deepening of the bureaucracy's counterrevolutionary collaboration with imperialism on a world scale.[1]

Two years later, in 1989, in an analysis of Gorbachev's policies titled *Perestroika Versus Socialism*, I wrote:

> During the past three years, decisive steps have been taken by Gorbachev to promote private ownership of the productive forces. The bureaucracy is ever more openly identifying its

---

1. International Committee of the Fourth International, *What Is Happening in the USSR: Gorbachev and the Crisis of Stalinism* (Detroit: Labor Publications, 1987), p. 12.

interests with the development of Soviet cooperatives organized along entirely capitalist lines. Thus, to the extent that the bureaucracy's own privileges are no longer bound up with, but are hostile to, the forms of state property, its relations with world imperialism must undergo a corresponding and significant change. The principal goal of Soviet foreign policy becomes less and less the defense of the USSR against imperialist attack, but rather more and more the mobilization of imperialist support—political and economic—for the realization of the domestic goals of *perestroika*, that is, the development of capitalist property relations within the Soviet Union. Thus, the counterrevolutionary logic of the Stalinist theory of socialism in one country finds its ultimate expression in the development of a foreign policy aimed at undermining Soviet state property and reintroducing capitalism within the USSR itself.[2]

I cannot claim exceptional credit for this appraisal of Gorbachev's policies, which was verified by subsequent developments. The perspective of the International Committee was based on the analysis of the contradictions of Soviet society and the counterrevolutionary trajectory of the Stalinist regime made by Trotsky a half century earlier in his book *The Revolution Betrayed*. Moreover, the ICFI's understanding of the post-Soviet process of capitalist restoration was facilitated by the fact that it proceeded along the lines anticipated by Trotsky.

The dissolution of the Soviet Union did not result, as Francis Fukuyama had predicted, in the "End of History," which the Rand Corporation analyst defined as "the end point of mankind's ideological evolution and the universalization of Western liberal democracy as the final form of human government."[3] It is quite clear that Fukuyama did not foresee the accession of Donald Trump to the American presidency.

In fact, neither in post-Soviet Russia nor in the advanced capitalist countries did developments conform to the schema of the sage from the Rand think tank. Within Russia, all the sunny predictions with which the restoration of capitalism had been justified were refuted by events. Rather than prosperity,

---

2. David North, *Perestroika Versus Socialism: Stalinism and the Restoration of Capitalism in the USSR* (Detroit: Labor Publications, 1989), p. 49.
3. *The National Interest*, 19 (Summer 1989), p. 3.

the fire sale of state assets to former Soviet bureaucrats and other criminal elements produced mass poverty and staggering levels of social inequality. Rather than witnessing a blossoming of democracy, the new Russian state rapidly assumed the form of an oligarchic regime. And the claim that Russia, once it had irrevocably repudiated its historical association with the October Revolution, would be welcomed by its new "Western partners" with tender embraces and integrated peacefully into the brotherhood of capitalist nations proved to be the most far-fetched and unrealistic of all the predictions.

Within the major imperialist countries, the events that followed the breakup of the Soviet Union—the succession of economic, geopolitical, and social crises that have characterized the last three decades—have substantiated the Marxist analysis of the contradictions that drive capitalism, as a world system, to destruction. The founding document of the Fourth International, written by Trotsky in 1938, defined the historical epoch as that of capitalism's "death agony" and described the contemporary situation on the eve of World War II:

> Mankind's productive forces stagnate. Already new inventions and improvements fail to raise the level of material wealth. Conjunctural crises under the conditions of the social crisis of the whole capitalist system inflict ever heavier deprivations and sufferings upon the masses. Growing unemployment, in its turn, deepens the financial crisis of the state and undermines the unstable monetary systems. ...
>
> Under the increasing tension of capitalist disintegration, imperialist antagonisms reach an impasse at the height of which separate clashes and bloody local disturbances... must inevitably coalesce into a conflagration of world dimensions. The bourgeoisie, of course, is aware of the mortal danger to its domination represented by a new war. But that class is now immeasurably less capable of averting war than on the eve of 1914.[4]

The present world situation bears more than just a disturbing resemblance to that described so acutely by Trotsky eighty-five years ago. His understanding of the world situation was derived from his analysis of the

---

4. Leon Trotsky, *The Death Agony of Capitalism and the Tasks of the Fourth International: The Transitional Program* (New York: Labor Publications, 1981), p. 1.

Preface

source of the crisis of capitalism: 1) the conflict between social production and private ownership of the means of production; and 2) the incompatibility of the capitalist nation-state system with the objective development of the world economy. Within the framework of capitalism, the crisis arising from these contradictions leads to the twin catastrophes of fascist barbarism and world war.

In his analysis of the fatal dynamic of global capitalism, Trotsky had placed central emphasis on the role of American imperialism. In 1928, writing from distant Alma Ata in Central Asia (to which he had been exiled by the Stalinist regime), he wrote:

> *In the period of crisis the hegemony of the United States will operate more completely, more openly, and more ruthlessly than in the period of boom.* The United States will seek to overcome and extricate herself from her difficulties and maladies primarily at the expense of Europe, regardless of whether this occurs in Asia, Canada, South America, Australia, or Europe itself, or whether this takes place peacefully or through war [emphasis in the original].[5]

In 1934, Trotsky described the trajectory of American imperialism in even sharper terms:

> U.S. capitalism is up against the same problems that pushed Germany in 1914 on the path of war. The world is divided? It must be redivided. For Germany it was a question of "organizing Europe." The United States must "organize" the world. History is bringing humanity face to face with the volcanic eruption of American imperialism.[6]

Trotsky mocked the penchant of the United States to sanctify its predatory policies with humanitarian phrases. He memorably described President Woodrow Wilson, in the aftermath of World War I, as "a philistine and hypocrite," an "oily Tartuffe" who "roams across blood-drenched Europe as the highest representative of morality, the Messiah of the American dollar,

---

5. Leon Trotsky, *The Third International After Lenin* (London: New Park Publications, 1974), p. 8.
6. Leon Trotsky, "War and the Fourth International", *Writings of Leon Trotsky [1933-34]* (New York: Pathfinder Press, 1975), p. 302.

chastises, pardons and settles the destinies of nations."[7] Now that Wilson's vicious racism has become well known, Trotsky's description of the once venerated American president, long praised as the icon of democratic liberalism, has become the consensus of the historical community.

But however apt his exposure of its hypocrisy, Trotsky did not explain the policies of American imperialism, or, for that matter, that of its German rival under Hitler, as merely criminal disruptions of an otherwise peaceful world. His indictment of the policies of these countries, and that of the other imperialist powers, was of a historical, rather than philistine moralistic character. The policy of invasion, annexations, and conquests was, and still is, rooted not in the madness of individual leaders, even in the case of a psychopath like Hitler, but in the desperate necessity to overcome the limits imposed by state borders on access to global resources and the world market. The relentless growth of imperialist militarism, leading inevitably toward world war, signified the historical bankruptcy of the nation-state system. As Trotsky foresaw in 1934, in an article originally published in the American journal *Foreign Affairs*:

> The struggle for foreign markets will become unprecedentedly sharp. Pious notions about the advantages of autarchy will at once be cast aside, and sage plans for national harmony will be thrown in the wastebasket. This applies not only to German capitalism, with its explosive dynamics, or to the belated and greedy capitalism of Japan, but also to the capitalism of America, which still is powerful despite its new contradictions.[8]

The contradictions discerned by Trotsky in the late 1920s and 1930s are now at a far more advanced, even terminal, stage of development. In the aftermath of the dissolution of the Soviet Union, the drive to "organize the world" in the interests of the global hegemony of the United States has assumed the form of a global rampage. The "volcanic eruption" of American imperialism, predicted by Trotsky almost ninety years ago, is well underway.

But the American volcano is not the only site of militaristic eruptions. A massive rise in military spending on an international scale is underway. The

---

7. Leon Trotsky, "Order Out of Chaos," *The First Five Years of the Communist International*, Vol. 1 (London: New Park Publications, 1973), p. 25.
8. Leon Trotsky, "Nationalism and Economic Life," available: https://www.marxists.org/archive/trotsky/1934/xx/nationalism.htm

gods of war are again athirst. The two main defeated powers of World War II are dropping their hypocritical pacifistic pretenses. Exploiting the opportunity provided by the Ukraine war, the German Bundestag has approved the tripling of the country's military budget. Japan, already the second largest military power in Asia, has announced a 26.3 percent increase in "defense" spending. They are determined not to be left out of the distribution of the spoils that will follow, in the aftermath of World War III, from a new redivision of the world, provided there is a world left to divide.

That the world is approaching the abyss of a global military cataclysm is now widely acknowledged in the capitalist media. After a year of propaganda relentlessly portraying the Russian invasion of Ukraine as an "unprovoked war," bourgeois commentators are now placing the war in a more realistic international context. The *Financial Times*' foreign policy specialist Gideon Rachman recently noted the "historical parallel" between the present situation and "the rise in international tensions in the 1930s and 1940s."

> The fact that the president of China and the prime minister of Japan paid simultaneous and competing visits to the capitals of Russia and Ukraine underlines the global significance of the Ukraine war. Japan and China are fierce rivals in east Asia. Both countries understand that their struggle will be profoundly affected by the outcome of the conflict in Europe.
>
> This shadow boxing between China and Japan over Ukraine is part of a broader trend. Strategic rivalries in Euro-Atlantic and Indo-Pacific regions are increasingly overlapping with each other. What is emerging is something that looks more and more like a single geopolitical struggle.[9]

Every historical personage is, of course, a product of his or her time. But Trotsky is a historical figure whose *active* influence upon contemporary events has extended far beyond his lifetime. His writings are studied not only for the insight they provide into the events of the first four decades of the last century, but also as analyses essential for understanding and intervening in present-day events.

In a massive 1,124-page study of *International Trotskyism* published in 1991 on the very eve of the dissolution of the USSR, the late Robert J.

---

9. "China, Japan and the Ukraine war," *Financial Times*, March 27, 2023.

Alexander, an anti-Marxist academic and long-time member of the US Council on Foreign Relations, expressed concern that the dissolution of the USSR might lead to the resurgence of Trotskyism as a mass movement. He wrote:

> As of the end of the 1980s the Trotskyists have never come to power in any country. Although international Trotskyism does not enjoy the support of a well established regime, as did the heirs of Stalinism, the persistence of the movement in a wide variety of countries together with the instability of the political life of most of the world's nations means that the possibility that a Trotskyist party might come to power in the foreseeable future cannot be totally ruled out.[10]

The ruling elites took Professor Alexander's warning seriously. They responded to the political danger on the left posed by the collapse of the Stalinist regimes by commissioning a series of slanderous pseudo-biographies of Trotsky. But the works of Professors Ian Thatcher, Geoffrey Swain, and Robert Service, despite initial rapturous reviews in the capitalist press, failed miserably. Their lies were comprehensively exposed by the International Committee. The biography written by the celebrated Professor Robert Service of Oxford University became a source of embarrassment for its publisher, Harvard University Press, after *The American Historical Review* acknowledged that my criticism of Service's biography as a "piece of hackwork" was "Strong words but justified."[11]

There is an historical materialist explanation for the persistence and growth of the international Trotskyist movement in the face of relentless persecution, spanning decades, by innumerable enemies. The basic objective economic and social forces that determined the general course of political events in Trotsky's lifetime, centered on the global class struggle of the bourgeoisie and proletariat, have not been superseded by history. Trotsky's Theory of Permanent Revolution remains the essential historic-strategic foundation of the struggle against capitalism by the international working class. He wrote in 1930:

---

10. Robert J. Alexander, *International Trotskyism 1929–1985: A Documented Analysis of the Movement* (Durham and London: Duke University Press, 1991), p. 32.
11. Review by Bertrand M. Patenaude in *The American Historical Review*, Vol. 116, No. 3 (June 2011), p. 902; cited in David North, *In Defense of Leon Trotsky* (Oak Park, MI: Mehring Books, 2013), pp. 243–48.

> The completion of the socialist revolution within national limits is unthinkable. One of the basic reasons for the crisis in bourgeois society is the fact that the productive forces created by it can no longer be reconciled with the framework of the national state. From this follow, on the one hand, imperialist wars, on the other, the utopia of a bourgeois United States of Europe. The socialist revolution begins on the national arena, it unfolds on the international arena, and is completed on the world arena. Thus, the socialist revolution becomes a permanent revolution in a newer and broader sense of the word; it attains completion only in the final victory of the new society on our entire planet.[12]

Far from his ideas being overtaken by events, the immense globally integrated development of the productive forces and the vast growth of the working class have further substantiated Trotsky's conception of socialist revolution as an interdependent process of international class struggle. The movement of history is now decisively intersecting with the strategic vision of the great Marxist theorist and revolutionary.

The present world situation is one that Trotsky would have no problem recognizing and analyzing. We are living in the final stage of the same historical epoch of imperialist war and socialist revolution. The historical problems with which Trotsky dealt—especially in the sixteen years between Lenin's incapacitating stroke and removal from political activity in 1923 and his own assassination in 1940—remain the unresolved existential political issues that confront the working class: imperialist war, the breakdown of democracy and resurgence of fascism, spiraling inflation, mass unemployment, poverty, the treachery of the existing mass labor organizations and their integration into the structures of the capitalist state.

This year marks the centenary of the founding of the Left Opposition in the Soviet Union. Trotsky's initial public critique, in the autumn of 1923, of the growth of bureaucratism in both the Soviet state and the Communist Party marked the beginning of the most politically consequential struggle of the twentieth century. The usurpation of political power by the Soviet bureaucracy, led by Stalin, was to have catastrophic consequences for the fate of the

---

12. Leon Trotsky, "What is the Permanent Revolution?," *The Permanent Revolution* and *Results and Prospects* (London: New Park Publications, 1972), p. 155.

international working class and the struggle for socialism. The political justification for this usurpation—which entailed the subordination of the working class to the bureaucracy, the destruction of all forms of workers' democracy, and, ultimately, the physical liquidation of Marxists within the USSR—was provided by the Stalinist dogma of "socialism in one country." This pseudo-theory, directed first and foremost against Trotsky's Theory of Permanent Revolution, sanctioned the repudiation of the perspective of international socialism upon which the October Revolution had been based.

A recently published volume devoted to a study of Trotsky's struggle against Stalinism begins with the following assertion: "For most of the last two decades of his life, the political and theoretical issue that concerned Leon Trotsky more than any other was the problem of Soviet bureaucracy."[13]

This statement is fundamentally incorrect. The problem of the Soviet bureaucracy was, for Trotsky, entirely secondary to the question of revolutionary internationalism. In fact, the actual nature of the Stalinist bureaucracy could only be understood within the context of the relationship of the Soviet Union to the international class struggle and the fate of world socialism. As a tendency that emerged within the Bolshevik Party—under conditions of the defeats suffered by the working class in Central and Western Europe in the aftermath of the October Revolution—Stalinism represented a nationalist reaction against Marxian internationalism. As Trotsky wrote just one year before his assassination, "It may be said that the whole of Stalinism, taken on the theoretical plane, grew out of the criticism of the theory of permanent revolution as it was formulated in 1905."[14]

The fight against the bureaucratic dictatorship was inextricably linked to the program of socialist internationalism. The same strategic principle applies to all political tasks in the present world situation. There are no national solutions to the great problems of the contemporary epoch.

Trotsky's Theory of Permanent Revolution provided the analysis of the objective dynamic of the international class struggle upon which the strategy of world socialist revolution had to be based. But Trotsky also explained that the victory of socialism would not be realized through the automatic working out of capitalist contradictions. These contradictions created only the objective conditions and potential for the conquest of power by the working class.

---

13. Thomas M. Twiss, *Trotsky and the Problem of Soviet Bureaucracy* (Chicago: Haymarket Books, 2014), p. 1.
14. Leon Trotsky, "Three Conceptions of the Russian Revolution", 1939, available: https://www.wsws.org/en/articles/2008/10/rrev-o21.html

But the transformation of potential into reality depended upon the conscious decisions and actions of the revolutionary party.

Trotsky's declaration in the 1938 founding document of the Fourth International that "The historical crisis of mankind is reduced to the crisis of the revolutionary leadership" was a summing up of the central lessons of the previous fifteen years of defeats suffered by the working class as a consequence of the opportunism and treachery of the Stalinist and Social Democratic parties and trade unions.

Events such as the defeat of the general strike in Britain in 1926, the crushing of the Shanghai working class by Chiang Kai-shek in 1927, the victory of the Nazis in Germany in 1933, the demoralization of the French working class in the aftermath of the mass strikes of 1936 by the politics of the Popular Front, the defeat of the Spanish Revolution in 1939, and, finally, Stalin's pact with Hitler and the outbreak of World War II provoked pessimism and disillusionment with the prospects for socialism among broad sections of the left-wing intelligentsia. Did these defeats not prove, they asked, that the working class is incapable of conquering and holding power?

Trotsky emphatically rejected the demoralization that motivated the question. The obstacle to the realization of socialism was not the "non-revolutionary" character of the working class, but, rather, the rottenness of the existing mass parties. But this raised a further question: Was it possible to build a party whose leaders would prove equal to the demands of the revolution? Those who denied this possibility were driven to the most pessimistic political conclusions, i.e., that the program of socialist revolution advanced an unrealizable utopia and that the position of humanity was, in essence, hopeless. "Not all our opponents express this thought clearly," Trotsky wrote in the autumn of 1939, "but all of them—ultra-lefts, centrists, anarchists, not to mention Stalinists and social-democrats—shift the responsibility for the defeats from themselves to the shoulders of the proletariat. None of them indicate under precisely what conditions the proletariat will be capable of accomplishing the socialist overturn."[15]

Trotsky had identified the source of the political demoralization of left intellectuals. The rejection of the revolutionary potential of the working class was the essential premise of the anti-Marxism of petty-bourgeois left academics in the aftermath of World War II. Directing their arguments against the

---

15. Leon Trotsky, "The USSR in War," *In Defence of Marxism* (London: New Park Publications, 1971), p. 15.

historical perspective of Trotsky (even if they did not openly acknowledge this), the Frankfurt School sought to disconnect Marxism from the working class. The post-modernists declared the end of "grand narratives" that explained history as an objective law-governed process and identified the working class as the central revolutionary force in society. The inevitable outcome of the regression in social thought was the total repudiation of Marxism and social revolution based on the working class. As two leading representatives of this regression, Ernesto Laclau and Chantal Mouffe, bluntly declared in 1985:

> At this point we should state plainly that we are now situated in a post-Marxist terrain. It is no longer possible to maintain the conception of subjectivity and classes elaborated by Marxism, nor its vision of the historical course of capitalist development...[16]

The anti-Marxist theoreticians have been refuted by events. Only the Trotskyist movement anticipated and has prepared for the global upsurge of class struggle that is now underway. Basing itself on the perspective of Permanent Revolution, the International Committee stated in 1988:

> We anticipate that the next stage of proletarian struggles will develop inexorably, beneath the combined pressure of objective economic tendencies and the subjective influence of Marxists, along an international trajectory. The proletariat will tend more and more to define itself in practice as an international class; and the Marxian internationalists, whose policies are the expression of this organic tendency, will cultivate this process and give it conscious form.[17]

The accelerating world capitalist crisis and global class struggle will provide the objective conditions for the socialist revolution and the overthrow of capitalism. "But," as Trotsky warned, "the great historic problem will not be solved in any case until the revolutionary party stands at the head of the proletariat."

---

16. Ernesto Laclau and Chantal Mouffe, *Hegemony & Socialist Strategy: Toward a Radical Democratic Politics* (London and New York: Verso, 1985) p. 4.

17. David North, Report to the 13th National Congress of the Workers League, *Fourth International*, July-December 1988, p. 39.

> The question of tempos and time intervals is of enormous importance; but it alters neither the general historical perspective nor the direction of our policy. The conclusion is a simple one: it is necessary to carry on the work of educating and organizing the proletarian vanguard with tenfold energy. Precisely in this lies the task of the Fourth International.[18]

The historical experiences of the past century thoroughly tested all political movements, parties, and tendencies that claimed to be leading the struggle against capitalism. But the upheavals of the twentieth century have exposed the counterrevolutionary role of the Stalinists, Social Democrats, Maoists, bourgeois nationalists, anarchists, and Pabloites. Only the Fourth International, led by the International Committee, has met the test of history. The international revolutionary socialist movement of the working class on every continent will develop on the theoretical and political foundations of Trotskyism, the Marxism of the twenty-first century.

* * * * *

This volume is dedicated to the memory of Wije Dias (August 27, 1941—July 27, 2022), a leading member of the International Committee of the Fourth International and general secretary of its Sri Lankan section for thirty-five years. Comrade Wije died in the midst of struggle, upholding in old age, and with undiminished passion, the ideals of his youth. His legacy—of courage, commitment to Trotskyist principles, and devotion to socialism—will provide an inspiring example to the working class in the great class battles that will decide the fate of mankind.

David North
Detroit
April 4, 2023

---

18. "Manifesto of the Fourth International on Imperialist War," *Writings of Leon Trotsky [1939–40]* (New York: Pathfinder Press, 1973, second edition, eighth printing), p. 290.

Tom Henehan

1

Leon Trotsky & the Development of Marxism

Foreword to the Turkish-language edition

In the process of writing, authors are often taken in a direction that they had not originally intended. This was the case in the writing of the essay, *Leon Trotsky and the Development of Marxism,* whose translation into Turkish by the comrades of Sosyalist Eşitlik I heartily welcome.

    I wrote this essay in the autumn of 1982 to commemorate the fifth anniversary of the political assassination of Tom Henehan, a leading member of the Workers League (predecessor organization of the Socialist Equality Party in the United States).

    On October 16, 1977, Comrade Henehan was murdered by two gunmen as he presided over a social event sponsored by the Young Socialists, the youth movement of the Workers League, in New York City. The attack was entirely unprovoked. The two assailants burst into the venue of the social event and deliberately created a commotion. As Henehan approached the entrance of the social club to determine what was happening, he was shot five times by one of the assailants. Another member of the Workers League, Jacques Vielot, was shot by a second assailant as he rushed to Tom's assistance. The two gunmen then fled the premises.

Originally published as the Preface to the 2021 Turkish-language edition of *Leon Trotsky & the Development of Marxism.*

Despite his own serious injuries, Vielot managed to drive Henehan, who was still conscious, to a nearby hospital. Though Tom was taken into an emergency room, the attending physicians, for reasons that were never explained, did not attempt surgery to stop his internal bleeding. Tom died in the emergency room approximately ninety minutes after arriving at the hospital. He was just twenty-six years old.

The murder of Tom Henehan was a political crime that deprived the American and international working class of a selfless, dedicated, and immensely capable fighter. Though he had been in the movement only four and half years, Tom was admired by his comrades in the Workers League and throughout the International Committee of the Fourth International. Born in Wisconsin on March 16, 1951 and raised in Michigan, he joined the Workers League in the spring of 1973 while still a student at Columbia University in New York. Tom's decision to join the Workers League came after the wave of student radicalism had subsided, and as affluent middle-class youth, having dabbled in protest politics, were turning to careerism and self-serving lifestyle and identity politics.

But Tom Henehan was attracted by the Workers League's political orientation to the working class and the emphasis it placed on the party's roots in the historical struggles of the world Trotskyist movement, dating back to the 1920s. His education as a Marxist took place as the Workers League was passing through a critical period in its own political development. In 1974, Tim Wohlforth, who had founded the Workers League in opposition to the Socialist Workers Party's break with the International Committee of the Fourth International, rejected the principles and program that he had defended for the previous fourteen years and rejoined the SWP. Wohlforth's renegacy found no support within the cadre of the Workers League, the youthful membership of which had been recruited and educated on the basis of the International Committee's opposition to the US Socialist Workers Party's abandonment of Trotskyism, exemplified in its reunification in 1963 with the Pabloite United Secretariat.

The Workers League responded to Wohlforth's betrayal by intensifying its study of the history of the Fourth International and assimilating the theoretical and political issues raised in the protracted struggle against Pabloite revisionism.

As the fifth anniversary of Comrade Henehan's assassination approached, it had been my intention to concentrate on his political work and pay tribute to his outstanding contribution to the building of the Workers League.

However, the review of Tom's life raised critical questions: How are those who join the Trotskyist movement educated? Through what process is a Marxist-Trotskyist cadre developed? What is the relationship between the daily activity of the revolutionary party and the history of the Fourth International?

These questions had acquired exceptional urgency in the context of a growing crisis in the International Committee of the Fourth International. In the weeks preceding the drafting of the essay commemorating the anniversary of Tom's assassination, I had begun work on an extensive critique of the drift of the Workers Revolutionary Party—at that time the most experienced and leading section of the International Committee—toward the opportunist politics of Pabloism.

The relations that the WRP had developed, starting in the mid-1970s, with a series of bourgeois-nationalist movements and regimes in the Middle East and Africa entailed a fundamental break with the strategic orientation defined by Trotsky in his Theory of Permanent Revolution. At the same time, the policies pursued by the WRP within Britain assumed a blatantly opportunist character; sycophantic apologies for the betrayals of the trade union bureaucracy were published with ever greater frequency in the party's organ, *News Line*.

The retreat of the Workers Revolutionary Party from the Trotskyist strategy of establishing the political independence of the working class, which its principal leaders—Gerry Healy, Michael Banda, and Cliff Slaughter—had defended against Stalinism and Pabloite opportunism in the 1950s and 1960s, was covered over with fraudulent invocations of dialectical materialism. What Healy called the "practice of cognition" was an eclectic combination of subjective impressionism and unrestrained pragmatism, which he attempted to endow with the appearance of profundity through the pretentious use of pseudo-Hegelian jargon. Moreover, the WRP leaders' focus on "philosophical method"—entirely unrelated to political analysis and which had absolutely nothing to do with Marxism—was aimed at undermining the study of Trotsky's writings and the critical documents that comprised the heritage of the International Committee of the Fourth International.

Once the drafting of the tribute to Henehan began, it was unavoidable that the theoretical and political issues with which I was preoccupied in the developing critique of the WRP would find expression. The tribute to Tom Henehan, five years after his death, required the defense of the principles, program, and genuine Marxist method upon which his own training as a revolutionary cadre had been based. Thus, the honoring of Tom's life assumed the form of an initial elaboration of a critique of the Workers Revolutionary Party's betrayal of Trotskyism. The articles did not specifically reference the Workers Revolutionary Party. But Healy, Banda, and Slaughter certainly did not fail to notice the political implications of my tribute to Tom Henehan, which was clearly directed against their opportunist falsification of Marxist theory. They would have been particularly offended by the following observation:

> Revisionists and political charlatans of all descriptions invariably base their politics and policies on the most immediate and practical needs of the hour. Principled considerations, i.e., those which arise out of a serious study of the history of the international workers movement, knowledge of its development as a law-governed process, and, flowing from that, a constant critical reworking of its objective experiences, are utterly foreign to these pragmatists. Their motto in politics is "anything goes—as long as it brings some success." Insofar as they evince an interest in history, it is simply to exploit a quotation torn out of context or to disguise their present opportunism with purely ceremonial references to the past achievements of the Trotskyist movement, or, what is more likely, of Trotsky as an individual.

Nor would Healy and Slaughter—the two principal exponents of the WRP's falsification of method—have been pleased with the following statement:

> Without a real knowledge of the historical development of the Trotskyist movement, references to dialectical materialism are not merely hollow; such empty references pave the way for a real distortion of the dialectical method. The source of theory lies not in thought but in the objective world. Thus the development of Trotskyism proceeds from the fresh experiences of the class struggle which are posited on the entire historically-derived knowledge of our movement.

Though my critique was directed against the WRP's distortion and falsification of dialectics, I was not unmindful of the danger that my criticism might be misrepresented and exploited in political bad faith by opponents of the International Committee to discredit dialectics and undermine the philosophical foundations of Marxist politics. Therefore, I emphasized the essential link between the dialectical method, applied in a manner consistent with the materialist conception of history, and the work of Leon Trotsky.

> Those who seriously and systematically study the writings of Leon Trotsky, and this is essential for the theoretical development of every cadre in the Workers League and the International Committee, will discover the enormous richness of the dialectical method. It would be wrong, of course, to mechanically reduce the whole content of the struggle waged by Trotsky against Stalinism to the question of dialectics versus metaphysics, independent of an examination of the social forces whose interests were, and continue to be, manifested through these historical battles. However, there is no question but that every stage in the development of the struggle against the Stalinist bureaucracy required a deepening of the dialectical materialist method against the subjective idealist metaphysics of the bureaucracy. Philosophy is partisan; that is, theory is a class question. Stalin's eclecticism and idealism, which made him initially vulnerable to the pressures of social forces hostile to the proletariat, became anchored, at a certain point in the development of the world crisis, in the material interests of the Soviet bureaucracy and, thus, of world imperialism.

I also sought to clarify the relationship of materialist dialectics to the work of the Bolshevik Party and the Communist International, founded in the aftermath of the 1917 October Revolution:

> Under the leadership of Lenin and Trotsky, the dialectical method, treated as a "dead dog" by Kautsky and the majority of the Social Democratic leaders, was revived, enriched, and restored to its rightful place in the Communist International—as the methodological foundation of the science of Marxist strategy, political perspectives and revolutionary action. In an epoch of civil wars, of abrupt "overnight" changes in the political situation, of day-to-day shifts in the relation of class forces on a world scale, of sudden movements on the political battlefield from left

to right and from right to left, only the dialectical method has been proven equal to the historical task of the proletariat. As Marx would have written: dialectics is not a lancet for academic debate but a weapon of class war. It is not the passion of the head; it is the head of revolutionary passion. It is in this spirit that the International Committee of the Fourth International trains the cadre of the world Trotskyist movement today.

The first two parts of *Leon Trotsky and the Development of Marxism* were published in the *Bulletin,* the twice-weekly organ of the Workers League, on October 15 and 19, 1982. On Friday, October 22, 1982, I personally informed Healy of my opposition to his idealist falsification of Marxist methodology. There immediately followed a series of explosive meetings with Healy.

Upon returning to the United States, I wrote the third and fourth parts of the essay, which were published in the November 23 and December 14, 1982 issues of the *Bulletin.* At this point the theoretical and political implications of the essay, i.e., its fundamental critique of the WRP's opportunist repudiation of the heritage of the Fourth International, was clearly understood by the WRP leaders. At a meeting held in London on December 18, 1982, Slaughter, who had expressed agreement with my criticisms of Healy's "practice of cognition" in October, abruptly reversed course and denounced me as an American pragmatist.

In response, I cited several passages in *Leon Trotsky and the Development of Marxism* devoted to the issue of method, and I asked that Slaughter explain precisely how they evinced sympathy for pragmatism. He chose not to take up the challenge.

The essay was never published in *News Line.* The opportunist degeneration of the Workers Revolutionary Party accelerated, culminating in the political disintegration of the organization and its break with the International Committee and Trotskyism in February 1986. In the aftermath of the split, the essay was widely circulated in the International Committee and published in the press of all its sections.

The older generation of comrades in the Socialist Equality Party and International Committee who worked with Tom and treasure his memory will share my satisfaction that this tribute has now found its way, through the efforts of a new generation of fighters for socialism, into the Turkish language. The emerging generation of Trotskyist revolutionaries throughout the world will draw inspiration from the example of Tom Henehan. This new edition testifies to the growing worldwide influence of the principles and program of the International Committee of the Fourth International that Tom sacrificed his life to defend.

David North,
October 5, 2021

I. Tom Henehan and the education of revolutionists

On October 16, 1977, Tom Henehan, a member of the Political Committee of the Workers League, was assassinated in New York while supervising a social activity that had been organized by the Young Socialists.

Two gunmen, Angelo Torres and Edwin Sequinot, entered the Ponce Social Club, where the YS dance was being held, and, with the assistance of a third man, Angelo Rodriguez, staged a provocation at the entrance to the dance hall.

Tom Henehan noticed the commotion and ran to the entrance. There he was shot five times by Torres. Another leading member of the Workers League, Jacques Vielot, was shot by Sequinot as he attempted to get at Torres.

Gravely wounded in the neck and chest, Tom was rushed to Wyckoff Heights Hospital by Vielot, who managed to drive to the hospital despite his own serious abdominal wounds.

Henehan was still conscious as he was wheeled into the hospital's Emergency Room. However, for reasons that have never been explained, the supervising surgeon chose not to attempt surgery to stop Tom's internal bleeding, though this is standard medical practice. Instead, he was left in the Emergency Room until he died of shock approximately ninety minutes after arriving at the hospital.

Several hours after Tom's death, which occurred shortly before 3 a.m., the surgeon had Vielot brought into the operating room to remove bullets that threatened his life. He survived and recovered fully.

A political murder

Tom Henehan was the victim of a political murder. His assassination came at a crucial point in the investigation conducted by the International Committee of the Fourth International into the circumstances surrounding the murder of Leon Trotsky in Mexico in August 1940. The investigation had just uncovered the fact that Joseph Hansen, the leader of the revisionist Socialist Workers Party, had secretly sought to establish, with the assistance of the US State Department, a confidential means of communicating with the Federal Bureau of Investigation in the weeks following the assassination of Trotsky. Only a few months before Tom's murder, Hansen had written that the continuation of the investigation would have "deadly consequences" for the International Committee.

Now Tom Henehan lay dead at the age of twenty-six years and seven months, a martyr of the Trotskyist movement who gave his life to liberate the working class from capitalist oppression. The capitalist press imposed a virtual blackout on all reporting of his murder. Neither the Socialist Workers Party nor the Stalinist Communist Party printed a word about Comrade Henehan's assassination in their newspapers. The SWP would not even issue a statement condemning his murder; instead they parroted the official police line by telling their members that the shooting of Tom was a "senseless killing."

The police in Brooklyn, New York—the site of the assassination—claimed that there had been only one gunman, Torres, and that he could not be found in spite of an "all points alert." As for Sequinot, the police released him from custody minutes after he had been identified by eyewitnesses as Torres' co-gunman.

For the next three years, the Workers League and the Young Socialists waged a tireless campaign in the labor movement to force the District Attorney's office in Brooklyn to apprehend Torres and Sequinot. Union officials representing several million trade unionists and tens of thousands of workers and youth sent letters and signed petitions demanding the arrest of Torres and Sequinot, much to the surprise of the police investigator who had told the Workers League just ten days after the shooting: "Henehan was just a commie and his death would be of interest only to other commies."

On October 15, 1980, Torres was arrested and booked for the murder of Tom Henehan and the shooting of Jacques Vielot. Official records obtained by the Workers League revealed that he had been arrested on a previous occasion by the police and quickly released, despite the outstanding warrant for the killing of Tom. Two months later, despite great reluctance, police also apprehended Edwin Sequinot. Both had been living in Brooklyn, at their home address, since the murder of Tom.

In July 1981, Torres and Sequinot went on trial for the murder of Henehan and the shooting of Vielot. Torres was found guilty of second degree murder and attempted murder, and was sentenced in August to twenty-five years to life imprisonment. Sequinot was found guilty of manslaughter and attempted murder, and was sentenced alongside Torres to a minimum of twenty-five years imprisonment.

However, as far as the Workers League is concerned, the investigation into the assassination of Tom Henehan is not over. The gunmen are in jail, but those who planned and ordered the killing have yet to be brought to justice. Based on the revolutionary strength of the working class, we are supremely confident that we shall expose every aspect of the conspiracy to murder Tom Henehan.

Five years after his death, the memory of Tom Henehan burns as brightly in the Workers League and every section of the International Committee as ever. There are hundreds of thousands of workers, youth, and anti-imperialist freedom fighters all over the globe who know of Tom Henehan's struggle and who are inspired by his life and his death.

Tom was only twenty-six when he died, and his activity inside the Workers League spanned just four and a half years. But no member of our movement who knew Tom can ever forget his determination, enthusiasm, and utter dedication. He possessed a great innate "feel" for the struggles of the labor movement and this enabled him to establish very close connections with a broad cross section of the working class, ranging from unemployed youth and shipyard workers in Brooklyn to coal miners in West Virginia.

The training of a revolutionary

But we cannot understand Tom Henehan's life and his role in the Workers League simply by adding up the sum of his personal qualities. As Mike Banda, General Secretary of the Workers Revolutionary Party in Britain, said at the memorial meeting held in New York City just six days after Tom's death: "Revolutionaries are not born. They are forged. They are trained out of the experiences of this movement, out of the intervention of its leadership, out of the whole struggle of past generations."

This was, of necessity, true for Tom as well. His political development was bound up with the historical struggles that have tempered the Trotskyist movement for nearly six decades and out of which the Workers League itself emerged. The real heart of cadre training is the conscious subordination of all who join the Party to the revolutionary principles through which the historical continuity of the Marxist movement is expressed. By "historical continuity," we have in mind the unbroken chain of political and ideological struggle by our *international* movement against Stalinism, Social Democracy, revisionism, and all other enemies of the working class.

The individual talents of different cadre are no substitute for this collective responsibility to assimilate and work off of the political and theoretical conquests of our movement historically. Lenin, Trotsky, the Bolshevik Party, and the Left Opposition are not merely great leaders and organizations of the past about whom we occasionally read and pay tribute to on special occasions. In all its theoretical and practical work, in the development of the dialectical materialist method, which makes possible the elaboration of scientific revolutionary perspectives, the International Committee carries forward and enriches the work of the great progenitors of our movement.

In 1916 Lenin characterized this epoch as that of imperialism, the highest and *final* stage of capitalism. In 1938 Trotsky reaffirmed this scientific analysis, defining this historical period as that of capitalism's *death agony*. All the vast political and economic changes on a world scale since Trotsky's death have confirmed time and again the historical validity of this analysis, and therefore the scientific character of the dialectical materialist method through which it was developed.

Sixty years of struggle

It is almost exactly sixty years since the political struggle which was to lead to the emergence of Trotskyism as the specific tendency representing the historical continuity of Marxism erupted inside the Politburo of the Russian Communist Party. In late 1922 Lenin was shocked to learn that, in his absence, Stalin and other Bolshevik leaders had supported the weakening of the state monopoly on foreign trade that was essential for the defense of the Soviet Union against world imperialism. Lenin saw in this opportunist decision a serious symptom of political degeneration within the Bolshevik leadership which reflected the growing bureaucratization of the state apparatus and the Party as a whole. Already gravely ill, having only partially recovered from a stroke in the spring of 1922 which had impaired his speech, Lenin turned to Trotsky for political support in the struggle to reverse the incorrect decision on the issue of the foreign trade monopoly.

On December 15, 1922, shortly before his departure to Gorkii (for the purpose of physical recuperation), Lenin wrote to Stalin:

> I am now through with putting my business in order, and am in a position to leave without worry. I have also come to an arrangement with Trotsky to stand up for my views of the foreign trade monopoly. There is only one thing that is worrying me extremely—it is that I am unable to speak at the Congress of Soviets ...
>
> I am resolutely opposed to any delay on the question of the foreign trade monopoly. If the idea should arise, for whatever reason (including the proposition that my participation in the question is desirable), to postpone it until the next plenum, I should most resolutely object to this, *because I am sure that Trotsky will be able to stand up for my views just as well as I myself* [emphasis added].¹

Confronted with the combined opposition of Lenin and Trotsky, Stalin and those who had voted with him against the foreign trade monopoly retreated. On December 21, 1922, Lenin wrote to Trotsky:

> It looks as though it has been possible to take the position without a single shot, by a simple manoeuvre. I suggest that we should not stop and should continue the offensive, and for that purpose put through a motion to raise at the Party congress the question of consolidating our foreign trade, and the measures to improve its implementation. This to be announced in the group of the Congress of Soviets. I hope that you will not object to this, and will not refuse to give a report in the group.²

The struggle over the question of the monopoly proved only to be a prelude to an even sharper struggle which almost immediately arose over the handling of the issues of Georgian nationality by Stalin and the head of the Cheka (secret police), F. Dzerzhinsky. On March 5, 1923, Lenin sent the following urgent note to Trotsky:

> It is my earnest request that you should undertake the defense of the Georgian case in the Party C.C. This case is now under

---

1. V.I. Lenin, "Letter to J.V. Stalin for members of the R.C.P.(B.) C.C.," *Collected Works*, Vol. 45 (Moscow: Progress Publishers, 1976), pp. 602–03.
2. "Letter to the Deputies," Ibid., p. 606.

"persecution" by Stalin and Dzerzhinsky, and I cannot rely on their impartiality. Quite to the contrary. I would feel at ease if you agreed to undertake its defence. If you should refuse to do so for any reason, return the whole case to me. I shall consider it a sign that you do not accept.[3]

Lenin, on the same day, then wrote a letter to Stalin threatening to break off all personal relations with him, on account of the rudeness with which Stalin had addressed Lenin's wife.

The final letter Lenin wrote that day was addressed to Georgian comrades who had been the victims of Stalin's bureaucratic abuse of authority:

I am following your case with all my heart. I am indignant over Orjonikidze's rudeness and the connivance of Stalin and Dzerzhinsky. I am preparing for you notes and a speech.[4]

However, before these notes could be written, Lenin suffered the massive stroke later that same day that incapacitated him and led to his death ten months later, on January 21, 1924.

These struggles were not a personal conflict between Lenin and Stalin. Without realizing it himself, Stalin was manifesting a process of bureaucratic degeneration within the Bolshevik Party that was the result of objective material pressures of world imperialism upon the first workers state. The economic backwardness of the Soviet Union, inherited from Tsarist Russia and intensified by a decade of imperialist war, revolutionary upheaval, and then struggle against counterrevolutionary forces, the delay in the extension of the socialist revolution into Western Europe, and the imperialist encirclement of the USSR: these were the conditions which gave rise to the growth of bureaucracy within the Soviet Union and the degeneration of the Bolshevik Party. Far from being an evil genius who masterminded his way to absolute power, it was the political weaknesses of Stalin that made him the instrument of bureaucratic reaction within the USSR.

The founding of the Left Opposition in the autumn of 1923 was the response of the most politically-developed Bolsheviks, led by Trotsky, to the increasing danger of degeneration within the Party leadership. Trotsky's

---

3. "To L.D. Trotsky," Ibid., p. 607.
4. "To J.V. Stalin," Ibid., p. 608.

initial analysis of these dangers, published under the title *The New Course*, provoked an outraged response among all those in the Party apparatus and state bureaucracy who felt, upon reading his articles, a sharp rebuke to their conservatism and implicit threat to their growing material privileges.

Socialism in One Country

The political significance of the growing polarization within the Bolshevik Party became clear when, in late 1924, Bukharin and Stalin advanced the novel proposition that socialism could be established in the USSR without the victory of the proletarian revolution in the advanced capitalist countries of Europe and the United States. This fundamental revision of Marxism, which separated the fate of the Soviet Union from the whole development of the World Socialist Revolution, reflected the growing preoccupation of an expanding bureaucratic elite with the defense of its own material privileges. Having adopted the position that socialism could be built in the Soviet Union without the overthrow of imperialism, the Stalinist faction moved inexorably—although, at first, unconsciously—toward a policy of accommodation with world capitalism. As Trotsky was to explain, if socialism could truly be built in one country, the international aims of the Soviet state would tend increasingly to focus not on world revolution—as that was no longer viewed as essential for the survival of the USSR—but on merely preventing direct military intervention by this or that capitalist state against the Soviet Union. This outlook set the stage for the destruction of the Third (Communist) International as a revolutionary force and its transformation into a compliant instrument of the foreign policy of the Soviet bureaucracy. This was the essential political content of the Stalinist bureaucracy's attack on the theory of Permanent Revolution, which, from 1925 on, was denounced again and again as the "original sin" of Trotskyism.

The concept of "Permanent Revolution," however, was not a subjective invention of Trotsky's mind. It was abstracted initially by Marx in 1850 from his analysis of the class relations in European society revealed in the course of the democratic revolutionary struggle of 1848. This concept was elaborated and enriched by Trotsky through his profound historical examination of the objective development of capitalist society, in which the *transition* from the era of *democratic* revolutions to *social* revolutions was carefully traced. Trotsky did not proceed from the concept to the external world. Rather, he explained how the concept reflected, at different stages in the development of the Marxist movement, the objective changes in the class struggle as a law-governed process.

Dialectics vs. metaphysics

In this objective exposition of the real historical development, Trotsky demonstrated the bankruptcy of the metaphysical mode of thinking, which, proceeding from formal logic, rigidly counterposed the democratic revolution to the socialist revolution.

Characteristic of all the denunciations of the theory of Permanent Revolution, especially in the course of the 1925–27 struggle over the policies of the Third International in China, was the theoretically stultifying and *politically disastrous* metaphysics of the Stalinist leaders—above all, of Stalin himself. These "epigones" argued: "China must complete the stage of the bourgeois-democratic revolution; China is waging a national struggle against imperialism; Chiang K'ai-shek is waging a progressive struggle against feudal warlords. Therefore, the Communist International and the Chinese Communist Party must support and subordinate itself to Chiang K'ai-shek and the bourgeois Kuomintang." As if to set a condition on what was essentially an utter betrayal of the independent interests of the Chinese working class, which doomed the revolution to a catastrophic defeat, the Stalinists asserted that the alliance was merely temporary.

Proceeding from a concrete analysis of the nature of the epoch, the relation of class forces on a world scale, and the specific features of Chinese society and the development of its revolution, Trotsky demonstrated how, in accordance with objective social laws, the "opposites" of the democratic-national revolution and social revolution became "identical" and were "transformed into one another."[5]

Thus, Trotsky explained:

> With regard to countries with a belated bourgeois development, especially the colonial and semi-colonial countries, the theory of the permanent revolution signifies that the complete

---

5. See Lenin's *Collected Works*, Vol. 38, p. 109: "*Dialectic*s is the teaching which shows how *Opposites* can be and how they happen to be (how they become) *identical*,—under what conditions they are identical, becoming transformed into one another,—why the human mind should grasp these opposites not as dead, rigid, but as living, conditional, mobile, becoming transformed into one another. [In reading] Hegel..."

and genuine solution of their tasks of achieving *democracy and national emancipation* is conceivable only through the dictatorship of the proletariat as the leader of the subjugated nation, above all of its peasant masses.[6]

Trotsky warned that:

> The theory of Stalin and Bukarin, running counter to the entire experience of the Russian revolution, not only sets up the democratic revolution mechanically in contrast to the socialist revolution, but also makes a breach between the national revolution and the international revolution.
>
> This theory imposes upon revolutions in backward countries the task of establishing an unrealizable regime of democratic dictatorship, which it counterposes to the dictatorship of the proletariat. Thereby this theory introduces illusions and fictions into politics, paralyses the struggle for power of the proletariat in the East, and hampers the victory of the colonial revolution.[7]

Trotsky summed up the theory of Permanent Revolution as follows:

> The conquest of power by the proletariat does not complete the revolution, but only opens it. Socialist construction is conceivable only on the foundation of the class struggle, on a national and international scale. This struggle, under the conditions of an overwhelming predominance of capitalist relationships on the world arena, must inevitably lead to explosions, that is, internally, to civil wars and externally to revolutionary wars.
>
> Therein lies the permanent character of the socialist revolution as such, regardless of whether it is a backward country that is involved, which only yesterday accomplished its democratic revolution, or an old capitalist country which already has behind it a long epoch of democracy and parliamentarism.

---

6. Leon Trotsky, *The Permanent Revolution* and *Results and Prospects* (London: New Park Publications, 1972), p. 152.
7. Ibid., p.156.

> The completion of the socialist revolution within national limits is unthinkable. One of the basic reasons for the crisis in bourgeois society is the fact that the productive forces created by it can no longer be reconciled with the framework of the national state. From this follow, on the one hand, imperialist wars, on the other, the utopia of a bourgeois United States of Europe. The socialist revolution begins on the national arena, it unfolds on the international arena, and is completed on the world arena. Thus, the socialist revolution becomes a permanent revolution in a newer and broader sense of the word; it attains completion only in the final victory of the new society on our entire planet.[8]

Between 1925 and 1927, the Left Opposition (which, in 1926, was joined by Zinoviev and Kamenev and became the United Left Opposition) waged a life-and-death struggle to save the Bolshevik Party from bureaucratic degeneration and, through this struggle, the Communist International as well. At stake historically was the fate of the Soviet Union and the entire international proletariat. In an atmosphere poisoned by increasingly vicious falsifications and ever more ominous forms of physical repression, Trotsky, with the simplicity of a genius, analyzed and summed up, in the concept "Permanent Revolution," all the fundamental features and general laws of the World Socialist Revolution. In his presentation of the "Basic Postulates" of the theory of Permanent Revolution, set out in fourteen points (see *The Permanent Revolution*, New Park, 1972, pp. 152–157), Trotsky advanced, not a set of inviolable and supra-historical formulas which were then to be mechanically imposed, but rather a dialectically developed theory to assist revolutionists in the scientific cognition of the concrete political tasks posed by the class struggle, from the standpoint of the independent revolutionary mobilization of the working class under the leadership of an international Marxist party.

The Sixth Congress

The expulsion of Leon Trotsky from the Russian Communist Party in November 1927 revealed the depth of its bureaucratic degeneration. The

---

8. Ibid., pp. 154–55.

internal purge of the Left Opposition was accompanied by the bureaucratic expulsion of leaders of the Communist International suspected of Trotskyist sympathies, or who evinced any trace of independent political thinking. The entire Sixth Congress of the Communist International, held in 1928, was held under the sign of the struggle against Trotskyism. However, Trotsky, now exiled to Asiatic and malaria-ridden frontiers of the Soviet Union, prepared a critique of the Sixth Congress' draft program. This document drew the balance sheet on all the political disasters which had been produced by the Stalinist leadership since the incapacitation of Lenin.

Accidentally, this document was translated into English and fell into the hands of a member of the American Communist Party delegation to the Sixth Congress, James P. Cannon. He secretly studied the document, found himself in agreement with its analysis and conclusions, smuggled it out of the Soviet Union at the conclusion of the Congress, and resolved to fight for its positions within the Communist Party. Supported by two other leading members in the Communist Party, Max Shachtman and Martin Abern, Cannon declared his support for Trotsky's position. No discussion, however, was permitted in the American Communist Party. A trial was hastily convened and Cannon, Shachtman, and Abern were expelled from the Communist Party.

The first issue of *The Militant*, established as the organ of the supporters of Trotsky expelled from the Communist Party, carried a letter by James P. Cannon, which declared:

> The struggle of the past five years has revolved around the living issues of the present period. It is our absolute conviction, based on the most objective study of all material we could secure—and carried on in the face [of] a previous prejudice—that on all of these basic questions of the period, the questions around which the whole life and future of the international Communist movement revolve—Trotsky has been in the main correct and the true defender of Leninism."[9]

In October 1938, six weeks after the founding of the Fourth International, Trotsky declared in a recorded speech:

---

9. James P. Cannon, *The Left Opposition in the U.S. 1928–32*, (New York: Monad Press, 1981), p. 43.

It is necessary to remark that the birth of the American group of Bolshevik-Leninists, thanks to the courageous initiative of Comrades Cannon, Shachtman, and Abern, didn't stand alone. It approximately coincided with the beginning of the systematic international work of the Left Opposition. It is true that the Left Opposition arose in Russia in 1923, but regular work on an international scale began with the Sixth Congress of the Comintern.[10]

II. Trotsky's dialectical method vs. Stalinist metaphysics

"Eclectics live by means of episodic thoughts and improvisations that originate under the impact of events," wrote Leon Trotsky in January 1932. "Marxist cadres capable of leading the proletarian revolution are trained only by the continual and successive working out of problems and disputes."[11]

Revisionists and political charlatans of all descriptions invariably base their politics and policies on the most immediate and practical needs of the hour. Principled considerations, i.e., those which arise out of a serious study of the history of the international workers movement, knowledge of its development as a law-governed process, and, flowing from that, a constant critical reworking of its objective experiences, are utterly foreign to these pragmatists. Their motto in politics is, "anything goes—as long as it brings some success." Insofar as they evince an interest in history, it is simply to exploit a quotation torn out of context or to disguise their present opportunism with purely ceremonial references to the past achievements of the Trotskyist movement, or, what is more likely, of Trotsky as an individual.

Thus, the objective significance of all the historical experiences through which the Trotskyist movement has passed, and submitted to Marxist analysis, is ignored. The lessons of the Chinese Revolution of 1925–27, the betrayal of the British General Strike in 1926, the defeat of the German proletariat, the treachery of Popular Frontism, the Moscow Trials, the crimes of the GPU, the assassination of Leon Trotsky—all these historical events are dismissed as "so much water under the bridge."

The whole development of Pabloism since the notorious Third World Congress of 1951 has proceeded entirely along these lines. Its "discovery" of

---

10. "The founding of the Fourth International," *Writings of Leon Trotsky [1938–39]* (New York: Pathfinder Press, 1974, second edition, ninth printing, 2023), p.107.
11. Leon Trotsky, "What Next?," *Germany 1931–1932*, (London: New Park Publications, 1970), p.52.

"self-reforming bureaucracies," "natural Marxists," "new-capitalism," and most recently, "revolutionists of action" and a "mass Leninist international" are all manifestations of the ideological and political betrayal of Trotskyist principles, and therefore of the working class.

Trotskyism as the development of Marxism

The history of Trotskyism cannot be comprehended as a series of disconnected episodes. Its theoretical development has been abstracted by its cadre from the continuous unfolding of the world capitalist crisis and the struggles of the international proletariat. Its unbroken continuity of political analyses of all the fundamental experiences of the class struggle, *over an entire historical epoch*, constitutes the enormous richness of Trotskyism as the *sole* development of Marxism after the death of Lenin in 1924.

A leadership which does not strive collectively to assimilate the *whole* of this history cannot adequately fulfill its revolutionary responsibilities to the working class. Without a real knowledge of the historical development of the Trotskyist movement, references to dialectical materialism are not merely hollow; such empty references pave the way for a real distortion of the dialectical method. The source of theory lies not in thought but in the objective world. Thus the development of Trotskyism proceeds from the fresh experiences of the class struggle which are posited on the entire historically-derived knowledge of our movement.

> Thus cognition rolls forward from content to content ... it raises to each next stage of determination the whole mass of its antecedent content, and by its dialectical progress not only loses nothing and leaves nothing behind, but carries with it all that it has acquired, enriching and concentrating itself upon itself...

Quoting this passage from Hegel's *Science of Logic*, Lenin, in his *Philosophical Notebooks*, wrote: "This extract is not at all bad as a kind of summing up of dialectics."[12] Nor is this extract bad "as a kind of summing up of" the constant dialectical development of Trotskyist theory.

---

12. V.I. Lenin, "Conspectus of Hegel's Science of Logic," *Collected Works*, Vol. 38 (Moscow: Progress Publishers, 1976), p. 230.

Between 1923 and 1933, the Left Opposition (which had been strengthened in 1928 by the formation of the International Left Opposition) fought for the reform of the Russian Communist Party and the Third (Communist) International (also known as the Comintern).

The basis for this policy did not lie in illusions about the nature of the Stalinist regime, which Trotsky then (up until 1933) characterized as *bureaucratic centrism*, but in the objective possibilities for a breakthrough in the proletarian revolution.

As a dialectical materialist, Trotsky always proceeded from the primacy of social being independent of social consciousness. The degeneration of the Bolshevik Party and of the Communist International during the 1920s was an objective manifestation of the setbacks suffered by the proletarian revolution during that decade. The tragic failure of the German revolution in 1923, due to the vacillations of the Communist Party leadership, led to the restabilization of European capitalism. Moreover, it weakened the position of the Comintern's European sections, temporarily strengthened the social democratic parties, and demoralized large sections of the Soviet working class which had counted on the support of the German revolution. The subsequent defeat of the Chinese revolution generated political indifference among Soviet workers, whose vanguard was acutely conscious of the isolation of the workers state and of the dangers of imperialist intervention.

Each setback for the international proletariat strengthened the bureaucracy, encouraged the growth of conservative tendencies within the working class, and speeded up the process of degeneration of the "Old Bolshevik" cadres in the party and state apparatus. In turn, this very process of degeneration led to the revisionist policies which directly contributed to new defeats of the international working class, which, as in a vicious cycle, intensified the isolation of the USSR and increased the power of the bureaucracy.

The struggle in the Comintern

As long as the possibility existed that a decisive section of the international working class could, despite the centrist mistakes and bureaucratic incompetence of its Stalinist leadership, find the road to power, Trotsky worked for the reform of the Comintern. There was, however, not a trace of fatalistic passivity in this policy. Through the tireless work of the International Left Opposition, Trotsky sought to explain to the revolutionary workers inside the official parties of the Comintern the deadly consequences of the Stalinist line, and to elaborate the correct policies that would, if adopted, lead to victory.

Despite the repression directed against him—he was expelled from the Soviet Union in January 1929 and deprived of his citizenship in 1932—Trotsky could not be swayed from this politically objective course. He recognized that the great struggle unfolding in Germany, whose decrepit Weimar Republic was caught between the anvil of fascist counterrevolution and the hammer of the socialist revolution, would decide the fate of the Communist International.

In Germany, the policies of the Comintern were leading to a catastrophe. Following the Sixth Congress and in the aftermath of the ignominious defeat in China produced by Stalin's right-wing opportunism, the Stalinists swung to an almost hysterical ultra-leftism that was, if anything, even more politically infantile than the ultra-leftism mocked less than a decade earlier by Lenin at the Third Congress of the Communist International.

This "ultra-leftism" was inaugurated by the Comintern when Stalin's henchman, V. Molotov, proclaimed the onset of the "Third Period," which was supposedly characterized by the unstoppable "revolutionary upsurge" and "radicalization of the masses." The latter slogan was elevated into an absolute principle which rendered any concrete analysis of the actual development of the class struggle in each country utterly superfluous. The "radicalization of the masses" became a pure metaphysical abstraction. No attempt was made to examine the concrete forms of this radicalization, the tempo of its development, the layers of the working class involved, etc. Neither the differentiation within the proletariat of each country nor the specific distinctions between the development of the workers movement in different countries was acknowledged. An abstract—and thus, non-dialectical—uniformity was imposed on the entire development of the international class struggle. On this basis, a set of bombastic formulas were declared to be universally valid: the "General Strike," the "Conquest of the Streets," and "No Alliances With the Reformists!"

Underlying this swing toward ultra-leftism was a deep-rooted skepticism within the Communist International toward its ability to break the stranglehold of Social Democracy over the working class. The necessity for patient political work among the masses, especially the powerful battalions organized within the trade unions, which had been especially stressed by Lenin at the Third and Fourth Congresses of the Communist International, was repudiated. Rather than exploit the contradictions within Social Democracy—that is, the conflict between its mass working class base and its political role as an agency of capitalism—the Stalinists, in practice, abstained from any sustained struggle to break the workers from their corrupt reformist leaders.

This took the following form in Germany. After the Wall Street crash of October 1929, the unfolding world depression devastated the German economy. The rise of mass unemployment and the ruination of the petty bourgeoisie led to the rapid growth of a mass fascist movement led by Adolf Hitler. Its recruits were drawn primarily from the ruined middle class and the destitute *lumpen*-proletariat.

Trotsky carefully analyzed the objective political and social content of fascism:

> Fascism is not merely a system of reprisals, of brutal force, and of police terror. Fascism is a particular governmental system based on the uprooting of all elements of proletarian democracy within bourgeois society. The task of Fascism lies not only in destroying the Communist advance guard but in holding the entire class in a state of forced disunity. To this end the physical annihilation of the most revolutionary section of workers does not suffice. It is also necessary to smash all independent and voluntary organizations, to demolish all the defensive bulwarks of the proletariat, and to uproot whatever has been achieved during three quarters of a century by Social Democracy and the trade unions. For, in the last analysis, the Communist Party also bases itself on these achievements.[13]

The central political task which confronted the German Communist Party was the mobilization of the working class against the fascist threat, and through this, to unite under its leadership the entire working class for the seizure of state power. To expose the reactionary nature of Social Democracy as a bulwark of the capitalist state it was necessary for the Communist Party to propose, before the entire working class, a *united front* of the two working-class parties in struggle against Hitler's brown shirts. Millions of German workers, loyal to the Social Democrats, wanted to fight the Nazis. The Social Democrats, on the other hand, were determined to contain the political struggle of the working class within the limits of the capitalist state.

---

13. Trotsky, "What's Next?," *Germany 1931–32*, p.48.

No struggle against Hitlerism which passed beyond those limits was permissible. Instead, the Social Democrats based their entire policy upon bankrupt appeals to the capitalist state to defend bourgeois democracy and to protect the working class against the fascist onslaught.

By calling for united action by the Communist and Social Democratic parties, the former would have been able to expose the cowardice of the reformists, their connections with the bourgeoisie, and their refusals to seriously fight Nazism. At the same time, the Communist Party would have attained enormous stature among Social Democratic workers as the only political force capable of defending their trade unions and democratic rights. The *tactic* of the United Front would have vastly strengthened the German working class, demoralized the petty bourgeois masses within Hitler's movement, discredited Social Democracy, and cleared the path to socialist revolution.

However, in accordance with the precepts of the "Third Period," the Stalinists embarked on the opposite course. They rejected any proposal for a United Front, and instead denounced the Social Democrats as "Social Fascists"; that is, they declared that the Social Democracy and fascism "are not antipodes, they are twins."[14] From this, the Stalinists established the rule that Social Democracy was as immediate and as great an enemy as the Nazis, and that united struggles by Communist and Social Democratic workers organizations against the fascists were impermissible.

How did the Stalinists arrive at this fatal political line? By means of purely formal logical deduction, the Stalinists insisted: 1) Fascism is an agency of the capitalist state; 2) Social Democracy is an agency of the capitalist class; 3) Therefore, fascism and Social Democracy are the same; 4) Ergo, Social Democracy is a variety of fascism, i.e., it is "Social-Fascism."

The theory of social fascism

The metaphysics of this argument consisted in the removal of all contradiction from the political categories with which the Stalinists pretended to deal. They ignored the fact that Social Democracy was not only an agency of capitalism, it was also a workers' party—i.e., it was an *Identity* of opposed determinations. Ultimately, fascism and Social Democracy served the same master, but they served capitalism in different ways. In order to carry out its

---

14. J.V. Stalin, *Works*, Vol. 6 (Moscow: Foreign Languages Publishing House, 1954), p. 294.

specific historical task, fascism had as its goal the liquidation not only of the Communist Party but also of Social Democracy. In order to defend capitalism, the fascists were called upon to destroy all elements of proletarian democracy, including the reformist organizations of the working class.

As Trotsky explained:

> The gist of this Stalinist philosophy is quite plain: from the Marxist denial of the *absolute* contradiction [between fascism and Social Democracy] it deduces the *general* negation of the contradiction, even of the *relative* contradiction. This error is typical of vulgar radicalism. For if there is no contradiction *whatsoever* between democracy and Fascism—even in the sphere of the *form* of the rule of the bourgeoisie—then these two régimes obviously enough must be equivalent. Whence the conclusion: Social Democracy=Fascism.[15]

Rather than finding a road to the Social Democratic workers and uniting the working class, the Stalinists deepened the divisions within the working class, alienated the Social Democratic workers, and played into the hands not only of the Social Democratic bureaucracy but of the fascists as well. On certain occasions, as in the politically-demented "Red Referendum" of 1931, the Stalinists collaborated with the Nazis against the Social Democrats, and thus squandered whatever credibility the German Communist Party retained in the eyes of Social Democratic trade unions.

Refusing to listen to the warnings of the International Left Opposition and its German Section,[16] the Stalinists replied with pathetic bluster. Their slogan became, "After Hitler, us!" They reassured the Stalinist rank-and-file that Hitler would not be able to remain in power very long, that his regime would collapse, and that the socialist revolution would soon follow.

Trotsky exposed that the political essence of this argument was "cowardice turned inside out," that is, a passive acceptance of the inevitability of a fascist victory. Politically bankrupt, the Stalinists implicitly relied on Hitler

---

15. Trotsky, "What's Next?," *Germany 1931–32*, p. 63.
16. It was established in the 1950s that the two leaders of the German section, Senin and Well, were Stalinist agents. In the 1940s, after emigrating to the United States, they became controllers of a GPU spy ring inside the Socialist Workers Party. Among their prime agents were Sylvia Caldwell, the secretary of SWP founder James P. Cannon, and Joseph Hansen, former secretary of Trotsky in Mexico and later, from 1959 on, the principal leader of the SWP.

to create, through his victory, the best conditions for the socialist revolution! In other words, the Stalinists relinquished to Hitler the task of developing revolutionary consciousness in the working class!

The combined treachery of the Stalinists and the Social Democrats demoralized and paralyzed the German working class. On January 31, 1933, despite the fact that the Nazis themselves had been steadily weakening over the previous months, Hitler came to power at the invitation of the democratic Weimar Republic. The German working class suffered the most catastrophic defeat in the history of the international workers movement without a shot being fired. In the weeks following Hitler's victory, the Social Democratic bureaucrats offered Hitler their most loyal collaboration. As for the Stalinists, their leaders were totally disoriented and paralyzed. Politically and morally discredited in the eyes of the German working class, the Communist Party disintegrated beneath the weight of fascist repression. As for the Social Democrats, despite their pledge of loyalty to the fascist regime, they, too, were outlawed. All independent working-class organizations in Germany were destroyed.

Trotsky wrote that the victory of Hitler meant the end of the German Communist Party:

> It must be said clearly, plainly, openly: Stalinism in Germany has had its August 4. Henceforth, the advanced workers will only speak of the period of the domination of the Stalinist bureaucracy with a burning sense of shame, with words of hatred and curses. The official German Communist Party is doomed. From now on it will only decompose, crumble, and melt into the void. German Communism can be reborn only on a new basis and with a new leadership.[17]

While pronouncing a political death sentence upon the German Stalinist party, Trotsky waited to see whether any section within the Communist International would speak up against the Stalinist betrayal. On April 7, 1933, the Executive Committee of the Comintern declared: "The political line ... followed by the CC of the German Communist Party, with Comrade

---

17. Leon Trotsky, "The Tragedy of the German Proletariat," *The Struggle Against Fascism in Germany* (New York: Pathfinder Press, 1971), pp. 501–02.

Thaelmann at its head, up to the Hitlerite coup, and at the moment when it occurred, was completely correct."[18]

This proclamation signified the utter political degradation of Stalinism. The acceptance of the German catastrophe without any protest meant that the Third International was finished historically as a revolutionary organization of the working class. Stalinism, Trotsky insisted, like Social Democracy in 1914, has passed decisively into the camp of bourgeois counterrevolution. The perspective of seeking to reform the Communist Parties and the Communist International no longer had any validity. The quantitative accumulation of political betrayals had produced a qualitative transformation of Stalinism itself. It had passed from bureaucratic centrism to conscious counterrevolution. On July 15, 1933, Trotsky wrote a historic statement: "It is Necessary to Build Communist Parties and an International Anew."

> Everything that has taken place since March 5: the resolution of the presidium of the ECCI on the situation in Germany; the silent submission of all the sections to this shameful resolution; the antifascist congress in Paris; the official line of the emigre Central Committee of the German Communist Party; the fate of the Austrian Communist Party; the fate of the Bulgarian Communist Party, etc.—all this testifies incontestably that the fate of not only the German Communist Party but also the entire Comintern was decided in Germany.
>
> The Moscow leadership has not only proclaimed as infallible the policy which guaranteed victory to Hitler, but has also prohibited all discussion of what had occurred. And this shameful interdiction was not violated, nor overthrown. No national congresses; no international congress; no discussion at party meetings; no discussion in the press! An organization which was not roused by the thunder of fascism and which submits docilely to such outrageous acts of the bureaucracy demonstrates thereby that it is dead and that nothing can ever revive it. To say this openly and publicly is our direct duty toward the proletariat and its future. In all our subsequent work it is necessary to take

---

18. Jane Degras, ed., *The Communist International 1919–1943, Documents*, Vol. 3 (Royal Institute of International Affairs, 1965), p. 259.

as our point of departure the historical collapse of the official Communist International."[19]

The defeat of the German working class was a world historical experience of the proletariat. There was not a trace of subjectivism in Trotsky's evaluation of the role of Stalinism. It was abstracted from the objective historical development of the class struggle, and in the further development of Trotsky's work, scientifically verified.

Objective social laws

It is of *decisive* importance to understand that Trotsky did not conclude his theoretical work on Stalinism once he had established, on the basis of the German events, its counterrevolutionary role. Nor did he rest content with pointing to the further development of Stalinist treachery after 1933—the Popular Front betrayals in France and Spain, the Moscow Trials, the Stalin-Hitler Pact—to substantiate his indictment of its counterrevolutionary role. *Trotsky set out to discover the objective social laws, from the standpoint of historical materialism, of the degeneration of the first workers state and of the transformation of the Stalinist bureaucracy into the principal agency of imperialism within the international workers movement.* Herein lay the great continuity of Trotsky's work with that of Marx, Engels, and Lenin.

In the aftermath of the collapse of the Second International in 1914, Lenin sought to establish the laws which were manifested in the transformation of the Second International into a bulwark of the imperialist order. As he later wrote, in 1920:

> Unless the economic roots of this phenomenon are understood and its political and social significance is appreciated, not a step can be taken toward the solution of the practical problems of the communist movement and of the impending social revolution.[20]

Accordingly, Lenin traced the degeneration of the Second International to the emergence of imperialism as a specific stage in the development of

---

19. Trotsky, "The Tragedy of the German Proletariat," *The Struggle Against Fascism in Germany*, p. 552.
20. V.I. Lenin, "Imperialism, the highest stage of capitalism," *Collected Works*, Vol. 22 (Moscow: Progress Publishers, 1974), p. 194.

capitalism (the transition from "free" competition to monopoly), in which the super-exploitation of the colonial masses created the super-profits which allowed for the cultivation and bribery of a labor bureaucracy and upper stratum of the working class, transforming them into "real *agents of the bourgeoisie in the working-class* movement, the labour-lieutenants of the capitalist class, real vehicles of reformism and chauvinism. In the civil war between the proletariat and the bourgeoisie they inevitably, and in no small numbers, take the side of the bourgeoisie, the 'Versaillais' against the 'Communards.'"[21]

By discovering the objective historical and economic laws which led Social Democracy into the camp of imperialism, Lenin proved scientifically the necessity for the building of a Third, *Communist* International and exposed the reactionary nature of all attempts to either revive the Second International or straddle the fence between Social Democracy and Communism.

The objective historical necessity for the life-and-death struggle against Stalinism and for the building of the Fourth International was established by Trotsky in *The Revolution Betrayed*. Alongside of Lenin's *Imperialism*, the book constitutes the greatest theoretical conquest of the dialectical materialist method in the twentieth century. It may be said (as Lenin said of Marx's *Capital*) that if Trotsky did not leave behind a *Logic*, he left behind the logic of this monumental analysis of the Stalinist bureaucracy. It is the essential theoretical foundation of the Fourth International and the irrefutable scientific answer to all revisionism.

The Revolution Betrayed uncovers the specific laws governing the emergence, growth, and inevitable destruction of the Soviet bureaucracy. Analyzing the contradictions which govern the existence of the bureaucracy as a privileged *caste* (not class) within a workers state, Trotsky established that the conquests of the 1917 October Revolution could be preserved and extended only through the *political revolution*, in which the Soviet workers overthrew the bureaucracy through a violent insurrection while preserving the nationalized property relations established by the Bolshevik revolution.

Trotsky provided not a formal, but rather a *dialectical* definition of the Soviet regime as *transitional*; that is, a contradictory social phenomenon, between capitalism, which had been overthrown, and socialism, whose construction in the USSR depended on the fate of the world revolution. As Trotsky explained:

---

21. Ibid.

> To define the Soviet regime as transitional, or intermediate, means to abandon such finished social categories as capitalism (and therewith "state capitalism") and also socialism. But besides being completely inadequate in itself, such a definition is capable of producing the mistaken idea that from the present Soviet regime *only* a transition to socialism is possible. In reality a backslide to capitalism is wholly possible ... In the last analysis, the questions will be decided by a struggle of living social forces, both on the national and the world arena.[22]

Trotsky acknowledged that

> Doctrinaires will doubtless not be satisfied with this hypothetical definition. They would like categorical formulae: yes—yes, and no—no. Sociological problems would certainly be simpler, if social phenomena had always a finished character. There is nothing more dangerous, however, than to throw out of reality, for the sake of logical completeness, elements which today violate your scheme and may tomorrow wholly violate it. In our analysis, we have above all avoided doing violence to a dynamic social formation which has had no precedent and knows no analogies. The scientific task, as well as the political, is not to give a finished definition to an unfinished process, but to follow all its stages, separate its progressive from its reactionary tendencies, expose their mutual relations, foresee possible variants of development, and find in this foresight a basis for action.[23]

Dialectical materialist method

And what is this if not the dialectical materialist method? In carefully studying *The Revolution Betrayed*, one cannot fail to be struck by the identity of method which guided Trotsky in his analysis of the Soviet Union, an entirely new social phenomenon—the first workers state in history—and that which guided Marx in his analysis of *Capital*. In the famous review of *Capital*

---

22. Leon Trotsky, *The Revolution Betrayed* (Detroit: Labor Publications, 1991), p. 216.
23. Ibid., pp. 216–17.

published by the *European Messenger* of St. Petersburg, which Marx cited in the Afterword of the Second Edition of Volume One, the writer noted:

> The one thing which is of moment to Marx [and to Trotsky—DN], is to find the law of the phenomena with whose investigation he is concerned; and not only is that law of moment to him, which governs these phenomena, in so far as they have a definite form and mutual connexion within a given historical period. Of still greater moment to him is the law of their variation, of their development, *i.e.*, of their transition from one form into another, from one series of connexions into a different one. This law once discovered, he investigates in detail the effects in which it manifests itself in social life. Consequently, Marx only troubles himself about one thing: to show, by rigid scientific investigation, the necessity of successive determinate orders of social conditions, and to establish, as impartially as possible, the facts that serve him for fundamental starting-points. For this it is quite enough, if he proves, at the same time, both the necessity of the present order of things, and the necessity of another order into which the first must inevitably pass over; and this all the same, whether men believe or do not believe it, whether they are conscious or unconscious of it. Marx treats the social movement as a process of natural history, governed by laws not only independent of human will, consciousness and intelligence, but rather, on the contrary, determining that will, consciousness and intelligence ... [24]

Virtually every word would be appropriate as a description of *The Revolution Betrayed*. Those who seriously and systematically study the writings of Leon Trotsky, and this is essential for the theoretical development of every cadre in the Workers League and the International Committee, will discover the enormous richness of the dialectical method. It would be wrong, of course, to mechanically reduce the whole content of the struggle waged by Trotsky against Stalinism to the question of dialectics versus metaphysics, independent of an examination of the social forces whose interests were, and continue to be, manifested through these historical battles. However,

---

24. Karl Marx, *Capital*, Vol. 1 (New York: International Publishers, 1967), p. 27.

there is no question but that every stage in the development of the struggle against the Stalinist bureaucracy required a deepening of the dialectical materialist method against the subjective idealist metaphysics of the bureaucracy. Philosophy is partisan; that is, theory is a class question. Stalin's eclecticism and idealism, which made him initially vulnerable to the pressures of social forces hostile to the proletariat, became anchored, at a certain point in the development of the world crisis, in the material interests of the Soviet bureaucracy and, thus, of world imperialism.

This was recognized by Trotsky. Class interests and philosophical method were, in his analysis, as dialectically related as the economic base of society to its ideological superstructure. Therefore, those in the petty-bourgeois minority of the Socialist Workers Party who claimed in 1940 that Trotsky "artificially" introduced dialectics into the discussion of "concrete" questions (i.e., the class nature of the Soviet state, the character of the SWP regime), merely demonstrated their own pragmatic superficiality and abysmal ignorance of Trotsky's life work.

From the standpoint of the unrelenting ideological struggle waged by Trotsky against the Stalinist bureaucracy and its leaders and apologists, the whole content of his writings between 1923 until his death on August 21, 1940, could be summed up, as Lenin summed up the forty-year correspondence of Marx and Engels, with the single word, "Dialectics."

III. The Fourth International and the problem of leadership

The founding of the Fourth International in September 1938 represented the culmination of Leon Trotsky's life as a Marxist and proletarian revolutionist. All the events since 1933, when, in the aftermath of the defeat of the German working class by the Nazis, he first issued the call for a new International, had fully confirmed his analysis of Stalinism as the principal and most deadly agency of imperialism within the international workers movement.

Trotsky's *Revolution Betrayed*, completed on the eve of the first round of the Moscow Trials in August 1936, which inaugurated the systematic physical extermination of the entire generation of Bolsheviks who had led the 1917 October Revolution, established the scientific foundations of the world revolutionary perspectives for which he fought.

The defense of the nationalized property relations established by the October Revolution and the regeneration of the USSR was shown to be possible only through the *political revolution*, the armed uprising of the Soviet masses against the counterrevolutionary Kremlin bureaucracy. This political revolution was shown, in turn, to be dependent upon and inseparable from the revival and upsurge of the international revolutionary struggles of the working class in the major capitalist countries and the oppressed colonial masses against world imperialism.

Thus, Trotsky's politics always took as their point of departure considerations of a scientific and principled character. The founding of the Fourth International arose out of objective historical necessity. On the other hand, those centrist elements who opposed the founding of the Fourth International invariably based their arguments on considerations of an utterly subjective nature.

While insisting that they did not disagree with Trotsky's assessment of Stalinism, centrists argued that the launching of the Fourth International was a futile venture. They claimed that the Trotskyist movement was too small and isolated to "proclaim" a new International—apparently forgetting that Lenin issued the call for a Third International when his voice was all but drowned out by the chauvinist proclamations of the leaders of the Second International during the first years of World War I. The centrists warned that the time was not "ripe" for founding the Fourth International, that a new world party could arise only out of great events.

Trotsky replied:

> The Fourth International has already arisen out of great events: the greatest defeats of the proletariat [Germany, Spain] in history. The cause for these defeats is to be found in the degeneration and perfidy of the old leadership. The class struggle does not tolerate an interruption. The Third International, following the Second, is dead for purposes of revolution. Long live the Fourth International.
>
> But has the time yet arrived to proclaim its creation? ... the sceptics are not quieted down. The Fourth International, we answer, has no need of being "proclaimed." It exists and it fights. It is weak? Yes, its ranks are not numerous because it is still young. They are as yet chiefly cadres. But these cadres are pledges for the future. Outside these cadres there does not exist a single revolutionary current on this planet really meriting the name. If our International be still weak in numbers, it is strong

in doctrine, program, tradition, in the incomparable tempering of its cadres. Who does not perceive this today, let him in the meantime stand aside. Tomorrow it will become more evident.[25]

Nature of the imperialist epoch

The difference between Trotsky and his centrist opponents on the question of founding the Fourth International was not merely one of timing. Underlying all the issues which separated them were fundamentally opposed conceptions of the nature of the imperialist epoch.

For the centrists, whose belief in the omnipotence of the existing bureaucracies in the workers movement always set the tone for their essentially verbal support for the socialist revolution, the defeats of the working class during the 1920s and 1930s were seen as a series of essentially unconnected episodes. Insofar as they attempted an explanation, the centrists attributed the defeats to any number of unfavorable objective circumstances. The role of proletarian leadership was only one of many factors. Lurking in the background of such superficial appraisals, though usually left unsaid, was the embittered opinion that the working class was the cause of it own misfortunes and incapable of overthrowing capitalism.

In contrast to this subjective perspective, which led directly to despair and capitulation, Trotsky, through an analysis of the entire historical experience of the working class since the advent of the imperialist epoch, arrived at the following conclusion:

> *The world political situation as a whole is chiefly characterized by a historical crisis of the leadership of the proletariat* [emphasis added].[26]

This passage—the opening sentence of the Transitional Program—is known, one can safely say, to all but the newest members of the Workers League and the sections of the International Committee. But what is, at first glance, *apprehended*, is not necessarily *comprehended*. The utter simplicity and clarity with which Trotsky presented the most profound ideas often leads the

---

25. Leon Trotsky, *The Death Agony of Capitalism and the Tasks of the Fourth International: The Transitional Program* (New York: Labor Publications, 1981), p. 42.
26. Ibid., p. 1.

inattentive reader to pass lightly over insights and truths arrived at by Trotsky after a lifetime of political struggles and sustained theoretical labors. Thus, in considering the significance of the Transitional Program's opening sentence, which immediately advances the fundamental reason for the existence of the Fourth International, it is necessary to understand Trotsky's (and Lenin's) conception of "the nature of the epoch."

A problem which frequently arises is that "the nature of the epoch" is approached simply from the standpoint of certain historically-given contradictions of the world capitalist system from which the inevitability of the socialist revolution is derived. But these contradictions are seen as something quite apart from the revolutionary practical activity of the working class and its conscious leadership. This is a mechanical and therefore false approach. While "objective" and "subjective" factors can be isolated and held apart in our thought for purposes of analysis, these factors are in constant dialectical interaction in the actual development of the class struggle.

Revolutionary leadership

The unique characteristic of this epoch—one in which all the economic prerequisites for the socialist revolution have long ago reached maturity—is the exceptional, i.e., decisive, role of revolutionary leadership. The social revolution is an objective necessity: the conflict between the productive forces and the social relations, between the bourgeois nation state and the world market, has built up the most acute revolutionary tensions within the very structure of capitalist society. But the inevitable explosion engendered by these continuously accumulating tensions can become the socialist revolution only through the conscious intervention of the revolutionary party based on Marxist theory.

However, the development of such a conscious leadership, capable of organizing and leading the assault against capitalist society, does not proceed in a straight line in conformity with the development of the objective contradictions of world imperialism. Sad to say, as the capitalist crisis worsens, the leadership of the proletariat does not automatically improve. The relationship between Party and Class is the most complex and contradictory of all social phenomena—not only because the working class itself is comprised of numerous layers whose political development proceeds unevenly, but also because the bourgeoisie itself intervenes continuously and relentlessly in this process. While sparing no resource to hold the mass of the exploited in utter ideological bondage, the bourgeoisie strives at every point to influence, if not directly control, the political development of the revolutionary vanguard.

The systematic and scientific study of this enormously complex relationship of Party and Class, the development of specific forms of theoretical, political, and organizational warfare against bourgeois domination of the workers movement, really began with the emergence of Bolshevism in Russia at the turn of the twentieth century.

Under the pressure of the First World War and the collapse of the Second International, Lenin was compelled to understand the historical and social roots of opportunism and to extend to the world arena the lessons of his fifteen-year struggle against opportunism in Russia.

Lenin established in 1916 that capitalism had been transformed into imperialism, the highest stage of capitalism on the eve of the socialist revolution. But while formulating the most concrete concept of imperialism ("the concentration of production and capital has developed to such a high stage that it has created monopolies ... the merging of bank capital with industrial capital ... the export of capital as distinguished from the export of commodities ... the formation of international monopolist capitalist associations ... the territorial division of the whole world among the biggest capitalist powers is completed..."[27]), Lenin did not stop at explaining the economic characteristics of this new historical stage. He analyzed the significance of this new epoch in relation to the development of the international workers movement and the worldwide struggle of the oppressed.

Lenin demonstrated that imperialism was synonymous with the corruption of the official leaderships of the working class (i.e., the Second International, the trade union bureaucracy in the United States) and their transformation into the open agents of the bourgeoisie. From this arose the necessity of founding the Third (Communist) International.

In keeping with the changed class relations engendered by imperialism—the unrelenting efforts of the bourgeoisie to subvert the leadership of the working class; the passage of the Second International into the imperialist camp—the Communist International was founded under the banner of ruthless and uncompromising ideological and political struggle against all forms of opportunism. Unlike the parties of the Second International, which not only accepted the presence of a right wing but actually allowed it to grow and exercise control over the organization as a whole, the new parties of the

---

27. V.I. Lenin, "Imperialism, the highest stage of capitalism," *Collected Works*, Vol. 22, p. 266.

Communist International were compelled to wage unceasing warfare against every opportunist element that reared its head.

There was to be no place for an official "opportunist" faction in the Communist International (also known as the Comintern). This was embodied in the twenty-one points for admission to the Third International that were debated and passed at its Second Congress in July–August 1920.

This demand for war against opportunism, written into the statutes of the Comintern, arose from the vast historical experience of the World War and the betrayal of the working class by the Second International. The great political development made by Trotsky himself between 1914 and 1917, when he shed the last vestiges of left centrism and completed his transformation into the revolutionary leader to whom Lenin was to refer as the best Bolshevik, occurred under the impact of the war. Except for Lenin, no other revolutionist made as profound an analysis of the collapse of the Second International.

Like Lenin, though independently of him, Trotsky dealt with the growth of opportunism as an objective social phenomenon. He related opportunism to the historically determined consolidation of the powerful national capitalist states during the latter half of the nineteenth century and the adaptation of the emerging labor movements to these states. As always in Trotsky's writings, a vast knowledge of historical processes provided the content of his theoretical analysis.

The development of the labor movement in England, France, and Germany, Trotsky explained, could not help but be bound up with the economic and political strengthening of the capitalist states of Europe. The historical maturation of these powerful states provided the foundation for the development of national labor movements and also, over a period of many decades, of "socialist" opportunism.

In examining the history of the greatest party of the Second International, the awesome German Social Democracy, Trotsky revealed the social and political mechanism of both its success and its ultimate degradation:

> Theoretically, the German labor movement marched under the banner of Marxism. Still in its dependence on the conditions of the period, Marxism became for the German proletariat not the algebraic formula of the revolution that it was at the beginning, but the theoretic method for adaptation to a national-capitalist state crowned with the Prussian helmet...

The great centralized trade unions of Germany developed in direct dependence upon the development of national industry, adapting themselves to its successes in the home and the foreign markets, and controlling the prices of raw materials and manufactured products. Localized in political districts to adapt itself to the election laws and stretching feelers in all cities and rural communities, the Social Democracy built up the unique structure of the political organization of the German proletariat with its many-branched bureaucratic hierarchy, its one million dues-paying members, its four million voters, ninety-one daily papers and sixty-five party printing presses. This whole many-sided activity, of immeasurable historical importance, was permeated through and through with the spirit of possibilism.

In forty-five years history did not offer the German proletariat a single opportunity to remove an obstacle by a stormy attack, or to capture any hostile position in a revolutionary advance. As a result of the mutual relation of social forces, it was constrained to avoid obstacles or adapt itself to them. In this, Marxism as a theory was a valuable tool for political guidance, but it could not change the opportunist character of the class movement, which in essence was at that time alike in England, France and Germany. ...

Marxism, of course, was not merely something accidental or insignificant in the German labour movement. Yet there would be no basis for deducing the social-revolutionary character of the party from its official Marxist ideology.

Ideology is an important, but not a decisive factor in politics. Its role is that of waiting on politics. That deep-seated contradiction, which was inherent in the awakening revolutionary class on account of its relation to the feudal-reactionary state, demanded an irreconcilable ideology which would bring the whole movement under the banner of social revolutionary aims. Since historical conditions forced opportunist tactics, the irreconcilability of the proletarian class found expression in the revolutionary formulas of Marxism. Theoretically, Marxism reconciled with perfect success the contradiction between reform and revolution. Yet the process of historical development is something far more involved than theorizing in the realm of pure thought. The fact that the class which was revolutionary in its tendencies was forced for several decades to adapt itself to the monarchical police state, based on the tremendous capitalist development of the country, in the course of which adaptation an organization of a million members was built up and a labour bureaucracy which led the entire movement was educated — this fact does not cease to exist and does not lose its weighty significance because Marxism anticipated the revolutionary character of the future movement. Only the most naive ideology could give the same place to this forecast that it does to the political actualities of the German labour movement.[28]

Revisionism was defeated in the German Social Democracy only in the domain of theory. But on the field of practice, it became entrenched and prospered. "The parliamentarians, the unionists, the comrades continued to live and to work in the atmosphere of general opportunism, of practical specializing and of nationalistic narrowness."[29]

Trotsky drew special attention to the political psychology of opportunism:

In default of revolutionary activity as well as the possibility for reformist work, the party spent its entire energy on building up the organization, on gaining new members for the unions and for the party, on starting new papers and getting new subscribers. Condemned for decades to a policy of opportunist waiting, the party took up the cult of organization as an end in itself. Never was the spirit of inertia so strong in the German Social Democracy as in the years immediately preceding the great catastrophe.[30]

Thus, the growth of opportunism was organically linked to the economic and social conditions of pre-1914 Europe, an epoch of "gradualism," of stability, of illusions in the historical viability of capitalism and bourgeois democracy. It was an epoch when the progress of the workers movement

---

28. Leon Trotsky, *The War and the International (1915)* (Oak Park, MI: Mehring Books, 2017), pp. 65–68.
29. Ibid., p. 68.
30. Ibid., p. 71.

was measured over decades, and when the task facing working class leaders seemed to be no more demanding than patiently guiding the movement along the familiar paths of union negotiations, parliamentary debates and holiday rallies.

All these time-honored tactics and staid routines were blown apart by the explosion of imperialist contradictions, whose subterranean development had gone unnoticed by virtually all the leaders of the Second International. Decades of "victory-crowned tactics" led, with the sudden outbreak of war in August 1914, to a political catastrophe of unprecedented historical magnitude. The utterly reactionary political physiognomy of men who had, for decades, claimed to be revolutionaries, was revealed within a few hours. Despite the anti-militarist and anti-imperialist resolutions that had been adopted by the Second International at its Stuttgart Congress in 1907 and at its Basle Congress in 1912, all the major sections of the International were swept along with the chauvinist tide and submitted to the ruling class of their countries.

The political spinelessness of the Second International's leadership was revealed by Victor Adler, the leader of the Austrian Social Democrats, shortly after his country's declaration of war on Serbia. Addressing the Bureau of the Workers' International in Brussels, which had met to discuss the imminent threat of a general European war, Adler stated:

> The war is already upon us. Up to now we have fought against war as well as we could. The workers also did their utmost against the war intrigues. But don't expect any further action from us. ... We have a state of emergency and martial law as a backdrop. I did not come here to address a public meeting, but to tell you the truth, that when hundreds of thousands are already marching to the borders and martial law holds sway at home, no action is possible here.[31]

This was the state of mind that prevailed throughout the International and led each section to vote war credits to finance the imperialist slaughter. Theoretically unprepared and politically bewildered by the abrupt change in the course of political development, the leaders of Social Democracy passed over, inexorably, into the camp of the class enemy.

---

31. Paul Frölich, *Rosa Luxemburg: Ideas in Action* (London: Pluto Press, 1972), p. 208.

"The mistake of the Revisionists," wrote Trotsky, "was not that they confirmed the reformist character of the party's tactics in the past, but that they wanted to perpetuate reformism theoretically and make it the only method of the proletarian class struggle. Thus, the Revisionists failed to take into account the objective tendencies of capitalist development, which by deepening class distinctions must lead to the Social Revolution as the one way to the emancipation of the proletariat."[32]

This historic betrayal by Social Democracy vindicated the profound revolutionary foresight embodied in Lenin's life-long struggle against all forms of revisionist opportunism. Only in Russia, beginning with the Second Congress of the Russian Social Democratic Labor Party (RSDLP), held in 1903, was the struggle against opportunism carried to the point of a split. In 1912, at the Prague Congress, Lenin completed the organizational break with Menshevism through the formal expulsion of the opportunists from the RSDLP. What set Lenin apart from all other leaders of the Social Democracy was his refusal to deal with opportunism as a legitimate tendency within the Marxist movement.

In the German Social Democratic Party, opportunist practice and the theoretical defense of Marxism by such leaders as Kautsky coexisted peacefully. However, it must be said that even in the domain of theory, the struggle was not pursued all too energetically. Kautsky took up the cudgels against Bernstein, who repudiated all the most fundamental propositions of Marxism, only at the insistence of Plekhanov. The latter's demand that Bernstein be expelled from the German party was rejected. The careful boundaries set upon the theoretical struggle against revisionism had definite political roots. Vigorous prosecution of the struggle against revisionism in theory would have led inevitably to direct conflict with opportunism in practice, i.e., with the trade union bureaucrats and parliamentarians whose influence and power within the party were considerable. Such a struggle would have revealed the contradictions within German Social Democracy far in advance of the outbreak of war in 1914.

Herein lay the political significance of Lenin's struggle against revisionism and opportunism. The same organic processes that were eroding the Social Democratic parties of western Europe found expression—though in different forms—within the Russian Social Democratic Labor Party. This was the political content of Menshevism. But that these organic tendencies, which

---

32. Trotsky, *The War and the International*, p. 68.

nourished revisionism, did not vanquish the Russian Social Democracy is explained by the war waged by Lenin against all forms of opportunism which tended to fortify or passively reflect bourgeois consciousness in the working class.

Thus, in the entire process of its ideological, political, and organizational development, Bolshevism proved to be the conscious expression of the proletariat's historical tasks in the new imperialist epoch of wars and revolutions.

In combating all forms of bourgeois ideology in the workers movement and in drawing the most uncompromising political and organizational conclusions from these struggles, Bolshevism gave a finished historical form to the proletariat's revolutionary role.

It was this which Trotsky himself came to realize in the aftermath of the collapse of the Second International. For all its profound insights into the origins of opportunism in the European labor movement, *War and the International* did not yet provide an answer to the fundamental question: exactly how are the organic tendencies toward opportunism, generated by the whole pressure of imperialism upon the workers movement and the systematic corruption of the existing leadership of the working class organizations, to be combated? The answer to this question was given in the theory and practice of Bolshevism.

As Trotsky later wrote:

> Gradually I reappraised my view of the relations between party and class and between revolutionary action and the proletarian organization. Under the impact of the social-patriotic treachery of international Menshevism, I came, step by step, to the conclusion that there was a need not only for ideological struggle against Menshevism (which I had earlier recognized—though to be sure with insufficient consistency) but also for an uncompromising organizational break with it. This reappraisal was not accomplished in one sitting. In my articles and speeches during the war one may find both inconsistency and backward steps. Lenin was absolutely right when he opposed any and every manifestation of centrism on my part, emphasizing them and even intentionally exaggerating them. But if the period of the war is taken as a whole, it becomes quite clear that the terrible humiliation of socialism at the beginning of the war was a turning point for me from centrism to Bolshevism—in all questions without

exception. And as I worked out a more and more correct, i.e., Bolshevik, conception of the relations between class and party, between theory and politics, and between politics and organization, my general revolutionary point of view toward bourgeois society was naturally filled with a more vital and realistic content.

From the moment when I clearly saw that a struggle to the death against defensism was absolutely necessary, Lenin's position came through to me with full force. What had seemed to me to be "splitterism," "disruption," etc., now appeared as a salutary and incomparably farsighted struggle for the revolutionary independence of the proletarian party. Not only Lenin's political methods and organizational techniques, but also his entire political and human personality appeared to me in a new light, in the light of Bolshevism, that is, in a truly Leninist light. One can understand and recognize Lenin for what he is only after becoming a Bolshevik.[33]

The advent of the imperialist epoch, the outbreak of World War I, and the disintegration, almost overnight, of the Second International lay bare, for the first time, an historical crisis of revolutionary leadership in the working class. In searching for the revolutionary answer to this crisis, Trotsky came to understand the political and historical implications of Bolshevism at a level exceeded only by Lenin himself. That is why, in 1917, Trotsky joined the Bolshevik Party, and was immediately propelled into the forefront of its general staff, and, in October, as chairman of the Military-Revolutionary Committee, organized the armed insurrection and the seizure of state power by the working class.

IV. The training of cadre and the conquest of power

At each of the first four congresses of the Communist International—those held while Lenin was still alive and politically active—Leon Trotsky insisted that the central historical lesson of the 1917 October Revolution and a fundamental characteristic of the imperialist epoch was the decisive role of

---

33. Leon Trotsky, "Our Differences," *Challenge of the Left Opposition [1923–25]* (New York: Pathfinder Press, 1975, 2017), pp. 342–43.

revolutionary Marxist leadership in the *preparation* of the socialist revolution and the seizure of state power by the working class.

Based on the concrete historical experience of the working class in Russia and on an international scale, Trotsky elaborated the conception that the fate of the socialist revolution for a number of years—and even for decades—can hinge on the decisions made by the leadership of a Marxist party in the course of a few days.

The concept of *cadre training* and of the role of the International was invested with a new historical content. In direct contrast to the outlook of the Second International—unstated but implicit in all its theoretical and practical work—the Communist International proceeded from the fundamental premise that the socialist revolution could not be left to the inexorable working out of abstractly conceived objective economic forces and social contradictions. The leaders of the revolutionary parties of the Comintern (as the Communist International was known) had to recognize that their subjective practice was a decisive *objective link* in the chain of historical events leading to the overthrow of capitalism.

Following this conception to its logical and most concrete conclusion, it meant that at a definite point, identified by Marxists, in the development of a revolutionary crisis in different capitalist countries, the question of the armed insurrection would arise as a specific item on the agendas of the leading committees of communist parties. Then, a definite date would have to be set and a plan of action prepared for the overthrow of the capitalist state.

The historic task of the Comintern was to train an international cadre in the leadership in its sections capable of fulfilling this task. From this standpoint, Trotsky conceived of the Communist International as a "school of revolutionary strategy." These conclusions, with which Lenin concurred, arose out of Trotsky's profound conception of the nature and tasks of the imperialist epoch. Like all the great masters of the dialectical materialist method, Trotsky's theoretical work always embodied a *summing up* of the living experiences of the class struggle, scientifically refracted through the concepts of historical materialism. He examined every important movement of the masses, always seeking to discover within each new form of the class struggle the operating dialectical laws governing the development of the socialist revolution. The method of Trotsky was that of Marx, who, as Lenin wrote, "studied the *birth* of the new society *out of* the old, and the forms of transition from the latter to the former, as a natural-historical process. He examined the actual experience of a mass proletarian movement and tried to draw practical lessons from it."[34]

The political work of the Bolshevik Party in 1917, from the time of Lenin's arrival in Petrograd in April through to the seizure of power in October, was conducted under the banner of the World Socialist Revolution. As Lenin told the delegates at the crucial April Conference of the Bolshevik Party, at which the decisive shift was made (in opposition to Stalin) from a policy of support to the bourgeois Provisional Government to the preparation of the seizure of power:

> The great honour of beginning the revolution has fallen to the Russian proletariat. But the Russian proletariat must not forget that its movement and revolution are part of a world revolutionary proletarian movement, which in Germany, for example, is gaining momentum with every passing day. Only from this angle can we define our tasks."[35]

The conception that socialism could be built in Russia independently of the overthrow of capitalism in Western Europe and throughout the world was never suggested in 1917. Within the leadership of the Bolshevik Party, it was an unchallengeable assumption and the basis of all its strategical considerations that the fate of the Russian Revolution depended upon events in the west. The greatest emphasis was placed, therefore, on the founding of the Third International to guide the victory of the World Socialist Revolution.

The revolutionary optimism of the Bolshevik leaders was justified. The Bolshevik victory landed like a stick of dynamite amid the explosive class contradictions that had been mounting throughout the imperialist war.

Revolution in Germany

In November 1918, revolution erupted in Germany, forcing the emperor to flee, raising the Social Democrats to power, and bringing about the end of World War I. In March 1919, a Soviet Republic was proclaimed in Hungary. Later that year, the great steel strike shook the United States. In September

---

34. V.I. Lenin, "The State and Revolution," *Collected Works*, Vol. 25 (Moscow: Progress Publishers, 1974), p. 430.

35. V.I. Lenin, Speech delivered to the seventh all-Russia conference of the RSDLP (B), *Collected Works*, Vol. 24, p. 227.

1920, an immense movement of the Italian working class culminated in the seizure of the factories and mills. In December 1920, Czechoslovakia was convulsed by mass strikes.

Despite the unprecedented historical magnitude of the revolutionary movement, especially in Europe, nowhere was the working class able to emulate successfully the example of the Soviet proletariat. In Germany, the uprising of the Spartakus movement was suppressed, and its leaders, Rosa Luxemburg and Karl Liebknecht, were murdered on January 15, 1919 with the approval of the Social Democratic regime. In March, the counterrevolution, with the blessings of the Second International, overthrew the Munich Soviet Government, and its leader, Levine, was executed. The Hungarian Soviet Republic, led by Bela Kun, was overthrown within a month. In Italy, the workers' offensive stopped short of a seizure of power. The fascists mounted a counter-offensive that was to bring Mussolini to power.

In 1919, the bourgeoisie of all the major European countries had thought that its overthrow was imminent. By the end of 1920, as the revolutionary wave receded, the bourgeoisie grew increasingly self-confident. *On the basis of the defeats inflicted upon the working class*, a period of political and economic stabilization set in. These developments, however tragic in their immediate consequences, were of enormous educational significance for the Communist International. They confirmed, from the side of the negative—that is, from adversity and disappointment—the essential historical significance of Bolshevism as the *indispensable* prerequisite for the victory of the socialist revolution; they deepened the theoretical insight of the Comintern into the dialectic of the imperialist epoch.

In a speech delivered in July 1921, at the very conclusion of the Third Congress of the Communist International, Trotsky spoke before the General Party Membership of the Moscow Organization:

> Some comrades have a far too simplified approach to the victory of the proletariat. There obtains today not alone in Europe but on a world scale a situation which permits us, from the standpoint of Marxism, to say with complete assurance that the bourgeois system has completely drained itself. The world productive forces cannot develop further within the framework of bourgeois society... But does this mean that the doom of the bourgeoisie is automatically and mechanically predetermined? No. The bourgeoisie is a living class which has risen on specific economic, productive foundations. This class is not a passive product of economic

development, but a living, dynamic, active historical force. This class has outlived itself, i.e., has become the most fearsome brake upon historical development. But this must not at all be taken to mean that this class is prone to historical suicide, that it is ready to say, "Since the scientific theory of historical development finds me reactionary, therefore I leave the scene." Of course, there cannot even be talk of this. On the other hand, the recognition by the Communist Party of the fact that the bourgeois class is condemned and subject to elimination is likewise far from sufficient to assure the victory of the proletariat. No, the bourgeoisie must still be defeated and overthrown!...

The bourgeoisie, even though it finds itself in a complete contradiction with the demands of historical progress, nevertheless still remains the most powerful class. More than that, it may be said that politically the bourgeoisie attains its greatest powers, its greatest concentration of forces and resources, of political and military means of deception, of coercion, and provocation, i.e., the flowering of its class strategy, at the moment when it is most immediately threatened by social ruin...

From a superficial standpoint there appears to be some sort of contradiction here: We have brought the bourgeoisie for judgment before the court of Marxism, i.e., the court of scientific knowledge of the historical process, and found it obsolete, and yet at the same time the bourgeoisie discloses a colossal vitality. In reality there is no contradiction here at all. This is what Marxism calls the dialectic...

Europe and the whole world are passing through a period which is, on the one side, an epoch of disintegration of the productive forces of bourgeois society, and, on the other side, an epoch of the highest flowering of the counter-revolutionary strategy of the bourgeoisie. We must understand this clearly and precisely. Counter-revolutionary strategy, i.e., the art of waging a combined struggle against the proletariat by every method from saccharine, professorial-clerical preachments to machine-gunning of strikers, has never attained such heights as it does today.[36]

---

36. *First Five Years of the Communist International*, Vol. 2 (London: New Park Publications, 1974), pp. 3–6.

This supremely conscious response of the world bourgeoisie to the October Revolution found its most brutal expression in the assassination of Luxemburg and Liebknecht. The one overriding lesson which the ruling class of *all* capitalist countries extracted from the victory of the October Revolution was that the emerging leaders and most promising cadre of the maturing social revolutions must be eliminated in advance of the future Octobers. Provocations, infiltrations, disruptions, assassinations: these methods became after 1917 the stock-in-trade of the world bourgeoisie.

The political conclusion drawn by Trotsky from this analysis sixty-one years ago has lost none of its relevance:

> The task of the working class—in Europe and throughout the world—consists in counterposing to the thoroughly thought-out counter-revolutionary strategy of the bourgeoisie its own revolutionary strategy, likewise thought out to the end.[37]

State-ism

Two interconnected characteristics, both bound up with the decay of the productive forces, the ever-more diseased nature of imperialist economic parasitism, were especially stressed by Trotsky: the phenomenon of *State-ism* and the putrefaction of bourgeois democracy.

In the Manifesto of the First Congress of the Comintern, Trotsky wrote:

> Finance capital, which plunged mankind into the abyss of war, itself underwent a catastrophic change in the course of this war. The dependency of paper money upon the material foundation of production has been completely disrupted. Progressively losing its significance as the means and regulator of capitalist commodity circulation, paper money became transformed into an instrument of requisition, of seizure and military–economic violence in general.
>
> The debasement of paper money reflects the general mortal crisis of capitalist commodity circulation. During the decades preceding the war, free competition, as the regulator of production and distribution, had already been thrust aside in the main

---

37. Ibid., p. 7.

fields of economic life by the system of trusts and monopolies; during the course of the war the regulating-directing role was torn from the hands of these economic groups and transferred directly into the hands of the military-state power. The distribution of raw materials, the utilization of Baku or Rumanian oil, Donbas coal, Ukranian wheat, the fate of German locomotives, freight cars and automobiles, the rationing of relief for starving Europe—all these fundamental questions of the world's economic life are not being regulated by free competition, nor by associations of national and international trusts and consortiums, but by the direct application of military force, for the sake of its continued preservation. If the complete subjection of the state power to the power of finance capital had led mankind into the imperialist slaughter, then through this slaughter finance capital has succeeded in completely militarizing not only the state but also itself; and it is no longer capable of fulfilling its basic economic functions otherwise than by means of blood and iron...

The state-ization of economic life, against which capitalist liberalism used to protest so much, has become an accomplished fact. There is no turning back from this fact—it is impossible to return not only to free competition but even to the domination of trusts, syndicates and other economic octopuses. Today the one and only issue is: Who shall henceforth be the bearer of state-ized production—the imperialist state or the state of the victorious proletariat?

In other words: Is all toiling mankind to become the bond slaves of victorious world cliques who, under the firm-name of the League of Nations and aided by an "international" army and "international" navy, will here plunder and strangle some peoples and there cast crumbs to others, while everywhere and always shackling the proletariat—with the sole object of maintaining their own rule? Or shall the working class of Europe and of the advanced countries in other parts of the world take in hand the disrupted and ruined economy in order to assure its regeneration upon socialist principles?[38]

---

38. *First Five Years of the Communist International*, Vol. 1, pp. 46–47.

It seems superfluous to comment on the exceptional applicability of this analysis to the conditions of present-day imperialism. One need only point out that compared to the gargantuan dimensions of contemporary imperialist state-ism, this phenomenon, in 1919, was merely in its larva stage. As for Trotsky's characterization of the financial and political life of imperialism, it could be mistaken for a summing up of the last decade:

> Capitalism has degenerated in the course of the war. The systematic extraction of surplus value from the process of production—the foundation of profit economy—seems far too boresome an occupation to Messrs. Bourgeois who have become accustomed to double and decuple their capital within a couple of days by means of speculation, and on the basis of international robbery.
>
> The bourgeois has shed certain prejudices which used to hamper him, and has acquired certain habits which he did not formerly possess. The war has inured him to subjecting a whole number of countries to a hunger-blockade, to bombarding from the air and setting fire to cities and villages, expediently spreading the bacilli of cholera, carrying dynamite in diplomatic pouches, counterfeiting his opponent's currency; he has become accustomed to bribery, espionage and smuggling on a hitherto unequaled scale. The usages of war have been taken over, after the conclusion of peace, as the usages of commerce. The chief commercial operations are fused nowadays with the functions of the state, which steps to the fore as a world robber gang equipped with all the implements of violence.
>
> The narrower the world's productive basis, all the more savage and more wasteful the methods of appropriation [of surplus value].[39]

The speeches and articles prepared by Leon Trotsky during the first four Comintern congresses are masterpieces of the political literature of Marxism. As examples of the historical materialist method in action, they rank with Marx's own historical address of May 1871 on the Civil War in France. Such works are ever green. But it must be emphasized that Trotsky is of our epoch,

---

39. Ibid., p. 138.

and his writings remain *irreplaceable* and *indispensable*, not only as the theoretical and political foundation of a Marxist strategy for the World Socialist Revolution but even for an intelligent understanding of the daily events of modern political life.

Marxism in the Imperialist Epoch

We are not simply paying tribute to the genius of Trotsky. What we consider essential is the historical content of his work and that of Lenin as the expression of the development of Marxism in the imperialist epoch. The split with the Second International was fundamental. The Bolsheviks declared war not only on its politics but on its philosophical outlook as well. If examined through the method of its leading theoretician, Kautsky, it is clear that the Second International's historic capitulation to imperialism was bound up with its vulgarization and revision of Marxism. Bolshevism's entire conception of Marxism—the only conception—could not be reconciled with its dissolution by Kautsky and other theoreticians of the Second International into a scholastic method of passive commentary on historical events. This method, despite its formal identification with Marxism, was fundamentally antithetical to its revolutionary essence. As Trotsky wrote:

> Kautsky is the founder and the most perfect representative of the Austrian forgery of Marxism. While the real teaching of Marx is the theoretical formula of action, of attack, of the development of revolutionary energy, and of the carrying of the class blow to its logical conclusion, the Austrian school was transformed into an academy of passivity and evasiveness ... and reduced its work to explaining and justifying, not guiding and overthrowing. It lowered itself to the position of a handmaid to the current demands of parliamentarism and opportunism, replaced dialectic by swindling sophistries, and, in the end, in spite of its great play with ritual revolutionary phraseology, became transformed into the most secure buttress of the capitalist State, together with the altar and throne that rose above it.[40]

---

40. Leon Trotsky, *Terrorism and Communism* (London: New Park Publications, 1975), p.183 [FN 40].

Characteristic of the leading theoreticians of the Second International, the "misfortune" of such thinkers as Plekhanov and Kautsky was their "inability to apply dialectics to the Bildertheorie [theory of reflection], to the process and development of knowledge."[41]

This "misfortune" permeated the theoretical work and political lives of the leaders of the Second International in Western Europe. While accepting the formal conclusions of the materialist conception of history, the study of its scientific concepts was detached from their philosophical moorings in the dialectical materialist theory of knowledge. The use of historical materialist concepts—such as *state, class, production relations, imperialism*—was relegated to the application of certain fixed formulas and definitions learned by rote.

Social practice

This method is the opposite of Marxism, which studies the historical evolution of all categories and concepts, not as products of the brain nor as emanations of an "absolute spirit," but as the reflections in the minds of social men of objective properties and relations existing within nature and society. These reflections arise not in the course of passive contemplation, but, as Marx proved, as a result of objective social practice, in the historically-determined interaction of man and nature. By placing social practice at the center of its theory of knowledge, having extracted the rational core of the Hegelian dialectic from its idealist form, Marx was able, for the first time in the history of philosophy, to establish scientifically the relation between matter and thought, object and subject, and practice and theory.

Man cognizes the world in the social process of changing it. The forms of his thinking are produced and conditioned by the growth of the productive forces and the social relations which arise therefrom. Man's cognition of the laws of nature *and* society, understood scientifically, as an historically developing *social* process, cannot be reduced to the one-sided (from object to subject), passive, and mirror-like reflection of nature in human thought. Cognition and practice constitute a unity of opposites, each influencing and shaping the other, in accordance with the dialectical laws governing the social process of production, which gives rise to the whole vast superstructure of ideology and politics.

---

41. Lenin, *Collected Works*, Vol. 38, p. 360.

The passive and contemplative "Marxism" of the Second International was not Marxism at all. It was a recrudescence of the old mechanical materialism that Marx himself had criticized and overthrown in his "Theses on Feuerbach":

> The chief defect of all previous materialism (that of Feuerbach included) is that things, reality, sensuousness are conceived only in the form of the *object, or of contemplation*, but not as *sensuous human activity, practice*, not subjectively ... Hence he [Feuerbach] does not grasp the significance of "revolutionary", of "practical-critical", activity.[42]

In his autobiography, *My Life*, recalling the deep political gulf he perceived between himself and the leaders of the Second International, even *before* 1914, Trotsky remarked about the Austrian Social Democratic leader, Karl Renner (later chancellor of Austria, and, finally, before his death at a suitably Biblical age, a staunch ally of the United States): He was "as far from revolutionary dialectics as the most conservative Egyptian pharoah."

This was not merely a passing observation. Trotsky had detected the connection between the passivity of the Social Democratic leaders, their incapacity for decisive revolutionary action, their distrust of the masses, their implicit faith in the durability of the capitalist order, and their indifference toward the dialectic, the mainspring of revolutionary Marxism. Renner, it might be noted, was a devout Kantian, the author of the *Theory of Capitalist Economy*, who attacked the dialectical method employed by Marx in *Capital*.

The method of thought with which Renner was identified had long before been criticized by Hegel, who noted the fundamental defect of Kantian philosophy and the old, mechanical materialism:

> Hitherto, the Notion of Logic has rested on the separation, presupposed once and for all in the ordinary consciousness, of the *content* of cognition and its *form* ... it is assumed that the material of knowing is present on its own account as a ready-made world apart from thought, that thinking on its own is empty and

---

42. Karl Marx, "Theses on Feuerbach," *Marx-Engels Collected Works*, Vol. 5 (London: Lawrence & Wishart, 2010), p. 3.

comes as an external form to the said material, fills itself with it and only thus acquires a content and so becomes real knowing.⁴³

Translated into ordinary English, Hegel's attack is directed against the mechanical conception, often mistaken for materialism, that ignores the active role of the forms of man's thinking, activated and applied in practice, in the cognition of the external world. It is this *active* side of cognition whose discovery Marx credited to idealism, principally that of Hegel. However, it was discovered only in an *abstract* form. That is, the only activity acknowledged by Hegel was the activity of pure thought, embodied in the logical categories and concepts, of which human activity was merely a predicate.

When reworked materialistically ("standing Hegel on his feet"), this "active side" of cognition, arising out of and guiding the objective social practice of men engaged in the class struggle, becomes the scientific method of both the analysis and revolutionary transformation of the world. "The philosophers have only *interpreted* the world in various ways; the point is to *change* it." This conclusion, drawn by Marx in his eleventh thesis on Feuerbach, is not, as academic falsifiers have at times suggested, a renunciation of philosophical work and a simple invocation of practical action. It is, rather, a concise summing up, on the basis of vast theoretical labors, of that essential relation between cognition and revolutionary practice, without which scientific knowledge of the objective world of the class struggle is impossible.

This issue is hardly the esoteric matter it might at first seem. Its "practical" implications were very much in evidence in all the struggles raging within the Bolshevik Party in 1917, as Lenin fought to orient the Bolshevik Party, against enormous opposition, to the seizure of state power. The high point of the political struggle within the Bolshevik Party came in October 1917, when Lenin's closest collaborators in the period of exile, Kamenev and Zinoviev, came out against the overthrow of the bourgeois Provisional Government.

Their arguments against a Bolshevik-led insurrection were quoted by Trotsky in *Lessons of October*:

> Whoever intends to do more than merely talk about an insurrection, is duty bound to weigh its chances soberly. And, here

---

43. G.W.F. Hegel, *Science of Logic* (New Jersey: Humanities Press, 1990) p. 44.

> we feel that it is our duty to say that at the present moment the greatest harm can result from underestimating the enemy forces and exaggerating our own. The forces of the enemy are greater than they appear. Petrograd will decide—but in Petrograd the enemies of the proletarian party have concentrated considerable forces: 5,000 Junkers, splendidly equipped and organized and, by virtue of their class position, eager and able to fight; and then the army headquarters; and then the shock troops, and then the Cossacks; and then a strong section of the garrison; and then there is a very strong section of the artillery deployed fanwise round Petrograd. Moreover, our enemies, with the help of the All-Russian Central Executive of the Soviets, will almost certainly attempt to bring troops from the front.[44]

The above paragraph is a classic example of the inability to grasp "the significance of 'revolutionary,' of 'practical-critical,' activity." The assessment of Zinoviev and Kamenev was based on an utterly one-sided, passive, and mechanical examination of the contending forces. The numerical strength of the enemy was summed up arithmetically. On the basis of a formal comparison, the position of the proletariat appeared hopeless.

> Two weeks prior to our bloodless victory in Petrograd—and we could have gained it even two weeks earlier—experienced party politicians saw arrayed against us the Junkers, eager and able to fight, and the shock troops, and the Cossacks, and a strong section of the garrison and the artillery, deployed fanwise and the troops arriving from the front. But in reality all this came to nothing; in round figures, zero ... Never tested in the fire of insurrection, these forces would have seemed immeasurably more terrible than they proved in action. Here is the lesson which must be burned into the consciousness of every revolutionist![45]

---

44. Leon Trotsky, "On the Current Situation," *Lessons of October* (London: New Park Publications), p. 36.
45. Ibid., p. 38.

Lessons of October

The "Lessons of October" were incorporated by Trotsky into the strategical revolutionary work of the Communist International. The recognition of the decisive role of revolutionary leadership and the indispensability of the dialectical method comprise the fundamental and interconnected themes of virtually all his great contributions to the training of its cadre—a training aborted by the growth of bureaucracy and the disorientation and, finally, the destruction of the Communist International. However, Trotsky's contributions remain a vast treasure of revolutionary experience, knowledge, and insights vital for the training of cadre today.

> While Marxism teaches that class relations arise in the process of production and that these relations correspond to a certain level of productive forces; while Marxism further teaches that all forms of ideology and, first and foremost, politics correspond to class relations, this does not mean that between politics, class groupings and production there exist simply mechanical relations, calculable by the four rules of arithmetic. On the contrary, the reciprocal relations are extremely complex. It is possible to interpret dialectically the course of a country's development, including its revolutionary development, only by proceeding from the action, reaction and interaction of all material and superstructural factors, national and worldwide alike, and not through superficial juxtapositions, or through formal analogies."[46]

Under the leadership of Lenin and Trotsky, the dialectical method, treated as a "dead dog" by Kautsky and the majority of the Social Democratic leaders, was revived, enriched, and restored to its rightful place in the Communist International—as the methodological foundation of the science of Marxist strategy, political perspectives, and revolutionary action. In an epoch of civil wars, of abrupt "overnight" changes in the political situation, of day-to-day shifts in the relations of class forces on a world scale, of sudden movements on the political battlefield from left to right and from right to left, only the dialectical method has been proven equal to the historical task of the proletariat.

---

46. *First Five Years of the Communist International*, Vol. l, p. 77.

As Marx would have written: dialectics is not a lancet for academic debate but a weapon of class war. It is not the passion of the head; it is the head of revolutionary passion. It is in this spirit that the International Committee of the Fourth International trains the cadre of the World Trotskyist movement today.

Вождь Красной армии.
Председатель Революционного Военного Совета Республики
и Народный Комиссар по военным и морским делам
Лев Давидович Троцкий.

2

An Intellectual Pygmy Denounces Trotsky

In periods of political reaction, innumerable forms of social backwardness, ignorance, and stupidity come into their own. All the official organs of public opinion exude an unpleasant smell. Enjoying the protection of the powers that be, reassured by the debased state of intellectual life, and reasonably confident that no one will have the opportunity to protest as they pass wind in public, contemporary "opinion makers" feel no shame about what they say or write.

One product of this foul climate is a vituperative denunciation of Leon Trotsky that appears unexpectedly in the midst of a review by Theodore Dalrymple of a new book by Christopher Hitchens. Published in the weekend edition of the *Financial Times*, Dalrymple's review objects bitterly to a chapter in Hitchens' book that offers a somewhat admiring portrait of Leon Trotsky.[1]

Dalrymple, who regularly contributes columns to the right-wing *Spectator* magazine in Britain, cannot abide Hitchens' acknowledgment that Trotsky was, at the very least, a great writer.

Despite the fact that Hitchens has broken with his radical past and repackaged himself as a supporter of the Bush administration and the war in Iraq, Dalrymple is angered by what he sees as Hitchens' lingering ambivalence toward the leader of the Russian Revolution.

Published on the World Socialist Web Site, August 2, 2005.
1. Theodore Dalrymple, "Reader, He Harried Me," *Financial Times*, July 30, 2005.

"Trotsky was a moral monster," thunders Dalrymple. To make favorable references to the literary skills of such a man, he proclaims, "is roughly the equivalent to making Hitler out to have been principally, and most memorably, a lover of animals, as indicated by his affection for his Alsatian, Blondi, or a lover of nature because he once posed for photographs in the open air dressed in lederhosen."

Dalrymple continues: "The fact that Trotsky was a talented phrasemaker or literary stylist is rather beside the point. He was a mass murderer who wanted to enslave the world all at once and forever, instead of steadily, bit by bit, as Stalin did. All this is ignored, in the name of a completely inadequate and fundamentally primitive theory."

An attack of this sort assumes that the reader knows absolutely nothing about the subject being dealt with. The comparison of Trotsky to Hitler is not only disgusting, it exhibits an abysmal ignorance of basic historical facts. No one perceived more clearly the dangers of fascism or did more to rally the German and international working class against this threat than Leon Trotsky. When no small number of British bourgeois politicians were coquetting with Hitler, looking upon him as a potential ally against the Soviet Union, Trotsky summed up the significance of Nazism:

> Fascism has opened up the depths of society for politics. ... Everything that should have been eliminated from the national organism in the form of cultural excrement in the course of the normal development of society has now come gushing out from the throat; capitalist society is puking up the undigested barbarism. Such is the physiology of National Socialism.[2]

Thirty or forty years ago, not to mention in his own lifetime, a description of Trotsky as a "talented phrasemaker" would have been read by a politically educated public as a rather crass understatement—something like describing Matisse, Picasso, or Rivera as gifted doodlers. Except among the politically pathological haters of Trotsky—the Stalinists and the fascist anti-Semites—it was commonly accepted that Leon Trotsky ranked among the greatest literary figures of the twentieth century. This was, by the way, the opinion of some of Trotsky's most brilliant contemporaries. We find,

---

2. Leon Trotsky, "What is National Socialism?," *The Struggle Against Fascism in Germany* (New York: Pathfinder, 2004), p. 468.

An Intellectual Pygmy Denounces Trotsky 61

for example, the following entry for June 3, 1931 in the diary of Walter Benjamin:

> The previous evening, a conversation with [Bertholt] Brecht, [Bernhard von] Brentano, and Hesse[-Burri] in the Café du Centre. The conversation turned to Trotsky; Brecht maintained that there were good reasons for thinking that Trotsky was the greatest living European writer. We exchanged episodes from his books.[3]

Brecht, Benjamin, Brentano, and Hesse-Burri understood what Dalrymple clearly doesn't: that there is a vast difference between being a "talented phrasemaker" and "the greatest living European writer." The former can help Madison Avenue sell products, or even satisfy the limited intellectual needs of an ill-informed consumer of newspaper columns. The latter exercises immense cultural and moral influence on humanity.

Trotsky's greatness as a writer expressed his stature as a thinker, a man whose ideas commanded the attention and respect of a worldwide audience long after he had lost all the overt trappings of political power.

One has only to read Dalrymple's clumsy reference to "a completely inadequate and fundamentally primitive theory" to recognize at once that he knows nothing of Trotsky's writings, and that he has not the slightest inkling of the issues at stake in Trotsky's struggle against Stalinism. Which of Trotsky's books has Dalrymple read? Of the scores of volumes attributed to Trotsky, one doubts that Dalrymple has read even one.

Let us compare Dalrymple's banal and imbecilic reference to Trotsky's "inadequate and fundamentally primitive theory" to a description of the latter's work in a book about Trotsky published thirty-two years ago by Prentice-Hall, which was then a leading supplier of text books used in an academic environment. Trotsky was included in its "Great Lives Observed" series. Describing Trotsky as "one of the giants of the first half of the twentieth century," the introduction to this volume offers this assessment of his theoretical work:

> His analysis of social forces in Imperial Russia and his development of the idea of "permanent revolution" suggest that as a

---

3. Walter Benjamin, *Selected Writings*, Volume 2, 1927–1934 (Cambridge, MA: Harvard University Press, 2001), p. 477.

Marxist thinker he could, on the power of his own creativity, go beyond the formulations of Marx and Engels. In that sense his theoretical contributions rank him with that old but brilliant coterie of Marxist theorists such as Plekhanov, Kautsky, Luxemburg, and for that matter Lenin himself.[4]

As for Dalrymple's characterization of Trotsky as a "moral monster," one must wonder what criteria he employs in arriving at this judgment. Trotsky was a revolutionist. He viewed class struggle not as one of many means that might be employed in the pursuit of political ends, but as an ontological reality of human society. Within this framework, he adhered to the sternest of moral codes: one in which the actions of the individual are judged in relation to the objective interests of the working class and its struggle against exploitation and all forms of oppression and injustice.

Trotsky—who sacrificed everything in defense of the revolutionary principles he proclaimed, who gave his own life in the fight against the Stalinist betrayal of the Russian Revolution—left behind a statement of his moral creed:

> A means can be justified only by its end. But the end in its turn needs to be justified. From the Marxist point of view, which expresses the historical interests of the proletariat, the end is justified if it leads to increasing the power of man over nature and to the abolition of the power of man over man.
>
> "We are to understand then that in achieving this end anything is permissible?" sarcastically demands the Philistine, demonstrating that he understood nothing. That is permissible, we answer, which really leads to the liberation of mankind. Since this end can be achieved only through revolution, the liberating morality of the proletariat of necessity is endowed with a revolutionary character. It irreconcilably counteracts not only religious dogma but every kind of idealistic fetish, these philosophic gendarmes of the ruling class. It deduces a rule for conduct from the laws of the development of society, thus primarily from the class struggle, this law of all laws.

---

4. *Great Lives Observed: Trotsky* (Englewood Cliffs, NJ: Prentice-Hall, 1973), p. 1.

> "Just the same," the moralist continues to insist, "does it mean that in the class struggle against capitalists all means are permissible: lying, frame-up, betrayal, murder, and so on?" Permissible and obligatory are those and only those means, we answer, which unite the revolutionary proletariat, fill their hearts with irreconcilable hostility to oppression, teach them contempt for official morality and its democratic echoers, imbue them with consciousness of their own historic mission, raise their courage and spirit of self-sacrifice in the struggle. Precisely from this it flows that not all means are permissible. When we say that the end justifies the means, then for us the conclusion follows that the great revolutionary end spurns those base means and ways which set one part of the working class against other parts, or attempt to make the masses happy without their participation, or lower the faith of the masses in themselves and their organization, replacing it by worship for the "leaders." Primarily and irreconcilably, revolutionary morality rejects servility in relation to the bourgeoisie and haughtiness in relation to the toilers, that is, those characteristics in which petty-bourgeois pedants and moralists are thoroughly steeped.[5]

It is, of course, possible to oppose on philosophical grounds Trotsky's rejection of Kant's categorical imperative as the basis for evaluating the legitimacy of one or another political action. Among Trotsky's most determined opponents was the American philosopher John Dewey. But it would have never occurred to Dewey, a man of the greatest intellectual integrity, to describe Trotsky as a "moral monster."

It would have been pointless and ethically impossible to serve as the chairman of a commission established to investigate the charges made by the Stalinist regime against Trotsky if the latter was, by the very nature of his political life, a moral criminal. Though he disagreed with the Marxian world view, Dewey understood all too well that issues of great principle were at stake in defending Trotsky's reputation, his "revolutionary honor," against false and baseless charges.

Such moral subtlety, not to mention personal integrity, is far beyond the intellectual horizon of Mr. Dalrymple.

---

5. Leon Trotsky, *Their Morals and Ours* (New York: Pathfinder Press, 2007), pp. 49–50.

Finally, the columnist fails to tell us who among the political leaders of the bourgeoisie, past and present, he counts among the paragons of morality. Perhaps Winston Churchill, who sent tens of thousands of youth to senseless deaths during World War I and sanctioned the use of poison gas against insurgent Iraqis in the 1920s? Or President Harry Truman, who issued the final orders for the dropping of two atomic bombs sixty years ago on the defenseless cities of Hiroshima and Nagasaki, killing nearly 200,000 human beings? Or, in a contemporary setting, Prime Minister Tony Blair, who, on the basis of out-and-out lies, took his country into a war that has cost tens of thousands of lives?

We wait, though not all too eagerly, for Mr. Dalrymple's answer.

10-ый год издания. — Май-июнь 1938 г.   Пролетарии всех стран, соединяйтесь!

БЮЛЛЕТЕНЬ ОППОЗИЦИИ

(БОЛЬШЕВИКОВ-ЛЕНИНЦЕВ)
Bulletin de l'Opposition (Bolcheviks-Léninistes)

ЛЕВ СЕДОВ — РЕДАКТОР-ИЗДАТЕЛЬ С ИЮЛЯ 1929 г. ПО ФЕВРАЛЬ 1938 г.

№ 66-67 АДМИНИСТРАЦИЯ и РЕДАКЦИЯ — ADMINISTRATION ET REDACTION:
« Bulletin de l'Opposition », Librairie du Travail
17, Rue de Sambre-et-Meuse - Paris (10°)
Подписная плата за 12 номеров — 34 фр. фр., за 6 номеров — 17 фр. фр. **Prix 6 fr.**

СОДЕРЖАНИЕ:

Агония капитализма и задачи Четвертого Интернационала.
Л. Т.: Продолжает ли еще "советское правительство" следовать принципам, усвоенным 20 лет тому назад?
Л. Троцкий: Шумиха вокруг Кронштадта.

Социальное страхование в СССР.
Вокруг процесса 21-го (Молчанов и др.).
Итоги разгрома «братских» компартий.
Уход из Коминтерна.
Жизнь Л. Д. Троцкого в опасности.

Агония капитализма и задачи Четвертого Интернационала *)
(Мобилизация масс вокруг переходных требований как подготовка к завоеванию власти)

Об'ективные предпосылки социалистической революции

Мировое политическое положение в целом характеризуется прежде всего историческим кризисом пролетарского руководства.

Экономическая предпосылка пролетарской революции давно уже достигла наивысшей точки, какая вообще может быть достигнута при капитализме. Производительные силы человечества перестали расти. Новые изобретения и усовершенствования не ведут уже к повышению материального богатства. Кон'юнктурные кризисы, в условиях социального кризиса всей капиталистической системы, обрушивают на массы все более тяжкие лишения и страдания. Рост безработицы углубляет, в свою очередь, финансовый кризис государства и подкапывает расшатанные денежные системы. Демократические правительства, как и фашистские, шествуют от одного банкротства к другому.

Сама буржуазия не видит выхода. В странах, где она уже оказалась вынужденной поставить свою последнюю ставку на карту фашизма, она теперь с закрытыми глазами скользит навстречу экономической и военной катастрофе. В исторически привилегированных странах, т.-е. в тех, где она еще может позволить себе в течение некоторого времени роскошь демократии за счет старых национальных накоплений (Великобритания, Франция, Соединенные Штаты и пр.), все традиционные партии капитала находятся в состоянии растерянности, граничащей моментами с параличем воли. «Нью Дил», несмотря на его показную решительность в первый период, представляет только особую форму растерянности, возможную в стране, где буржуазия успела накопить неисчислимые богатства. Нынешний кризис, еще далеко не сказавший своего последнего слова, успел уже показать, что политика «Нью Дил» в Соединенных Штатах, как и политика Народного фронта во Франции, не открывают никакого выхода из экономического тупика.

Нисколько не лучше картина международных отношений. Под возрастающим давлением капиталистического распада империалистские антагонизмы достигли той грани, за которой отдельные столкновения и кровавые вспышки (Абиссиния, Испания, Дальний Восток, Центральная Европа...) должны неминуемо слиться в мировой пожар. Буржуазия отдает себе, разумеется, отчет в смертельной опасно-

---

*) Программа действия, предложенная к обсуждению Международным Секретариатом секции IV Интернационала.

Bulletin of the Opposition, 1938

3

The Classical Marxism of Leon Trotsky

On September 3, 1938, the Fourth International held its founding congress in a suburb of Paris. The conference agenda allowed for only one day of official proceedings, owing to, according to the minutes, "the illegal circumstances under which the congress was held..." The "illegal circumstances" to which the minutes referred were those created by the relentless persecution of the Trotskyist movement by the police of the bourgeois-democratic state in France, the armed gangs of fascists acting with legal impunity in much of Europe, and above all, the ruthless assassins of the Soviet secret police, the GPU, working to carry out Stalin's instructions that Leon Trotsky and his closest collaborators be physically eliminated.

The siege conditions under which the congress was held were reflected in the remarks with which Pierre Naville, then a supporter of the Fourth International, opened the meeting:

> Owing to the tragic death of Klement there would be no formal report: Klement had had a detailed, written report in preparation which was to have been circulated, but it had disappeared with the rest of his papers. The present report would be only a summary.[1]

Lecture at the University of Michigan on November 1, 2008, commemorating the seventieth anniversary of the founding of the Fourth International. Published on the World Socialist Web Site, November 3, 2018.

The deceased to whom Naville was referring was Rudolf Klement, the late secretary of the Fourth International, who had been abducted and murdered by Stalinist agents in July 1938, less than two months before the conference. He was the fourth leading figure in the Trotskyist movement to have been murdered in the year immediately preceding the founding congress: (1) Erwin Wolf in September 1937; (2) Ignace Reiss in September 1937 in Switzerland; (3) Leon Sedov, the son of Trotsky, in February 1938 in Paris; and (4) Rudolf Klement. What Naville did not, and could not, know was that a GPU agent who had played a key role in the organization of these four assassinations—Mark Zborowski—was in attendance at the congress, acting as the representative of the Russian section of the Fourth International.

These assassinations were inextricably linked to the campaign of political genocide directed against the remnants of revolutionary workers, socialist intellectuals, and Bolshevik leaders who had played a decisive role in the October 1917 Revolution. Directed by Stalin, the three frame-up trials held in Moscow between August 1936 and March 1938 were the public manifestation of a massive operation aimed at the total destruction of Trotskyist, i.e., Marxist, influence in the USSR.

Contemporary bourgeois historians insist, with few exceptions, that the Stalinist terror had little to do with Trotsky and Trotskyism. Stalin, they claim, had no reason to fear Trotsky, whom he had expelled from the USSR in 1929, and whose influence was negligible. This superficial appraisal has been challenged by the late Soviet/Russian historian, General Dmitri Volkogonov, who, despite his own hostility to Trotsky, emphasized that Stalin was tormented by the "ghost" of the exiled revolutionary:

> Trotsky was no longer present, yet Stalin grew to hate him even more in his absence, and Trotsky's spectre frequently returned to haunt the usurper... He thought of Trotsky when he had to sit and listen to Molotov, Kaganovich, Khrushchev and Zhdanov.
>
> Trotsky was of a different caliber intellectually, with his grasp of organization and his talents as a speaker and writer. In every way he was far superior to this bunch of bureaucrats, but he was also superior to Stalin and Stalin knew it. "How could

---

1. Will Reissner, ed., *Documents of the Fourth International, The Formative Years 1933–1940* (New York: Pathfinder Press, 1973), p. 284.

I have let such an enemy slip through my fingers?" he almost wailed. On one occasion he confessed to his small circle that this had been one of the biggest mistakes of his life...

The thought that Trotsky was speaking not only for himself, but for all his silent supporters and oppositionists inside the USSR, was particularly painful to Stalin. When he read Trotsky's works, such as *The Stalin School of Falsification, An Open Letter to Members of the Bolshevik Party*, or *The Stalinist Thermidor*, the Leader almost lost his self-control... Stalin read the translation of *The Revolution Betrayed* in a single night, seething with bile. It was the last straw. For some years he had been nurturing two decisions in his mind, and now he proposed to have them carried out. First, he must at all costs remove Trotsky from the political arena... Second, he was now even more convinced on the need for a determined and final liquidation of all potential enemies inside the country.[2]

Trotsky understood very well the physical power of his enemies and the scale of the dangers that confronted him and his supporters. But he conducted his work with extraordinary confidence in the ultimate victory of the Fourth International as the instrument of world socialist revolution. Celebrating the founding of the Fourth International, he declared on October 18, 1938:

> The hangmen think in their obtuseness and cynicism that it is possible to frighten us. They err! Under blows we become stronger. The bestial politics of Stalin are only politics of despair. It is possible to kill individual soldiers of our army, but not to frighten them. Friends, we will repeat again in this day of celebration ... *it is not possible to frighten us*.[3]

The origins of the Fourth International lay in the struggle initiated by Trotsky and the Left Opposition in October 1923 against the increasing bureaucratization of the Soviet state and the Communist Party of the Soviet Union. This political struggle began even before Stalin emerged as Trotsky's

---

2. Dmitri Volkogonov, *Stalin: Triumph and Tragedy* (New York: Grove Weidenfeld, 1988), pp. 254–60.
3. Leon Trotsky, "The founding of the Fourth International," *Writings of Leon Trotsky [1938–39]* (New York: Pathfinder Press, 1974, second edition, ninth printing, 2023), pp. 109–10.

principal opponent and the leader of the Communist Party. For Trotsky, Stalin's rise to power was not the cause of the degeneration of the Soviet state and the Communist Party, but rather a political manifestation of the strengthening of political reaction within the USSR, as a result of the defeats suffered by the working class in Western Europe in the aftermath of the October Revolution. For Lenin and Trotsky, the fate of socialism within the Soviet Union depended upon the victory of the world socialist revolution. The idea that socialism could develop within Russia alone, an isolated and economically backward state, was incompatible with the most basic premises of Marxist theory.

Stalin's claim, in late 1924, that socialism could be built in one country—that is, that the Soviet Union could achieve socialism apart from the outcome of the struggles of the international working class beyond the borders of the USSR, especially in Western Europe and North America—revealed the essentially nationalist orientation, perspective, and program of the ruling bureaucracy. By "socialism," the bureaucracy, led by Joseph Stalin, meant a system of national economic autarchy which safeguarded the income and privileges it enjoyed on the basis of state ownership of the means of production.

The bureaucracy's persecution of Trotsky and the Left Opposition entailed the falsification and repudiation of the Marxist and internationalist foundations of the Bolshevik Party. Ever more openly and crassly, the Stalinist regime subordinated the interests of the international revolutionary movement to the needs of the bureaucracy. The result of its betrayal of the program of world socialist revolution was a series of political defeats for the international working class—in Britain in 1926, in China in 1927, and, most disastrously, in Germany in 1933. Stalin's catastrophic misdirection of the German Communist Party made possible Hitler's rise to power in January 1933. This event, in turn, set into motion the chain of events which led to World War II and the deaths of tens of millions of people.

In the aftermath of Hitler's victory, Trotsky and the International Left Opposition altered their previous policy, which had been oriented toward the reform of the Communist Party of the Soviet Union and the Third (Communist) International. Trotsky now called for the construction of a new International and for a *political revolution* in the USSR. He defined the Stalinist bureaucracy within the USSR as an agency of imperialism within the workers movement.

The years between 1933 and 1938 were devoted primarily to the theoretical and political preparation of the founding congress of the Fourth

International. Writing in 1935, Trotsky evaluated this work as the most important of his life—even more important than his role in the organization of the October Revolution and the founding and leadership of the Red Army. In justifying this assessment, Trotsky argued that if he had been absent in 1917, Lenin's leadership would have been sufficient to overcome the political opposition in the Bolshevik Party and carry through the decision to take power. But now, in the 1930s, there was no one else capable of educating a new cadre of revolutionaries and preserving the continuity of the Marxist movement. Trotsky acknowledged that he was, at this point in time, indispensable, and that he would need five years to ensure the continuity of the heritage of Marxism. Trotsky, when he made that assessment, had exactly five years to live—and he succeeded in realizing this goal.

It is necessary to understand why Trotsky's work was indispensable. Reference to his genius is insufficient. Three elements of his intellectual and political personality must be stressed.

First, Trotsky was the last great representative of "classical Marxism," that is, the representative of a theoretical and political school and tradition that traced itself directly back to Marx and Engels, and which trained and inspired the mass revolutionary workers movement that emerged in the last decades of the nineteenth century. As explained in *The Historical and International Foundations of the Socialist Equality Party*, Trotsky embodied "a conception of revolutionary theory, rooted philosophically in materialism, directed outward toward the cognition of objective reality, oriented to the education and political mobilization of the working class, and strategically preoccupied with the revolutionary struggle against capitalism."[4]

Second, Trotsky grasped, more profoundly than any other political thinker of the twentieth century, the global dimensions and dynamics of the socialist revolution, the dialectical interaction of international socioeconomic processes and historically-determined national conditions. This understanding found expression in the theory of permanent revolution, first formulated by Trotsky in response to the problems raised by the 1905 Revolution in Russia, in which the relation between traditional bourgeois-democratic tasks and the implicitly socialist strivings of the working class, in a backward country, emerged in a manner that contradicted existing conceptions and required a new theoretical paradigm.

---

4. *The Historical and International Foundations of the Socialist Equality Party* (Oak Park, MI: Mehring Books, 2008), p. 59.

Third, Trotsky assimilated the essential political lessons of Lenin's struggle against Menshevik opportunism and centrism in the years between the split of 1903 and the revolutionary dénouement of 1917. Having crossed swords with Lenin over questions of political principle in that crucial formative period, Trotsky came to understand and appreciate Lenin's extraordinary foresight in opposing all forms of opportunism in the Russian Social Democratic Labor Party and, later, after the outbreak of the imperialist war in 1914, within the Second International. The lessons that Trotsky drew from this historical experience formed an essential political foundation for the struggle to build the Fourth International.

Each of these elements of Trotsky's intellectual and political itinerary are deserving of detailed elaboration. But time demands a more concentrated approach. Let us, therefore, focus on the question of "classical" Marxism. Even among those who are familiar with, and place high value on, Trotsky's powers as a revolutionary strategist, it is all too rare that one finds sufficient appreciation of the theoretical foundations of his political thought. Notwithstanding Trotsky's insistence on dialectical materialism as the mainspring of revolutionary thought, even sympathetic commentators view such professions of philosophical commitment to be arcane and insubstantial. For example, a noted scholar and specialist on Trotsky's social and political thought, after citing a passage in which Trotsky expounds the basic elements of dialectical materialism, asks with evident exasperation: "What, however, did all this have to do with the study of society and the formulation of Marxist revolutionary policy and strategy?"[5] The question betrays inadequate understanding of the relationship between philosophical outlook and method, on the one hand, and political thought and practice on the other. It also indicates a limited appreciation of the content and implications of the confrontation, with which Trotsky was extremely familiar, between Marxian materialism and various schools of philosophical idealism.

While a great deal has been written about the political struggles within the many conflicting tendencies of the European (and especially Russian) socialist movement prior to World War I, far less attention has been paid to the theoretical conflicts. Even the conflict against the revisionism of Eduard Bernstein has been examined largely from the standpoint of political program

---

5. Baruch Knei-Paz, *The Social and Political Thought of Leon Trotsky* (Oxford: Oxford University Press, 1978), pp. 487–88.

and perspective. The differences in these spheres were, of course, of immense and enduring significance. But another aspect of this crucial conflict between Marxism and revisionism needs to be stressed—that is, the philosophical dimensions of the struggle.

Examined from this standpoint, Bernstein, a neo-Kantian, was part of a broader intellectual tendency whose opposition to Marxism was rooted philosophically in various currents of subjective idealism.

Briefly stated, these tendencies rejected philosophical and historical materialism, which asserts the primacy of matter over consciousness. On this basis, they rejected the conception that the development of human society, including its intellectual development, proceeded in accordance with laws related to the economic structure of society.

There was no more determined advocate of the materialist conception of history than Trotsky, whose theoretical education—beginning in the late 1890s—proceeded in constant conflict with the increasingly influential schools of subjective idealist and irrationalist thought. Near the end of his long revolutionary career, Trotsky offered the following explanation of Marx's materialist outlook:

> Having established science as cognition of the objective recurrences of nature, man has tried stubbornly and persistently to exclude himself from science, reserving for himself special privileges in the shape of alleged intercourse with supersensory forces (religion), or with timeless moral precepts (idealism). Marx deprived man of these odious privileges definitely and forever, looking upon him as a natural link in the evolutionary process of material nature; upon human society as the organization of production and distribution; upon capitalism as a stage in the development of human society...
>
> It is utterly impossible to seek the causes for the recurrences in capitalist society in the subjective consciousness—in the intentions or plans—of its members. The objective recurrences of capitalism were formulated before science began to think about them seriously. To this day the preponderant majority of men know nothing about the laws that govern capitalist economy. The whole strength of Marx's method was in his approach to economic phenomena, not from the subjective point of view of certain persons, but from the objective point of view of the

development of society as a whole, just as an experimental natural scientist approaches a beehive or an ant-hill.

For economic science the decisive significance is how people act, not what they themselves think about their actions. At the base of society is not religion and morality, but nature and labor. Marx's method is *materialistic* because it proceeds from existence to consciousness, not the other way around. Marx's method is *dialectic*, because it regards both nature and society as they evolve, and evolution itself as the constant struggle of conflicting forces.[6]

In the world of political struggle, the application of Marx's materialist outlook required that revolutionary policy be based, first and foremost, upon an analysis of objective socioeconomic conditions. The revolutionary party had to base its actions, not on the prevailing moods and illusions of the masses, but on the really existing level of the socioeconomic contradictions of capitalism. The moods of the masses were themselves a distorted reflection of objective conditions. The revolutionary party could overcome these moods only to the extent that it fought within the working class for a correct understanding of the capitalist crisis and its political implications.

In discussions between Trotsky and his American supporters, held in May 1938 on the eve of the founding congress of the Fourth International, Trotsky stressed this objective starting point of the revolutionary program:

> The political backwardness of the American working class is very great. This signifies that the danger of a fascist catastrophe is very great. This is the point of departure for all our activity. The program must express the objective tasks of the working class rather than the backwardness of the workers. It must reflect society as it is, and not the backwardness of the working class. It is an instrument to overcome and vanquish the backwardness. That is why we must express in our program the whole acuteness of the social crises of the capitalist society, including in the first line the United States. We cannot postpone or modify objective conditions which don't depend on us. We cannot guarantee that

---

6. Leon Trotsky, "Marxism in Our Time," *The Essential Marx*, Leon Trotsky, ed. (Mineola, NY: Dover, 2006), pp. 2–4.

the masses will solve the crisis; but we must express the situation as it is, and that is the task of the program.[7]

These words are invested with acute relevance in the present situation. What should be the starting point of revolutionary politics today—the objective nature and implications of the unfolding crisis of American and world capitalism, whose depth and severity are without equal since the Great Depression of the 1930s, or the prevailing and confused state of political consciousness that exists among masses of workers? Should we adapt our program to the present-day illusions among workers in the electoral rhetoric of Barack Obama? Or should we expose the poison hidden within the honeyed phrases, and prepare the masses for the great social conflicts that will inevitably be generated by the intensification of the economic crisis?

The election will be concluded in three days. Whichever of the two bourgeois parties wins the presidential and congressional elections will then confront the consequences of the spiraling economic disaster. If, as now seems likely, Obama emerges as president-elect, he will assume central responsibility for pursuing the national and international interests of the American ruling class. How long, do you imagine, will he be able to preserve the illusion that the crisis affects all classes of the population in the same way, that the "American people are in this together," that "sacrifices" can and will be "shared," and that the interests of the poor are the same as the interests of the rich? How long will it be before the irrepressible determination of the financial aristocracy to exploit the opportunities created by the crisis for its own maximum enrichment becomes painfully obvious to the masses of workers? Or, for that matter, the powerlessness of a President Obama to control these strivings, even if he wanted to?

It is worth recalling Trotsky's comments in 1939 on the Roosevelt administration's New Deal, which is generally portrayed by historians as the apex of governmental radicalism. Trotsky noted rather sardonically the generally ineffectual character of Roosevelt's confrontations with the American bourgeoisie:

> Today monopolists are the strongest section of the ruling class. No government is in any position to fight against monopoly in general, i.e., against the class by whose will it rules. While attacking

---

7. Leon Trotsky, "The political backwardness of American workers," *The Transitional Program for Socialist Revolution* (New York: Pathfinder Press, 2001), pp. 189–90.

one phase of monopoly, it is obliged to seek an ally in other phases of monopoly. In union with banks and light industry it can deliver occasional blows against the trusts of heavy industry, which, by the way, do not stop earning fantastic profits because of that.[8]

Will the same fate befall President Obama? Will the walls of American capitalism tumble before the rhetorical trumpets of Mr. "Yes We Can"? No, they won't. As a matter of fact, his performance during the infamous bank bailout crisis, not to mention that of Senator McCain, provided an indication of how an Obama administration will react when confronted with the demands of the ruling aristocracy.

In the final analysis, the policies of an Obama administration will be determined by the objective conditions confronting American capitalism. And it is at this point that a clear distinction must be made between the United States in the era of Roosevelt and the United States in the era of Obama. Three quarters of a century have passed since Franklin Roosevelt first took the oath of office and proclaimed that the United States had nothing to fear but fear itself. He spoke as the leader of a capitalist nation which, for all its economic problems, still retained at its disposal colossal resources. In comparison to the industrial might of the United States, all other nations were dwarfs. Those days have long passed. The United States has for decades been in economic decline. It has accumulated massive debts as its industries have decayed. Indeed, the essential source of the economic crisis can be located in the separation of the process of wealth accumulation from the material processes of production. On the eve of the explosion of the economic crisis, the US financial industry accounted for 40 percent of all profits!

A President Obama will not have a "New Deal" to offer the American working class—though one should recall that Roosevelt's New Deal proved incapable of ending the Depression. The economic crisis was "solved" by World War II. Moreover, whatever gains were achieved during the 1930s were the product, not of government reforms and handouts, but of immense social struggles by the working class—such as the Toledo Auto-Lite strike, the Minneapolis and San Francisco general strikes, the Flint sit-down strike, and other powerful and bloody battles.

What, then, are the prospects for socialism in the United States? This was a question about which Trotsky, a keen observer of American society and its

---

8. Trotsky, "Marxism in Our Time," *The Essential Marx*, p. 27.

economic and political structures, thought a great deal. He understood very well the power and influence of capitalist ideology in the so-called "Land of Unlimited Opportunity." He wrote in 1939:

> In the United States, where a man who owns a million is referred to as being "worth" a million, market concepts have sunk in deeper than anywhere else. Until quite recently Americans gave very little thought to the nature of economic relations. In the land of the most powerful economic system economic theory continued to be exceedingly barren. Only the present deep-going crisis of American economy has bluntly confronted public opinion with the fundamental problems of capitalist society.[9]

The process of economic, social, and political enlightenment was pre-empted by the Second World War, from which the United States emerged victorious, not only militarily and politically, but also economically. What need was there to continue questioning the legitimacy of capitalism, when 75 percent of industrial production was located in the United States, and where the dollar was "as good as gold." Moreover, the post-war anti-communist witch-hunts were aimed at constricting intellectual life in the United States and delegitimizing, if not completely criminalizing, the Marxist critique of American capitalism. More recently, the collapse of the Stalinist regimes in the USSR and Eastern Europe, in the late 1980s and early 1990s, was hailed as definite proof of the irrevocable triumph of capitalism, and even of the "End of History."

But what remains of capitalist triumphalism today, in the aftermath of the catastrophic failure of the economic system? Little more than a month ago, pleading for public support for a bailout of the banks, President Bush declared before a nationwide audience that the capitalist system in the United States stood on the brink of collapse. Two days later, he told members of his cabinet and congressional leaders that, "This sucker is going down!" The entire ideology of American capitalism—of the infallibility of the market, of the absolute independence of the market from the state—lost all credibility. The high prophet of the cult of the market, Alan Greenspan—hailed as the "Maestro" of the Federal Reserve—appeared before a congressional committee as a shuffling and bewildered old man, on the verge of senility, confessing amazement that markets had failed to behave as he believed they would.

---

9. Ibid., p. 2.

And against the backdrop of this crisis, the dreaded "S" word has made its reappearance in American political life. An unguarded reference by Obama to sharing the wealth, by which he meant absolutely no harm, has been seized upon by McCain and Palin as proof that Obama is planning to introduce socialism into America. Senator Biden was asked on television whether Obama was, in fact, a closet-Marxist! These episodes reveal the fears lurking within the ruling class. Obama and Biden are taunted by their desperate Republican opponents for planning to "share the wealth." The Democratic candidates indignantly deny the accusation. But will masses of American workers, under conditions of mounting unemployment and mass foreclosures, agree that "sharing the wealth" is really such a bad idea?

Social being determines social consciousness. Conditions of crisis not only discredit old ideologies. They give rise to conceptions that are in alignment with objective reality. It will not be possible to maintain the semi-official ban on Marxism in discussions of the crisis of American and world capitalism. As Trotsky foresaw, objective events will force a profound shift in political life. What he wrote in 1939 acquires extraordinary relevance in the present situation:

> Partial reforms and patchwork will do no good. Historical development has come to one of those decisive stages when only the direct intervention of the masses is able to sweep away the reactionary obstructions and lay the foundations of a new regime. Abolition of private ownership in the means of production is the first pre-requisite to planned economy, i.e., the introduction of reason into the sphere of human relations, first on a national and eventually on a world scale... Liberated humanity will draw itself up to its full height.[10]

---

10. Ibid., p. 43.

4

Trotsky's Victory over Stalinism: Seventy-five Years of the Fourth International 1938–2013

Seventy-five years ago, on September 3, 1938, the Fourth International was founded at a conference held on the outskirts of Paris. The work of the conference had to be completed within one day due to precarious security conditions. During the twelve months that preceded the conference, the Trotskyist movement had been under relentless attack. Though he lived in exile in Mexico, Leon Trotsky was viewed by the Stalinist regime in the Soviet Union as its most dangerous political opponent. Stalin was determined to destroy the international movement that Trotsky had created during the decade that followed his expulsion from the Soviet Communist Party in 1927 and his deportation from the USSR in 1929.

In September 1937, Erwin Wolf, a political secretary of Trotsky, was murdered by agents of the Soviet secret police, the GPU. During that same month, Ignace Reiss, who had defected from the GPU and declared his loyalty to the new International being founded by Trotsky, was assassinated in Lausanne, Switzerland. In February 1938, Leon Sedov—Trotsky's eldest son and most important political representative in Europe—was murdered by the GPU in Paris. And in July 1938, only six weeks before the founding

---

Published on the World Socialist Web Site, September 4, 2013.

conference, Rudolf Klement—the leader of the movement's International Secretariat—was kidnapped from his apartment in Paris and murdered.

Sedov, Wolf, and Klement were elected honorary presidents of the conference, and the French Trotskyist Pierre Naville informed the delegates that "Owing to the tragic death of Klement there would be no formal report; Klement had had a detailed, written report in preparation which was to have been circulated, but it had disappeared with the rest of his papers. The present report would be merely a summary."[1]

The hellish conditions in which the conference was held reflected the political situation that confronted the international working class. Fascist regimes held power in Germany and Italy. Europe teetered on the brink of war. The infamous Munich conference at which British and French imperialism surrendered Czechoslovakia to Hitler—with the acquiescence of the capitalist government in Prague—was to be held only several weeks later. The Spanish revolution, having been misled and betrayed by its Stalinist and anarchist leaders, was rapidly approaching defeat after more than two years of civil war. In France, the Popular Front government of 1936–38 had done everything in its power to politically demoralize the working class. In the Soviet Union, the terror that had been unleashed by Stalin in 1936 had annihilated virtually the entire generation of Old Bolsheviks. The betrayals of the Stalinists and social democrats had sabotaged the only means by which the outbreak of a second imperialist world war could have been prevented—that is, the socialist revolution of the working class.

The crisis of leadership

The main task facing the delegates attending the founding conference was the adoption of a document that had been drafted by Leon Trotsky. It was titled "The Death Agony of Capitalism and the Tasks of the Fourth International." Its opening sentence, among the most significant and profound in the annals of political literature, stated: "The world political situation as a whole is chiefly characterized by a historical crisis of the leadership of the proletariat."[2]

---

1. Will Reissner, ed., *Documents of the Fourth International: The Formative Years 1933–40* (New York: Pathfinder Press, 1973), p. 285.
2. Leon Trotsky, *The Death Agony of Capitalism and the Tasks of the Fourth International: The Transitional Program* (New York: Labor Publications, 1981), p. 1.

With these words Trotsky summed up not only the situation as it existed in 1938, but also the central political problem of modern history. The objective prerequisites—i.e., the international development of the productive forces, the existence of the revolutionary class—for the replacement of capitalism by socialism were present. But revolution was not merely the automatic outcome of objective economic conditions. It required the politically conscious intervention of the working class in the historical process, based on a socialist program and armed with a clearly elaborated strategic plan. The revolutionary politics of the working class could not be *less conscious* than the counterrevolutionary politics of the capitalist class it sought to overthrow. Herein lay the historic significance of the revolutionary party.

But the decisive role of the revolutionary party, which had been positively demonstrated in October 1917—when the Russian working class, under the leadership of the Bolshevik Party of Lenin and Trotsky, overthrew the capitalist class and established the first workers state in history—was confirmed in the negative by the defeats of the 1920s and 1930s. A series of revolutionary opportunities had been lost by the false policies and deliberate betrayals carried out by the mass social democratic and Communist (Stalinist) parties that commanded the allegiance of the working class.

The political bankruptcy and reactionary role of the social democratic parties of the Second International had been laid bare as early as 1914, when they repudiated their own internationalist programs and supported the war policies of their own national ruling classes. The Communist (or Third) International had been formed in the aftermath of the October Revolution, in opposition to the betrayal of the social democracy.

But the growth of the state bureaucracy within the Soviet Union and the political degeneration of the Russian Communist Party had far-reaching consequences for the Communist International. In 1923, the Left Opposition had been formed under Trotsky's leadership to combat the bureaucratization of the Russian Communist Party. But the bureaucracy, which found in Stalin a dedicated representative of its interests and privileges, fought back savagely against its Marxist opponents. In 1924, Stalin and Bukharin proclaimed the program of "socialism in one country," which repudiated the program of socialist internationalism—that is, of permanent revolution— upon which Lenin and Trotsky had based the Bolshevik conquest of power in October 1917. The Stalin-Bukharin program provided an anti-Marxist theoretical justification for the practical subordination of the interests of the international working class to the national interests of the Soviet bureaucracy.

The impact of this fundamental revision of Marxist theory on the practice of the Third International and its affiliated parties was catastrophic. In the course of the 1920s, those leaders of national Communist parties who failed to fall in line with the dictates of Moscow were bureaucratically removed and replaced with compliant and incompetent factotums. Disoriented by the policies formulated by Stalin—who ever more openly viewed the Third International not as a party of world socialist revolution, but rather as an instrument of Soviet foreign policy—the Communist parties staggered from one disaster to another. The defeat of the British General Strike in 1926 and, one year later, the defeat of the Chinese Revolution, were critical milestones in the degeneration of the Third International.

In 1928, having been exiled to Alma Ata in Central Asia, Trotsky wrote *The Draft Program of the Communist International: A Criticism of Fundamentals* on the eve of the organization's Sixth Congress. This document was a detailed elaboration of the theoretical and political causes of the defeats suffered by the Communist parties during the preceding five years. The main target of Trotsky's critique was the Stalin-Bukharin theory of "socialism in one country." He wrote:

> In our epoch, which is the epoch of imperialism, i.e., of *world* economy and *world* politics under the hegemony of finance capital, not a single communist party can establish its programme by proceeding solely or mainly from conditions and tendencies of developments in its own country. This also holds entirely for the party that wields the state power within the boundaries of the USSR. On August 4, 1914, the death knell sounded for national programmes for all time. The revolutionary party of the proletariat can base itself only upon an international programme corresponding to the character of the present epoch, the epoch of the highest development and collapse of capitalism. An international communist programme is in no case the sum total of national programmes or an amalgam of their common features. The international programme must proceed directly from an analysis of the conditions and tendencies of world economy and of the world political system taken as a whole in all its connections and contradictions, that is, with the mutually antagonistic

interdependence of its separate parts. In the present epoch, to a much larger extent than in the past, the national orientation of the proletariat must and can flow only from a world orientation and not *vice versa*. Herein lies the basic and primary difference between communist internationalism and all varieties of national socialism.[3]

Trotsky's emphasis on the primacy of a world orientation arose not simply from general theoretical considerations, but from his analysis—which he developed in 1923–24—of the global implications of the emergence of the United States as the principal imperialist power.

Trotsky was barred from attending the sessions of the Communist International. His writings were already proscribed within all the Communist parties. However, through some fortuitous bureaucratic mishap, Trotsky's *Criticism of the Draft Program* was translated into English and came into the possession of James P. Cannon, who was attending the Sixth Congress as a delegate of the American Communist Party. Persuaded by Trotsky's analysis, Cannon, with the assistance of a Canadian delegate, Maurice Spector, smuggled the document out of the Soviet Union. On the basis of the analysis presented in the *Criticism of the Draft Program*, Cannon—joined by Max Shachtman, Martin Abern, and several other leading members of the Communist Party—began the fight for Trotsky's ideas outside the Soviet Union. Soon expelled from the Communist Party, Cannon and Shachtman formed the Communist League of America, which played a critical role in the emergence of the International Left Opposition.

When it was formed in 1923, the aim of the Left Opposition was the *reform* of the Communist Party on the basis of the program of revolutionary internationalism, and the reestablishment of open debate within the party in accordance with the principles of democratic centralism. With the establishment of the International Left Opposition, which rapidly gained adherents throughout the world, Trotsky sought to achieve the reform of the Communist International. As long as there remained the possibility that the disastrous policies of Stalin might be reversed through the growth of opposition within the Soviet Communist Party and the Third International, Trotsky refrained from issuing the call for a new International.

---

3. Leon Trotsky, *The Third International After Lenin* (London: New Park Publications, 1974), pp. 3–4.

The rise of fascism in Germany

The situation in Germany between 1930 and 1933 weighed heavily in Trotsky's calculations. With the collapse of the German economy in the aftermath of the Wall Street crash of 1929, Hitler's National Socialist (Nazi) party emerged as a mass force. Whether or not Hitler came to power depended on the policies of the two mass organizations of the German working class, the Social Democratic Party (SPD) and the Communist Party (KPD). These two parties commanded the allegiance of millions of German workers and possessed the power to defeat the Nazis.

Having been exiled in 1929 to the island of Prinkipo, off the coast of Turkey, Trotsky wrote voluminously, analyzing the German crisis and appealing for united action by the two working-class parties to stop Hitler's march to power. But the SPD, subservient to the bourgeois state and opposed to any politically independent action by the working class, would not countenance even a defensive struggle against the Nazis. The fate of the German working class was, instead, to be left in the hands of the corrupt and criminal bourgeois politicians of the Weimar regime who were scheming to bring Hitler to power. As for the KPD, it adhered blindly to the Moscow-dictated definition of the Social Democracy as "social fascist"—that is, the political equivalent of the Nazi party. The Stalinists rejected Trotsky's call for a United Front of the KPD and SPD against Hitler. In a political prognosis that must be counted among the most disastrous miscalculations in history, the Stalinists—justifying their own passivity—proclaimed that a Nazi victory would soon be followed by a socialist revolution that would bring the Communist Party to power. "After Hitler, us" was the Stalinist slogan.

The tragic denouement came on January 30, 1933. Appointed chancellor by the aged President von Hindenburg, Hitler came to power legally, without a shot being fired. Both the SPD and KPD, organizations with millions of members between them, did nothing to oppose the Nazis' triumph. Within days, the Nazis, now in control of the state apparatus, set their terror into motion. Within months, the SPD, the KPD, the trade unions, and all other mass working class organizations were smashed. The twelve-year nightmare, which would cost the lives of millions, including the vast majority of European Jewry, had begun.

Trotsky waited several months after Hitler's accession to power to see whether the German catastrophe would evoke protests and opposition within either the remnants of the KPD or the Third International. But the opposite occurred. The Stalinist organizations, within Germany and in the International, reaffirmed the correctness of the political line that had been dictated by the Soviet bureaucracy.

The outcome in Germany convinced Trotsky that there existed no possibility for the reform of the Communist International. Therefore, in July 1933, Trotsky issued a public call for the formation of the Fourth International. This fundamental shift in policy in relation to the Third International led Trotsky to a further conclusion. If the possibility of reforming the Communist International did not exist, the perspective of reform was no longer valid for the Communist Party of the Soviet Union. To change the policies of the Stalinist regime would require its overthrow. However, as this overthrow would be aimed at defending, rather than replacing, the nationalized property relations established in the aftermath of October 1917, the revolution advocated by Trotsky would be of a *political* rather than a *social* character.

The events between 1933 and 1938 confirmed the correctness of Trotsky's new course. During the five years that followed Hitler's conquest of power, the Stalinist regime emerged as the most dangerous counterrevolutionary force within the international workers movement. The defeats that were caused by the policies of the Kremlin bureaucracy were not the outcome of mistakes, but rather of conscious policies. The Stalinist regime feared that the success of social revolution in any country might inspire a reawakening of the revolutionary fervor of the Soviet working class.

Arguments against the founding of the Fourth International

As Trotsky worked systematically for the formal establishment of the Fourth International, he encountered two major forms of opposition.

The first was that of tendencies and individuals who refused to draw any conclusions of a principled character from the international experience of the class struggle and the betrayals of Stalinism and Social Democracy. While occasionally expressing sympathy and even agreement with one or another aspect of Trotsky's analysis, they refused to commit themselves and their organizations to the fight for a new revolutionary International. In effect, these tendencies—which Trotsky designated "centrist"—sought to find a safe middle ground between revolution and counterrevolution. Underlying their unprincipled political maneuvering were opportunist calculations. They were determined to prevent international principles from impinging on their national tactics. The parties that exemplified this form of national opportunism were the German Socialist Workers Party (SAP), the Spanish Workers Party of Marxist Unification (POUM), and the British Independent Labour Party (ILP). The latter organization, led by Fenner Brockway (later Lord Brockway), played a major role in the establishment of the so-called London Bureau.

The second argument against the formation of the Fourth International was that its proclamation was premature. An International, it was claimed, could arise only out of "great events," by which was meant a successful revolution. At the founding conference, this position was advanced by a Polish delegate, identified in the minutes as Karl, who argued that a new International could be created only in a period of "revolutionary upsurge." The conditions of "intense reaction and depression" were "circumstances wholly unfavorable for the proclamation of the Fourth." The delegate stated that "the forces constituting the Fourth were disproportionately small in relation to its tasks," and that "It was therefore necessary to wait for a favorable moment and not be premature."[4]

As he drafted the founding document of the Fourth International, Trotsky anticipated the arguments of the Polish delegate:

> Skeptics ask: But has the moment for the creation of the Fourth International yet arrived? It is impossible, they say, to create an International "artificially"; it can arise only out of great events, etc., etc. All of these objections merely show that skeptics are no good for the building of a new International. They are good for scarcely anything at all.
>
> The Fourth International has already arisen out of great events: the greatest defeats of the proletariat in history. The cause for these defeats is to be found in the degeneration and perfidy of the old leadership. The class struggle does not tolerate an interruption. The Third International, following the Second, is dead for purposes of revolution. Long live the Fourth International![5]

In October 1938, Trotsky recorded a speech in which he welcomed, with evident emotion, the founding of the Fourth International.

---

4. *Documents of the Fourth International*, pp. 296–97.
5. Trotsky, *The Death Agony of Capitalism and the Tasks of the Fourth International: The Transitional Program*, p. 42.

> Dear friends, we are not a party like other parties. Our ambition is not only to have more members, more papers, more money in the treasury, more deputies. All that is necessary, but only as a means. Our aim is the full material and spiritual liberation of the toilers and exploited through the socialist revolution. Nobody will prepare it and nobody will guide it but ourselves. The old Internationals—the Second, the Third, that of Amsterdam, we will add to them also the London Bureau—are rotten through and through.
>
> The great events which rush upon mankind will not leave of these outlived organizations one stone upon another. Only the Fourth International looks with confidence at the future. It is the World Party of Socialist Revolution! There never was a greater task on the earth. Upon every one of us rests a tremendous historical responsibility.[6]

With the perspective afforded by three quarters of a century, it is possible to judge whether history has vindicated Trotsky's appraisal. What remains of the old organizations—Stalinist, social democratic, and centrist—whose political shipwreck was foretold by Trotsky? The Second International exists only as a center of anti-working-class operations and conspiracies directed by the CIA and various other state intelligence agencies. The Third International was officially dissolved by Stalin in 1943. The Stalinist parties throughout the world continued to orbit around the Kremlin bureaucracy for several more decades, until the dissolution of the USSR in 1991 swept them into the garbage dump of history.

The Russian Communist Party, though much reduced in size, continues to exist. It holds demonstrations in Moscow alongside Russian nationalists and fascists, where placards bearing the portrait of Stalin are waved alongside banners that have the swastika emblazoned upon them. And it is true that the "Communist Party" holds power in China, where it presides over the second largest capitalist economy in the world, whose police state regime guarantees that super-profits extracted from the working class are transferred to the transnational corporations of the United States and Europe.

---

6. Leon Trotsky, "The founding of the Fourth International," *Writings of Leon Trotsky [1938–39]* (New York: Pathfinder Press, 1974, second edition, ninth printing, 2023), p. 108.

The political struggle within the Fourth International

The Fourth International, the sole revolutionary organization, has successfully navigated the shoals and rapids of such an extended period of history. Of course, it has passed through intense political struggles and splits. The internal conflicts reflected the vicissitudes of the class struggle under continually changing international socioeconomic conditions and the realignment of social forces—not only within the working class, but also among different layers of the middle class—under the impact of these changes.

Political cynics, who ferment in abundance in the bubbling miasma of ex- and pseudo-left academics, are fond of pointing to the splits within the Fourth International. Such people, who submit in silence to the crimes of the capitalist parties to which they give their vote year after year, understand nothing of the class dynamics of politics. Nor, on a personal level, can they understand why anyone, anywhere, would conduct a determined and uncompromising political struggle over matters of principle.

Fifteen years after the founding of the Fourth International, in November 1953, the emergence of a pro-Stalinist tendency led to a split in which fundamental questions of class orientation, historical perspective, and political strategy were involved. The combined pressure of the post-war restabilization of capitalism, the political influence of the Stalinist bureaucracy, and the increasing political self-consciousness of a growing middle class found expression in the development of a new form of opportunism. This new opportunism, known as Pabloism (derived from its best-known exponent, Michel Pablo), rejected Trotsky's characterization of the Soviet bureaucracy and Stalinism as counterrevolutionary. It envisaged the realization of socialism in a process that was to unfold in the course of centuries, through revolutions led by the bureaucracy and its affiliated Stalinist parties. It even suggested that a nuclear world war would create the conditions for the victory of socialist revolution. The Pabloite theory also attributed revolutionary capacities denied by Trotsky to numerous bourgeois national and petty-bourgeois radical movements, especially in the colonial and "Third World" countries.

The essential content of Pabloism's revision of Marxist theory and the Trotskyist perspective was its rejection of the central role of the working class in the socialist revolution. The International Committee of the Fourth International was formed in 1953, at the initiative of James P. Cannon, to fight against the influence of Pabloite opportunism, whose political logic and practice would lead, unless opposed, to the liquidation of the Fourth International as a revolutionary working-class party.

The political struggle against the influence of Pabloism raged within the Fourth International for more than thirty years. This struggle was brought to a successful conclusion in 1985 when the orthodox Trotskyists of the International Committee regained the political leadership of the Fourth International. The factors that contributed to this victory were the deepening global crisis of capitalism, the deep crisis of the Stalinist bureaucracy, and the evident bankruptcy of all labor organizations based on a national reformist program.

However, these objective conditions alone would have been insufficient. The defeat of the revisionists and opportunists by the orthodox Trotskyists of the International Committee was achieved because the latter consciously based their work on the vast political and theoretical legacy of Trotsky and the Fourth International. This legacy, which had been developed and built upon over decades, was an inexhaustible source of political strength. In the final analysis, the development of the world crisis of capitalism and the class struggle unfolded in accordance with the perspective developed by Trotsky and the Fourth International.

Seventy-five years—three quarters of a century—is a substantial period of time. Obviously, much has changed since the time of the Founding Congress of the Fourth International. But the basic structures and contradictions of capitalist society persist. For all the technological innovations, the situation that confronts modern capitalism appears no less desperate than it was in 1938. In fact, it is worse. When Trotsky wrote the founding document of the Fourth International, the world bourgeoisie was plagued by an intractable economic crisis, abandoning democracy, and racing toward war. Today, as we celebrate seventy-five years since the founding of the Fourth International, global capitalism is... plagued by an intractable economic crisis, abandoning democracy, and racing toward war.

The words of Trotsky, written seventy-five years ago, retain an extraordinary immediacy:

> All talk to the effect that historical conditions have not yet "ripened" for socialism is the product of ignorance or conscious deception. The objective prerequisites for the proletarian revolution have not only "ripened"; they have begun to get somewhat rotten. Without a socialist revolution, in the next

historical period at that, a catastrophe threatens the whole culture of mankind. The turn is now to the proletariat, i.e., chiefly to its revolutionary vanguard. The historical crisis of mankind is reduced to the crisis of the revolutionary leadership.[7]

---

7. Trotsky, *The Death Agony of Capitalism and the Tasks of the Fourth International: The Transitional Program*, pp. 1–2.

5

Why the GPU Assassinated Trotsky

On August 21, 1940, Leon Trotsky died from wounds inflicted the previous day by an agent of the Soviet Union's secret police, known then as the GPU. The assassination occurred in the context of a historically unprecedented wave of political reaction. In Europe, fascist regimes held power in Germany, Italy, and Spain. The Second World War had begun nearly a year earlier with the Nazi invasion of Poland on September 1, 1939, just days after the signing of the Stalin-Hitler Pact. The lives of tens of millions were to be destroyed in the ensuing paroxysm of imperialist violence. This was the terrible consequence of the deliberate sabotage of the revolutionary struggles of the working class by the mass social-democratic and Stalinist parties in the years that preceded the outbreak of the Second World War.

The assassination of the greatest and last surviving leader of the 1917 October Revolution marked the climax of the Stalinist regime's eradication of the heroic generation of socialist workers and intellectuals who had secured the victory of the Bolshevik revolution, founded the Soviet Union as the first workers state in history, and posed before the international working class the overthrow of capitalism and imperialism as a realizable strategic objective.

By the time Trotsky was assassinated, Stalin's regime of bureaucratic terror had already murdered hundreds of thousands of revolutionists within the USSR. The frame-up trials held in Moscow between 1936 and 1938, which

---

Published on the World Socialist Web Site, September 30, 2015, commemorating the seventy-fifth anniversary of the assassination of Trotsky.

doomed dozens of the principal leaders of the Bolshevik Party, were the public manifestation of a broader wave of murderous terror. Stalin's homicidal rampage was not confined to Old Bolsheviks whom he perceived as a direct political threat to his regime.

The Stalinist terror was nothing less than a war to extirpate the entire Soviet culture, which had developed in the aftermath of the October Revolution and was profoundly influenced by socialist internationalism. Writers, musicians, painters, mathematicians, physicists, biologists, economists, and engineers were persecuted, sent to brutal prison camps, tortured, and slaughtered. Members of foreign Communist parties, on the mere suspicion of harboring sympathy for Trotsky, were shot en masse. Entire party leaderships were liquidated.

The monstrous crimes committed by the Stalinist regime were carried out under the banner of the "Struggle against Trotskyism." The unrelenting campaign of hate directed against Trotsky was not only the expression of Stalin's obsessive desire for revenge against his unyielding political opponent. More significantly, Trotsky represented, in the history he personified and the program for which he fought, the conscious socialist-internationalist negation of Stalin's bureaucratic-nationalist regime.

It is a commonplace among most contemporary academics that Trotsky represented no threat to the Stalinist regime. Such cynical appraisals are contradicted by a study of Stalin's personal archive. Though Trotsky was in exile, without any of the external trappings of power, his specter haunted Stalin. Stalin's biographer, General Dmitri Volkogonov, has recounted that Stalin had a "special cupboard in his study" where he kept "virtually all of Trotsky's works, heavily scored with underlinings and comments. Any interview or statement that Trotsky gave to the Western press was immediately translated and delivered to Stalin." Describing the dictator's fear of Trotsky, Volkogonov wrote:

> The thought that Trotsky was speaking not only for himself, but for all his silent supporters and the oppositionists inside the USSR, was particularly painful to Stalin. When he read Trotsky's works, such as the *Stalinist School of Falsification*, *Open Letter to the Members of the Bolshevik Party*, or *The Stalinist Thermidor*, the Leader almost lost his self-control.[1]

---

1. Dmitri Volkogonov, *Stalin: Triumph and Tragedy* (London: Weidenfeld and Nicolson, 1991), p. 256.

Why the GPU Assassinated Trotsky

For Stalin, the threat posed by Trotsky was not limited to hidden and potential opposition within the Soviet Union. Trotsky's struggle for the Fourth International—that is, to reestablish socialist internationalism as the program of the working class in all countries—was seen by Stalin as the most dangerous threat to the nationalist policies pursued by the Kremlin in the interests of the ruling bureaucracy.

The assassination of Trotsky in August 1940 was prepared over many years through the infiltration of the international Trotskyist movement in Europe and the United States by agents of the GPU. In the initial stage of their activity, the Stalinist agents sought to disrupt, through factionalism and intrigues, the activities of the small Trotskyist organizations that were part of the International Left Opposition, the predecessor of the Fourth International.

Among the first and most significant of these agents were the Sobolovecius brothers—known as Senin and Well—who wreaked havoc within the German section of the Left Opposition, thus undermining its political effectiveness during the two crucial years that preceded Hitler's rise to power in 1933. Following the political catastrophe in Germany, Senin and Well would continue to play a central and deadly role in GPU operations against the Trotskyist movement, both in Europe and the United States.

Of all the GPU agents, the most notorious was Mark Zborowski, an émigré from Poland who infiltrated the Trotskyist movement in France. With the unflagging assistance of his collaborator, Lola Dallin (who once described herself as his "Siamese Twin"), Zborowski, using the party name "Etienne," successfully wormed his way into the leadership of the Fourth International. He became the ever-present political assistant of Leon Sedov, Trotsky's eldest son and the leader of the Fourth International in Europe. In November 1936, with information provided by Zborowski-Etienne, the GPU was able to steal a valuable portion of Trotsky's archive that had been secretly stored in a research center in Paris. However, in the aftermath of the first trial in Moscow, at which Trotsky and Sedov were sentenced to death *in absentia*, the Kremlin demanded that its agents find the means to carry out the sentences.

While the Stalinist regime sought to justify its persecution of Trotsky by slandering him as an agent of imperialism, the ruling elites in the capitalist countries left no doubt as to where their sympathies lay in Stalin's war against the persecuted revolutionary. In the United States, the Moscow correspondent of the *New York Times*, Walter Duranty, vouched for the legal integrity of the frame-up trials. Countless liberal intellectuals, in the interest of strengthening ties between the American Communist Party and the Roosevelt administration, went to extraordinary lengths to justify the murder of Old Bolsheviks in Moscow and lend credence to the preposterous accusations against Trotsky.

When the first trial began in August 1936, Trotsky was living in exile in "democratic" Norway. His efforts to expose the frame-up were blocked by that country's Social-Democratic government, which was anxious to avoid giving offense to Stalin. Trotsky and his wife, Natalia Sedova, were placed under house arrest and denied all contact with the press and their own supporters. Trotsky was denied the right to communicate with his closest political assistants. For a time, the Norwegian Social-Democratic regime even toyed with the idea of returning Trotsky to the Soviet Union. Finally, with the assistance of the great painter Diego Rivera, the left nationalist government of Lazar Cárdenas granted Trotsky asylum in Mexico, where the aged but still vigorous revolutionist arrived in January 1937.

Trotsky immediately set about to organize a great "counter-trial." Its purpose was not only to refute Stalin's charges but also to expose the proceedings as a criminal frame-up. In a public statement denouncing the trial, recorded on film, Trotsky declared:

> Stalin's trial against me is built on false confessions, extorted by modern Inquisitorial methods, in the interests of the ruling clique. *There are no crimes in history more terrible in intention and execution than the Moscow trials of Zinoviev-Kamenev and of Pyatakov-Radek.* These trials develop not from communism, not from socialism, but from Stalinism, that is, from the unaccountable despotism of the bureaucracy over the people!
>
> What is my principal task now? To reveal the *truth*. To show and to demonstrate that the true criminals hide under the cloak of the accusers.[2]

Trotsky's appeal led to the formation of an international commission of inquiry, chaired by the celebrated American liberal philosopher, John Dewey. In April 1937, members of the commission traveled to Mexico where they held public hearings at which Trotsky answered questions dealing with all aspects of his political principles, ideas, and activities. He

---

2. Leon Trotsky, "Speech for a Newsreel, January 30, 1937," *Writings of Leon Trotsky [1936-37]* (New York: Pathfinder Press, 1978), p. 179.

testified for eleven days. The commissioners then returned to the United States, where they pored over the evidence and finally rendered their verdict in December 1937. They found Trotsky not guilty and denounced the trials in Moscow as a frame-up.

The Stalinist regime responded to Trotsky's exposure of the Moscow Trials by escalating its attacks on the Fourth International. In July 1937, the German Trotskyist Erwin Wolf, one of Trotsky's most capable secretaries, was kidnapped while on assignment in Spain. He was subsequently tortured and murdered. In September 1937, Ignace Reiss—who had defected from the GPU, denounced Stalin, and declared his support for the Fourth International—was tracked down by the Stalinist secret police and murdered in Switzerland. The circumstances of Reiss' murder raised suspicions that he had been betrayed by an agent planted by the GPU inside the Paris center of the Fourth International. The principal target of these suspicions was Mark Zborowski-Etienne. However, with the assistance of Lola Dallin, who wrote regularly to Natalia Sedova in Mexico and portrayed herself and Zborowski as selfless comrades and assistants of Leon Sedov, the accusers of the GPU agent were kept on the defensive.

In February 1938, Sedov suddenly fell ill with what appeared to be a routine appendicitis. He was transported to a hospital, the Clinic Mirabeau, chosen by Lola Dallin. It was known to be infested with anti-Bolshevik Russian émigrés as well as GPU agents. Zborowski informed the GPU of Sedov's illness and whereabouts. Following a routine operation, Sedov appeared to be recovering. But he suddenly took a turn for the worse, fell into a delirium, and died in agony.

The physical cause of Sedov's death was never precisely determined. The available evidence indicates that he was the victim of either a peritonitis attack caused by deliberate medical malpractice, or poisoning. But while the means employed to bring about Sedov's death remain unknown, there is no reason to doubt, to quote the words of the old Trotskyist Georges Vereeken (1896–1978), "that Trotsky's son was deliberately handed over to the GPU killers by Zborowski."[3]

Following the murder of Leon Sedov, Zborowski and Dallin sent a tender message of condolence to his bereaved parents. However, suspicions against both Zborowski and Dallin mounted, and an effort was made by

---

3. Georges Vereeken, *The GPU in the Trotskyist Movement* (London, New Park Publications, 1976), p. 291.

Trotsky to establish a commission of inquiry. It is believed that Rudolf Klement, the secretary of the Fourth International, was in possession of an appeal from Trotsky for the creation of a commission when he suddenly disappeared from his Paris apartment in July 1938, just six weeks before the founding congress of the Fourth International was to be held. Klement's decapitated torso was eventually pulled out of the Seine River. Within the space of one year, four major figures in the Fourth International had been murdered. In each case, the GPU assassination squads acted with information provided by Zborowski-Etienne. And with both Sedov and Klement murdered, Zborowski participated in the founding congress of the Fourth International as the official Russian delegate.

As the GPU murdered his closest collaborators and supporters, the preparations for Trotsky's assassination intensified. Seeking information about and access to Trotsky, the GPU successfully placed an agent in the New York headquarters of the Socialist Workers Party (SWP) in 1938. The agent was a young member of the Communist Party by the name of Sylvia Franklin, who was married to a Stalinist agent named Zalmond Franklin. Louis Budenz—the editor of the Stalinist *Daily Worker* who was also heavily engaged in anti-Trotskyist espionage operations—introduced Franklin to one of the top Soviet GPU operatives in the United States, Gregory Rabinowitz (alias "John"), who selected her for the assignment. She adopted the party name Sylvia Caldwell, and soon managed to become the personal secretary of SWP national secretary James P. Cannon. In that position, she had access to all communications between Cannon and Trotsky. She systematically copied documents in Cannon's office and turned them over to the GPU.

Another critical step in the conspiracy against Trotsky was taken when Budenz, again working with Rabinowitz, carefully stage-managed the rekindling of a friendship between Ruby Weil, a member of the Communist Party, and an old acquaintance named Sylvia Ageloff, who had become active in the Trotskyist movement. Weil accompanied Ageloff on a trip to Europe in 1938, and it was there that Weil introduced Ageloff to Ramon Mercader, alias "Frank Jacson," the future assassin of Leon Trotsky.

The GPU also planted agents inside Trotsky's villa in Coyoacan. Many years later, in May 1956, in the course of a US Senate investigation into Soviet espionage, an American ex-GPU agent by the name of Thomas L. Black testified that he was selected by Rabinowitz to take part in the conspiracy against Trotsky. He told the Senate committee:

First, I was to go to Coyoacan, and there would be other Soviet agents in Trotsky's household, and I asked him who they would be. He said that I would find out that when the time came.[4]

Asked if he knew the nature of the planned assignment, Black replied: "To arrange for the assassination of Trotsky."[5]

As it turned out, Black did not travel to Mexico and participate in the assassination. However, agents were already in place in Coyoacan, and—as subsequent evidence eventually confirmed—at least one other American GPU operative in the SWP was sent down to Mexico from New York in the spring of 1940 to participate in the assassination conspiracy.

Trotsky was not unaware of, let alone indifferent to, the Stalinist efforts to murder him and strangle the Fourth International. In November 1937, he wrote "An Open Letter to All Workers' Organizations."

> Never before has the labor movement had in its own ranks so vicious, dangerous, powerful, and unscrupulous an enemy as Stalin's clique and its international agents. Remissness in the struggle against this enemy is tantamount to betrayal. Only windbags and dilettantes but not serious revolutionists can confine themselves to pathetic outbursts of indignation. It is necessary to have a plan and an organization. It is urgent to create special commissions which would follow the maneuvers, intrigues, and crimes of the Stalinists, warn the labor organizations of danger in store, and elaborate the best methods of parrying and resisting the Moscow gangsters.[6]

This passage refutes the absurd and lying claim—propagated by the SWP in the aftermath of the assassination—that Trotsky emphatically opposed any discussion of, let alone counter-measures against, the danger posed by the GPU to the Fourth International. The historical record establishes that

---

4. "Scope of Soviet Activity in the United States," Hearings Before the Subcommittee to Investigate the Administration of the Internal Security Act and Other Internal Security Laws of the Committee on the Judiciary, United States Senate, April 27 and May 17, 1956. https://archive.org/stream/ScopeOfSovietActivityInTheUnitedStates
5. Ibid.
6. Leon Trotsky, "It Is High Time to Launch a World Offensive Against Stalinism: An Open Letter to All Workers' Organizations," *Writings of Leon Trotsky [1936-37]* (New York: Pathfinder Press, 1978), p. 179.

Trotsky actively sought to expose and counteract the operations of the GPU. These efforts, however, were frustrated by agents already positioned inside the Fourth International.

In late 1938, Alexander Orlov, who had occupied a high position in the GPU, defected from the Soviet Union. He was intimately familiar with the murderous operations of the GPU against the Fourth International. Though his motivations remain unclear, Orlov sent Trotsky a secret communication that identified a certain "Mark" as an agent of the GPU. Though he did not know the last name of the agent, it was clearly Zborowski-Etienne. Trotsky—who did not know of Orlov—immediately sought to make contact with the unknown correspondent. The effort, for reasons that remain unclear, was not successful.

Several months later, Orlov sent a second and even more detailed denunciation of the agent in Paris. The letter also warned Trotsky that a female GPU agent would come to Mexico and attempt to poison him. Shortly afterwards, in the summer of 1939, Lola Dallin arrived in Mexico. Trotsky confronted her with the letter. In testimony later given to a Senate subcommittee, Dallin claimed that she persuaded Trotsky that the letter was a GPU hoax. She told Trotsky: "See how they work? They want that you should break with the only people that are left over in France, Russians, let us say, in France, in Paris."⁷ Despite Dallin's attempt to discredit the warning, Trotsky attempted again, but without success, to make contact with its anonymous author.

As for Dallin, upon returning to Paris, she immediately—according to her Senate testimony—warned Zborowski of the messages Trotsky had received. This information effectively rendered useless Trotsky's proposal that his followers in Paris secretly track Zborowski's movements.

In the early morning hours of May 24, 1940, a Stalinist raiding party armed with machine guns, led by the painter and fanatical Stalinist David Alfaro Siqueiros, was able to enter the grounds of Trotsky's villa on the Avenida Viena. They did not need to scale the walls of the villa or use explosives to blow the front gate open. The gate was opened for them by Robert Sheldon Harte, a twenty-five-year-old Stalinist from New York City who had gained admission to the SWP. Owing to the indifference to security

---

7. "Scope of Soviet Activity in the United States:," Hearing Before the Subcommittee to Investigate the Administration of the Internal Security Act and Other Internal Security Laws, March 2, 1956, Google Books, p. 137. Available: https://books.google.com/books?id=4GBHKfJ_uqkC&pg=PA101-IA10&lpg=PA101-IA10&dq=senate+subcommittee+

that characterized the SWP leadership, Harte—whose personal and political background was all but unknown—was soon sent to serve on Trotsky's guard detail.

Miraculously, Trotsky and Natalia managed to survive the assault by slipping under the bed as the assassins sprayed their bedroom with machine gun fire. The raid exposed the utter lack of preparation by Trotsky's guard detail. After the raiding party retreated from the villa, believing that it had accomplished its mission, Trotsky was the first to walk out onto the grounds. He had to search for his guards. None of them had fired their weapons. The few who had attempted to fight back were unable to do so because their machine guns jammed, apparently because they were using the wrong ammunition.

Almost immediately, well-grounded suspicions were raised about the role of Sheldon Harte in the assault. He disappeared with the raiding party, and eyewitness accounts indicated that Harte had left the villa of his own volition. A picture of Stalin was discovered in Harte's New York apartment. A dictionary in his possession bore the signature of Siqueiros. Several weeks after the raid, Harte's body was discovered. Members of the Siqueiros gang had executed him. At that point, Trotsky did not accept the allegations against Harte. But the peculiar and highly suspicious aspects of Harte's behavior did not allow Trotsky to categorically declare the dead man's innocence. He left open the possibility that Harte may have been involved in the attempt on his life. In any event, documents discovered after the dissolution of the Soviet Union have irrefutably established that Harte was, indeed, a Stalinist agent. He had been murdered because Siqueiros doubted that he could be trusted with information relating to the organization and execution of the raid.

In the final weeks that remained of his life, Trotsky devoted his immense reserves of energy to the exposure of the Stalinist murder machine. He wrote two major documents relating to the May 24th raid: "Stalin Seeks My Death," completed on June 8, 1940, and "The Comintern and the GPU," completed on August 17, 1940, just three days before his assassination.

On August 20, 1940, shortly after five in the afternoon, Frank Jacson arrived unexpectedly at the villa on the Avenida Viena. Following his previous visit, on August 17, Trotsky had expressed displeasure with Jacson's odd behavior. He voiced doubts about Jacson's claim that he was a Frenchman. Except for his relationship with Sylvia Ageloff, the nature of his interest in the Fourth International remained entirely unknown and unexamined.

But no notice was taken of Trotsky's concerns, and Jacson was admitted into the compound. Though it was a warm and sunny day, Jacson was carrying a raincoat, in which he concealed an alpenstock, an automatic firearm, and a large dagger. In violation of the most elementary security procedures, Jacson was permitted to accompany Trotsky alone into his study. Minutes later, while Trotsky reviewed an article written by Jacson, the assassin struck Trotsky from behind with the alpenstock. Jacson had expected that the blow to the head would immediately render Trotsky unconscious. But Trotsky screamed, rose from his chair, and fought back against his assassin. Guards ran into the study and disarmed Jacson.

Trotsky gradually lapsed into unconsciousness as he was driven to the hospital. He died twenty-six hours after the assault, on August 21, 1940. He was two months short of his sixty-first birthday.

The assassination of Trotsky was a devastating blow to the international working class. To the extent that any one man or woman can be described as politically indispensable to the cause of socialism, Trotsky was such a person. He embodied a vast and unequalled political experience. With the possible exception of Lenin, there was no other figure who played such a monumental role in the political history of the twentieth century. Moreover, seventy-five years after his death, Trotsky remains an extraordinarily contemporary figure. He has not yet passed entirely into history. He is as much a figure of the present as he is of the past. The writings of Trotsky, his theoretical and political conceptions, his revolutionary internationalism, still speak with immense power to the problems of the world in which we live today. Trotsky remains the great voice of the unfinished revolutionary tasks bequeathed by the twentieth century to the twenty-first.

6

Lenin, Trotsky, and the Marxism of the October Revolution

I am pleased to have had the opportunity to attend the Leipzig Book Fair, and also to speak here at the University of Leipzig. At the book fair, Mehring Books, the publishing arm of the International Committee of the Fourth International, presented its two-volume collection of lectures and essays marking the centenary of the Russian Revolution. The title of the two-volume work is *Why Study the Russian Revolution?*[1] I am confident that the material in them answers the title's question.

In brief, the central theses advanced are, first, that the Russian Revolution was the most significant event of the twentieth century; and, second, that the lessons of this revolution must be studied if the global crisis that now confronts humanity in the twenty-first century is to be resolved on a progressive basis—that is, through the ending of the capitalist system, the establishment of workers' power, and the democratic, egalitarian, and scientific reorganization of the world economy on a socialist basis.

The October Revolution was the culmination of the massive social uprising of the working class and oppressed masses of Russia in 1917. It was, and remains,

---

Lecture given at the University of Leipzig in Germany on March 16, 2018. Published on the World Socialist Web Site, March 19, 2018.

1. International Committee of the Fourth International, *Why Study the Russian Revolution Volume I & Volume II* (Oak Park MI: Mehring Books, 2018).

unique in one fundamental sense: it was the first, and remains to this day, the only revolution carried out consciously by the working class, led by a Marxist party acting on the basis of an international socialist program and perspective.

If I may be permitted to quote from my first lecture on the Russian Revolution, delivered in March 2017 and published in the first volume of *Why Study the Russian Revolution?*

> The Russian Revolution demands serious study as a critical episode in the development of scientific social thought. The historical achievement of the Bolsheviks in 1917 both demonstrated and actualized the essential relationship between scientific materialist philosophy and revolutionary practice.[2]

The evolution of the Bolshevik Party vindicated Lenin's statement in *What Is to Be Done?* "Without revolutionary theory there can be no revolutionary movement." As Lenin continuously insisted, Marxism is the most highly developed form of *philosophical materialism*, which critically reworked and assimilated the genuine achievements of classical German idealism, chiefly that of Hegel (that is, dialectical logic and the recognition of the active role of historically evolving social practice in the cognition of objective reality).

In no other revolution was there such a conscious and explicit relationship between Marxist theory and the revolutionary practice of the working class. In order to explain, more precisely, the nature of this relationship, it is necessary to take note of the significant historical anniversaries that we are marking in 2018.

This year marks the 200th anniversary of the birth of Karl Marx. It also marks the 170th anniversary of the publication of the *Communist Manifesto*. Of all the great philosophers, none speaks to our own time so powerfully and directly as Karl Marx. His work does not require "retranslation" into a comprehensible modern language. In a letter to Lassalle in May 1858, Marx noted, "Even in the case of philosophers who give systematic form to their work, Spinoza for instance, the true inner structure of the system is quite unlike the form in which it was consciously presented by him."[3]

---

2. David North, "Why Study the Russian Revolution?," Ibid., p. 19.
3. Karl Marx, Letter to Ferdinand Lassalle, *Marx-Engels Collected Works*, Vol. 40 (New York: International Publishers, 1983), p. 316.

In Marx, by contrast, there is a remarkable correspondence between the "true inner structure" of the philosopher's system and the form in which it found expression. Beginning with his critique of Hegel's *Philosophy of Law*, Marx set out to liberate theoretical thought from the mystical obfuscations of philosophical idealism. There is a wonderful moment in Raoul Peck's film, *The Young Marx*, when Engels says, to the not entirely congenial revolutionary journalist, "You are the greatest materialist philosopher of our age. You are, my dear man, a genius."

Engels is referring specifically to Marx's *Critique of Hegel's Philosophy of Law*. In this work, written in 1843, Marx draws attention to the central problem of Hegel's philosophical idealism:

> Not the logic of the matter, but the matter of logic is the philosophical element. The logic does not serve to prove the state, but the state to prove the logic.[4]

That is, Hegel derived the state and its laws from the movement of pure thought, from the self-movement of the abstract categories of Logic. This was an inversion, in the realm of idealist philosophy, of the actual relationship between matter and consciousness. The critique of Hegel's system required a return to philosophical materialism, which asserts the primacy of matter over consciousness; that consciousness is derived from and reflects the movement of a material universe. Marx's critique of Hegel's idealism—what Engels praises, in the scene to which we have just referred, with the well-known phrase, "Placing Hegel on his feet,"—established the theoretical foundation for the revolution in social, historical, and political thought that was accomplished jointly by Marx and Engels between 1844 and 1847.

In *The German Ideology*, written in 1845 (though not published for eighty years), Marx and Engels contrasted their materialist philosophy to the idealism of the Young Hegelians, who followed in their deceased master's footsteps:

> In direct contrast to German philosophy which descends from heaven to earth, here it is a matter of ascending from earth to heaven. That is to say, not of setting out from what men say,

---

4. Karl Marx, "Contribution to the Critique of Hegel's Philosophy of Law," *Marx-Engels Collected Works*, Vol. 3 (New York: International Publishers, 1975), p. 18.

imagine, conceive, nor from men as narrated, thought of, imagined, conceived, in order to arrive at men in the flesh; but setting out from real, active men, and on the basis of their real life-process demonstrating the development of the ideological reflexes and echoes of this life-process.[5]

The outcome of this work was the elaboration of the materialist conception of history, its application to the scientific study of the laws of motion of the modern capitalist system, and, on this theoretical foundation, the conscious political organization of the international working class, and the development of the strategy and tactics of the world socialist revolution. Marx concisely summarized his materialist conception of history in the "Preface to a Critique of Political Economy," written in 1859:

> In the social production of their existence, men inevitably enter into definite relations, which are independent of their will, namely relations of production appropriate to a given stage in the development of their material forces of production. The totality of these relations of production constitutes the economic structure of society, the real foundation, on which arises a legal and political superstructure and to which correspond definite forms of social consciousness. The mode of production of material life conditions the general process of social, political and intellectual life. It is not the consciousness of men that determines their existence, but their social existence that determines their consciousness.[6]

Throughout his life, Marx insisted on the materialist foundations of his theoretical work. In his Afterword to the first volume of *Das Kapital*, published in 1867, Marx explained:

> My dialectic method is not only different from the Hegelian, but is its direct opposite. To Hegel, the life-process of the human brain, *i.e.*, the process of thinking, which, under the name of

---

5. Karl Marx and Frederick Engels, "The German Ideology," *Marx-Engels Collected Works*, Vol. 5 (New York: International Publishers, 1976), p. 36.
6. Karl Marx, "Preface to a Critique of Political Economy," *Marx-Engels Collected Works*, Vol. 29 (New York: International Publishers, 1987), p. 263.

"the Idea," he even transforms into an independent subject, is the demiurgos of the real world, and the real world is only the external, phenomenal form of "the Idea." With me, on the contrary, the ideal is nothing else than the material world reflected by the human mind, and translated into forms of thought.[7]

Marx resisted all efforts to reconcile his materialist philosophy with Hegelian or any other variation of philosophical idealism. In 1868, in a letter to his good friend Ludwig Kugelmann, Marx explicitly refuted the claim of the young professor Eugen Dühring that *Das Kapital* was based on a Hegelian schema:

He [Dühring] knows full well that my method of exposition is *not* Hegelian, since I am a materialist, and Hegel an idealist. Hegel's dialectic is the basic form of all dialectic, but only *after* being stripped of its mystical form, and it is precisely this which distinguishes *my* method.[8]

Marx and Engels' application of the materialist conception of history in their analyses of the economic and social contradictions of the capitalist system are being substantiated, as never before, in the contemporary world. The global expansion of capitalism, particularly during the past quarter-century, has created a state of permanent and continuously intensifying crisis. It has become something of a cliché to state that Fukuyama's "End of History" thesis—proclaimed in the aftermath of the dissolution of the USSR and the Stalinist regimes in Eastern Europe—has been refuted by events. All the contradictions exposed by Marx now manifest themselves with unprecedented intensity. The accumulation of wealth is accompanied by an extraordinary degree of social inequality. A few dozen people in the world control and dispose of more wealth than three-quarters of the planet's entire population. The real state of capitalist society exceeds in its injustices, its fixation with the mindless accumulation of personal riches, the clumsiest of populist caricatures. In every critical social sphere—education, health care, housing, and a secure old age—capitalist society is moving backward, renouncing even the limited reforms of the past century.

---

7. Karl Marx, *Capital* Vol. 1 (London: Lawrence & Wishart, 1974), p. 29. Citation is from the 1873 Afterword to the Second German Edition.
8. Karl Marx to Ludwig Kugelman, *Marx-Engels Collected Works*, Vol. 42 (New York: International Publishers, 1987), p. 544.

The descriptions given by the ruling elites of the present state of the world speak for themselves. The possibility of a cataclysmic war between nuclear armed powers is widely acknowledged.

And yet, in the midst of global crisis, the intellectual representatives of petty-bourgeois pseudo-left politics, occupying prominent positions in the academic world, proclaim the death of Marxism. Countless professors, obsessed with issues of race, gender, ethnicity, psychology, environmentalism, and, of course, sexuality, assert that Marxism cannot provide a guide to the problems of the present. Answers must be found outside the theoretical framework of Marxism.

In a volume that bears the imposing title, *Critical Companion to Contemporary Marxism*, the authors state:

> We are no longer dealing with a crisis *within* Marxism between various interpretations, provoking expulsions and splits ... We face a crisis that involves Marxism's very existence, capped as it is by the disappearance of the institutions, party or other, that officially referred to it, and by its erasure from the cultural sphere, the collective memory, and individual imaginations.[9]
>
> The most important authors we present, from Bourdieu, via Habermas and Foucault, to Derrida, can in no way be identified as Marxists. Such figures, along with others, simply seem to us to be indispensable to any reconstruction. They represent other elements in our culture, which cannot be assimilated to Marxism, but which are nevertheless precious to us.[10]

A more appropriate title of this volume would be *Companion for Contemporary Anti-Marxists*. The publishers, editors, and contributors are seeking to resolve the "crisis of Marxism" on the basis of its liquidation into various forms of idealist, irrationalist, and explicitly anti-Marxist thought.

Involved in this project are not only incorrect theoretical conceptions. Underlying the anti-Marxist theoretical conceptions are reactionary political positions, rooted in the interests of sections of the petty bourgeoisie—its

---

9. Jacques Bidet and Stathis Kouvelakis, eds., *Critical Companion to Contemporary Marxism* (Chicago: Haymarket Books, 2009), p. 5.
10. Ibid., p. 7.

more affluent sections—that are hostile to the entire theoretical and political legacy of the October Revolution.

For example, a leading academic representative of the contemporary pseudo-left, Alain Badiou, wrote in 2008:

> Marxism, the workers' movement, mass democracy, Leninism, the party of the proletariat, the socialist state—all the inventions of the 20th century—are not really useful to us anymore.[11]

The pseudo-leftist celebrity and intellectual charlatan Slavoj Žižek states in his latest book *Lenin 2017: Remembering, Repeating, and Working Through*:

> Let's face it: today, Lenin and his legacy are perceived as hopelessly dated, belonging to a defunct 'paradigm'. Not only was Lenin understandably blind to many of the problems that are now central to contemporary life (ecology, struggles for emancipated sexuality, etc.), but also his brutal political practice is totally out of sync with current democratic sensitivities, his vision of the new society as a centralised industrial system run by the state is simply irrelevant, etc.?[12]

None of these critics of Marxism offers any credible theoretical and political alternative. The same Monsieur Badiou, who proclaimed that Marxism and other "inventions" of the twentieth century "are not really useful to us anymore," wrote just two years later: "[T]he majority of the political categories movement activists are trying to use to think and transform our current situations are, as they now stand, largely inoperative." The title of this essay is, appropriately, "Our Contemporary Impotence."[13]

In discussing the intellectual bankruptcy of the contemporary pseudo-left, I cannot avoid calling attention to yet another anniversary. This year

---

11. Alain Badiou, "The Communist Hypothesis," New Left Review, No. 49, Jan./Feb. 2008. Available: https://newleftreview.org/issues/ii49/articles/alain-badiou-the-communist-hypothesis
12. Slavoj Žižek, *Lenin 2017: Remembering, Repeating, and Working Through* (New York, Verso, 2017), p. xiv.
13. Alain Badiou, "Our contemporary impotence," *Radical Philosophy* 181, Sept./Oct. 2013, p. 43, available: https://www.radicalphilosophy.com/article/our-contemporary-impotence.

marks the fiftieth anniversary of 1968, a year that witnessed massive social upheaval on a world scale—from the struggle waged against American imperialism in Vietnam and the mass student protests throughout the world against this neocolonial war, to the events of May-June 1968 that threatened the survival of capitalism in France, and the anti-Stalinist Prague Spring in Czechoslovakia.

In that critical year, what were the theoretical works that influenced politically-radicalized youth, students, and broad sections of the left intelligentsia? Of course, Marxism was very much "in the air." But it was a "Marxism" that was, in its theoretical foundations and political orientation, profoundly different from the Marxism that formed the basis of the practice of the Bolshevik Party. It was not the school of Marx, Engels, Lenin, and Trotsky that influenced the Generation of 1968, but the Frankfurt School of Max Horkheimer, Theodore Adorno, Walter Benjamin, Wilhelm Reich, and, most popular of all, Herbert Marcuse.

Two characteristics of the Frankfurt School need to be stressed: First, its indifference, and even explicit hostility, to the working class and the development of its struggle against the capitalist system. The essential element of the historical pessimism and skepticism of the Frankfurt School was its rejection of the classical Marxist conception of the decisive revolutionary role of the working class in the struggle against capitalism. This pessimism can be politically explained as a demoralized reaction to the defeats suffered by the German working class between 1918 and 1933. For intellectuals such as Horkheimer and Marcuse, these defeats were not to be explained as the outcome of the errors and betrayals of the political parties of the working class—that is, of the Social Democratic and Communist parties—but as the demonstration of the non-revolutionary character of the working class.

As early as 1927, in an essay titled "The Impotence of the German Working Class," Max Horkheimer wrote: "The capitalist process of production has thus driven a wedge between the interest in socialism and the human qualities necessary to its implementation."[14]

The political pessimism of the Frankfurt School was intensified by the catastrophe of 1933 and the horrors of Nazism and the Second World War. What little remained of the Marxism of the Frankfurt School academics served as little more than window dressing for their accommodation to the post-World War Two imperialist order and, especially in the case of Horkheimer and

---

14. Max Horkheimer, *Dawn & Decline: Notes 1926–1931 and 1950–1969* (New York: Seabury Press, 1978), p. 62.

Adorno, the reconstruction of the bourgeois democratic state under the aegis of Konrad Adenauer ("Der Alte"), Ludwig Erhard ("Der Dicke"), and even Kurt Georg Kiesinger ("Der Nazi"). Herbert Marcuse attempted to maintain a more critical and radical attitude to capitalist society. But his rejection of the working class as a revolutionary force was no less explicit:

> Now to the question of the working class. I said, and I still say it today, that the American working class is not a revolutionary class. ... I said that in the present situation, in view of the fact that the American working class is not a revolutionary class, it so happens that the political consciousness, the radical political consciousness, is concentrated among minority nonintegrated groups such as the students, such as the black and brown minorities, such as women and so on.[15]

As I have already stated, the theoretical conceptions developed in opposition to Marxism are, in the final analysis, rooted in definite social and political interests. The theoreticians of the Frankfurt School expressed the outlook of sections of the German petty bourgeoisie. Moreover, the main representatives of the Frankfurt School showed no interest in, let alone active political support for, Trotsky's struggle against the Stalinist regime in the Soviet Union. This is a political fact that is, without question, of great importance in understanding the evolution of the Frankfurt School. However, it would be wrong to neglect consideration of its theoretical-philosophical roots. An examination of the theoretical influences that found expression in the Frankfurt School is necessary, not only to understand this intellectual tendency and its many offshoots, but also to identify its essential difference from the Marxism of Bolshevism and the October Revolution.

Marxism played an immense role in the development of the German workers movement. It provided the theoretical foundation for the development of the SPD as the mass party of the German working class. It is unquestionable that the advanced sections of the working class were educated on the basis of Marxism, and that Marxism also influenced broad sections of the petty-bourgeois intelligentsia. But it must be stressed that the relation of the petty-bourgeois intelligentsia to Marxism was frequently ambivalent and even hostile. This

---

15. Debate between Herbert Marcuse and Raymond Aron, available: https://www.nytimes.com/1972/08/15/archives/marx-and-paramarx-on-capitalist-contradictions.html

is a complex subject, which has been the subject of extensive historical study. Only a brief overview of this issue is possible within the framework of this lecture.

It is a striking historical coincidence that, at precisely the point when the Social Democratic Party emerged from illegality in 1890, with virtually unchallengeable authority within the working class, sections of the petty-bourgeois intelligentsia expressed increasing dissatisfaction with the Marxist foundations of the movement. Specifically, the philosophical materialism of Marxism, its insistence on the primacy of matter over consciousness, on the law-governed character of social development, and the dominant influence of economic forces, aroused increasing objection within sections of the petty-bourgeois periphery of the SPD. Marxism, they argued, placed excessive emphasis on the law-governed character of social processes, of objective necessity over subjective initiative, and of conscious motivation over unconscious and even irrational impulses. Marxian determinism, rooted in philosophical materialism, discouraged the individual expression of free will and personal initiative.

In opposition to Marxist materialism, with its insistence on the primacy of socioeconomic forces and processes and its elevation of scientific knowledge and objective truth over intuition and subjective will, political and intellectual tendencies drew inspiration not from Marx, but from Schopenhauer and Nietzsche. One such tendency was represented by the well-known anarchist, Gustav Landauer. He declared himself a bitter enemy of Marxist materialism:

> We perceive the coming condition of things as possible or even as necessary because we love it and desire it. Man is the measure of all things and there is no objective knowledge in which concepts are a mirror of the objects perceived. ...
>
> It would be much more worthwhile if socialists would first give unconstrained expression to their will and then make clear why they believe that the thing is also capable of realization. But to proclaim the unconditional necessity, founded upon nature, of a definite course ... is to cripple the driving power of the movement through a ... superstition that everything will develop by itself. ...[16]

---

16. Gustav Landauer, „Dühringianer und Marxisten", *Der Sozialist*, October 1892, cited in Eugene Lunn, *Prophet of Community, The Romantic Socialism of Gustav Landauer* (Berkeley: University of California Press, 1973), p. 61.

> Marxism ... must be told to its face that it is the plague of our age and the curse of the socialist movement![17]

The views expressed by Landauer emerged in the context of an intellectual environment in which substantial sections of the bourgeois and petty-bourgeois intelligentsia and especially artists were increasingly drawn to the exploration of the unconscious. Even as science was making extraordinary advances, these layers were seized by the conviction that the key to an understanding of reality and ultimate truth lay in the exploration of subjective experience.

This was by no means a tendency that found expression only in Germany and Austria. It was a broad-based intellectual phenomenon, which found a response throughout Europe, including Russia. The implications of this assault on philosophical materialism were far-reaching. It raised the following questions: were the program, strategy, and tactics of the socialist parties, and the practice of the working class, to be based on a scientific analysis of an objective reality that exists independently of consciousness, or on the basis of intuition and subjective will? Were the goals and actions of the working class to be based on an understanding of objective laws of social development or, as George Sorel and others urged, on psychologically provocative myths?

Two prominent figures in the Bolshevik faction of the Russian Social Democratic Party, Alexander Bogdanov and Anatoly Lunacharsky, under, to a not inconsiderable extent, the influence of Nietzsche, argued that Marxism had to be revised in a manner that would infuse the struggle for socialism with a far greater emotional content. Lunacharsky even proposed the development of a new socialist religion, which would sustain the revolutionary movement with faith and enthusiasm, and thereby counter the pessimism and demoralization that followed the defeat of the 1905 Revolution. Lunacharsky declaimed: "Let us adore the potential of mankind, our potential and represent it in an aureole of glory, the more strongly to love it." As one historian noted in a study of Nietzsche's influence on Russian socialists, Lunacharsky's "preaching has the manufactured enthusiasm and false cheerfulness of scoutmasters whipping up support for an unpopular but necessary chore: Lunacharskii frequently expresses the conviction that in the current social crisis only the enthusiasm produced by his

---

17. Gustav Landauer, „Aufruf zum Sozialismus", 1908–1911, cited in ibid., p. 201.

religion can provide the strength and motivation needed for the victory of socialism."[18]

Lenin, bemused by Lunacharsky's religious ecstasy, began referring to him as "the blessed Anatole." But Lenin did not limit himself to endowing his erratic comrade with a humorous nickname. Recognizing the dangerous political implications of the development of subjective and irrationalist tendencies within the socialist movement, Lenin wrote his greatest theoretical treatise, *Materialism and Empirio-Criticism*. There is no other work by Lenin that has provoked such outrage as his intransigent defense of philosophical materialism. Not even *What Is to Be Done?* has been so bitterly denounced. *Materialism and Empirio-Criticism*, it is claimed, is a work of "vulgar materialism," which impermissibly simplifies the relationship between matter and consciousness, promoting the "crude" conception that consciousness is merely a reflection of the material world, and that human thought and practice are nothing more than a programmed response to material stimuli. It is even claimed that Lenin, when he wrote *Materialism and Empirio-Criticism*, had not yet studied Hegel and was not familiar with dialectics.

Such descriptions of *Materialism and Empirio-Criticism* unscrupulously distort Lenin's text, not to mention his intellectual biography. One will find in *Materialism and Empirio-Criticism* numerous passages in which Lenin brilliantly illuminated the relationship between materialism and dialectical logic. But he certainly did insist on the primacy of matter over consciousness, and on the objective existence of a material world independent of thought. Lenin's profound respect for Hegel's *Logic* was always tempered by his criticism of its idealist foundations. To the very end of his life, Lenin remained firmly committed to the defense of the theoretical method and heritage of Karl Marx and Friedrich Engels. The recognition of the objective world, existing independently of consciousness, formed the essential basis of a materialist epistemology. And this materialist epistemology was, in turn, the theoretical foundation for the development of a scientifically grounded program and perspective upon which to base the practice of the working class. In a critical passage of *Materialism and Empirio-Criticism*, Lenin wrote:

> The highest task of humanity is to comprehend this objective logic of economic evolution (the evolution of social life) in its

---

18. Aileen Kelly, "Empiriocriticism: A Bolshevik Philosophy?," *Cahiers du Monde russe et soviétique*, Vol. 22, No. 1 (January-March 1981), p. 104.

general and fundamental features, so that it may be possible to adapt *to it* one's social consciousness and the consciousness of the advanced classes of all capitalist countries in as definite, clear and critical a fashion as possible.[19]

What this means is that the working class must understand the laws of historical and social development, and it must be able to correctly analyze objective developments in order to conduct a revolutionary struggle against capitalism and change the world. It is on this basis that the great Russian Marxists—above all, Lenin and Trotsky—prepared for and led the working class to power in October 1917.

Lenin's commitment to materialism was not of a merely abstract and intellectual character. The defense of materialism was inseparably bound up with the fight to develop a correct appraisal of political developments, define precisely the tasks of the working class, and provide a correct political and practical orientation. The essential link between philosophical materialism and the political orientation of the working class was repeatedly stressed by Lenin. In his 1913 essay, "The Three Sources and Three Component Parts of Marxism," Lenin wrote:

> The philosophy of Marxism is *materialism*. Throughout the modern history of Europe, and especially at the end of the eighteenth century in France, where a resolute struggle was conducted against every kind of medieval rubbish, against serfdom in institutions and ideas, materialism has proved to be the only philosophy that is consistent, true to all the teachings of natural science and hostile to superstition, cant and so forth. The enemies of democracy have, therefore, always exerted all their efforts to "refute", undermine and defame materialism, and have advocated various forms of philosophical idealism, which always, in one way or another, amounts to the defence or support of religion.[20]

An examination of the work of Lenin and Trotsky in the years prior to 1917 reveals an intense and unrelenting focus on issues of political

---

19. V. I. Lenin, "Materialism and Empirio-Criticism," *Collected Works* Vol. 14 (Moscow: Progress Publishers, 1968), p. 325.
20. V. I. Lenin, "Three Sources and Three Component Parts of Marxism," *Collected Works* Vol. 19 (Moscow: Progress Publishers, 1968), p. 24.

perspective and analysis. The Marxism of Lenin and Trotsky, rooted methodologically in dialectical and historical materialism, was occupied, above all, with understanding the dynamics of the escalating crisis of the world capitalist system, and the implications of that crisis within Russia. Again, to quote Lenin, this time from his biographical-theoretical essay on Karl Marx, written in 1913:

> Only an objective consideration of the sum total of the relations between absolutely all the classes in a given society, and consequently a consideration of the objective stage of development reached by that society and of the relations between it and other societies, can serve as a basis for the correct tactics of an advanced class.[21]

Notwithstanding the differences that existed between Lenin and Trotsky before 1917, their work was concentrated on the development of the strategic orientation of the socialist movement.

With the outbreak of war in 1914, Lenin's study of the world crisis acquired an extraordinary depth and intensity, with far-reaching consequences for the orientation of the Bolshevik Party in 1917. The theoretical work that underlay the writing of *Imperialism* in 1915–16 led to the crucial shift in Bolshevik strategy, which found expression in Lenin's *April Theses*. Though he had followed a different political path, Trotsky's extraordinary role in 1917 was prepared by his development, during the previous twelve years, of his theory of permanent revolution.

There can be no revolution without will, that is, without the highest degree of subjective determination. But will and determination must be guided by a correct appreciation of objective reality, upon which the practice of the socialist movement must be based. From a theoretical standpoint, the rejection of the glorification of subjective will as a basis for political action separates Marxism from countless varieties of petty-bourgeois radical politics, including anarchism and Maoism, and, of course, the most counterrevolutionary of mass middle-class movements, fascism. At a speech before the Third Congress of the Communist International in 1921, Trotsky explained:

---

21. V. I. Lenin, "Karl Marx," *Collected Works* Vol. 21 (Moscow: Progress Publishers, 1964), p. 75.

> If we detach the subjective from the objective aspect, this philosophy leads logically to pure revolutionary adventurism.
>
> And I believe that we have learned in the great school of Marxism to unite dialectically the objective with the subjective. That is, we have learned to base our action not only on this or that expression of subjective will but also on the conviction that the working class must hew to this subjective will of ours and that the will to action of the proletariat is determined by the objective situation.[22]

Two years later, when Trotsky was already engaged in the struggle against the growth of the bureaucracy in the Soviet Union, he brilliantly explained the relationship between the scientific appraisal of objective reality and subjective will in the work of Lenin:

> Leninism is, first of all, realism, the highest qualitative and quantitative appreciation of reality, from the standpoint of revolutionary action. Precisely because of this it is irreconcilable with the flight from reality behind the screen of hollow agitationalism, with the passive loss of time, with the haughty justification of yesterday's mistakes on the pretext of saving the tradition of the party.
>
> Leninism is genuine freedom from formalistic prejudices, from moralizing doctrinalism, from all forms of intellectual conservatism attempting to bind the will to revolutionary action. But to believe that Leninism signifies that 'anything goes', would be an irremediable mistake.[23]

We live in a world of extraordinary complexity. The vast and immensely powerful productive forces, global in scope, appear to overwhelm humanity. Certainly, they overwhelm the ruling class, which does not know how to, and —on account of the economic logic of the capitalist system—cannot develop and make socially progressive use of these forces. This is the essential problem that underlies the unending series of economic crises, intensifying

---

22. Leon Trotsky, "Summary of Discussion on World Economic Crisis," available: https://www.marxists.org/archive/trotsky/1921/trotsky03.htm
23. Leon Trotsky, *The New Course* (London: New Park Publications, 1943), p. 42.

social dislocation, and the mounting danger of a Third World War, fought with nuclear weapons.

The working class, by virtue of its objective position in the global productive forces, can solve the historical problem that eludes the bourgeoisie. But it can only accomplish this to the extent that it is able to align its subjective consciousness with objective reality. The revolutionary Marxist party is the essential political instrument for the achievement of this alignment of consciousness and reality, of objective political necessity with mass revolutionary practice. This alignment was achieved in 1917. It must be achieved again, and the accomplishment of this task is the central objective of the International Committee of the Fourth International.

7

Trotsky and Trotskyism in the Contemporary World

First, I would like to thank the Socialist Equality Party for inviting me to Sri Lanka to deliver two lectures on the occasion of the eightieth anniversary of the Fourth International. Actually, we are celebrating this year a double anniversary, for the SEP is also marking the fiftieth anniversary of its own founding, as the Sri Lankan section of the Fourth International, in 1968. The principled and courageous struggle that the SEP has waged, over a period of a half century, for the unity of all sections of the working class in Sri Lanka, regardless of ethnic or religious background, is well known to, and has inspired, socialists throughout the world.

The focus of my lectures in Colombo and Kandy will be a major event in the political history of the twentieth century: the founding of the Fourth International by Leon Trotsky in September 1938. It was the culmination of the struggle that Trotsky had begun fifteen years earlier, in 1923, when he founded the Left Opposition to fight against the bureaucratic degeneration of the Bolshevik Party and the Soviet regime, in which Stalin was coming to play an increasingly powerful and treacherous role. This struggle assumed international dimensions, as the Stalinist regime—under the false and anti-Marxist

---

David North delivered these remarks at a press briefing in Colombo's National Library Conference Hall on Monday, October 1, 2018. Published on the World Socialist Web site, October 2, 2018.

banner of socialism in one country—subordinated the struggle for world socialism to the defense of the material interests and privileges of the ruling bureaucracy within the Soviet Union.

Stalin's nationalist repudiation of the revolutionary internationalist program of Marxism led to a series of crushing defeats of the working class, such as in China in 1927 and Germany in 1933. In fact, it was the rise of the Nazis to power in Germany in January 1933—the consequence of the disastrous policies pursued by the Stalinists—that directly precipitated Trotsky's call for the formation of a new revolutionary international. The events that followed—such as the Stalinist betrayal of the Spanish Revolution and Stalin's launching, in 1936, of the counterrevolutionary terror that swept through the Soviet Union—confirmed the correctness of Trotsky's call for the Fourth International.

These events are, without question, of great historical significance, and it is certainly appropriate to devote lectures to their review and analysis. But, you might justly ask, in what way are the events that transpired so many years ago of contemporary interest? And why should workers, students, and intellectuals, who are not presently involved in the activities of the Fourth International, attend these lectures?

In answering these legitimate questions, allow me to recall the world situation that existed in 1938. The capitalist system was in the grip of a global economic crisis that had begun a decade earlier, with the Wall Street crash of 1929. The Great Depression inflicted massive suffering on the working class in the advanced capitalist countries. Democracy was in retreat throughout the world. To sustain its political rule in the face of mounting social anger, the ruling elites created various forms of authoritarian regimes, of which the Nazi Third Reich was only the most brutal. The foreign policy of the imperialist powers assumed an increasingly militaristic character, which found expression, first of all, in savage colonialist wars. The Japanese imperialists seized Manchuria in 1932. Mussolini invaded Ethiopia in 1935. Great power conflicts were intensifying relentlessly, and it was apparent that humanity was about to be plunged into a second world war, even more terrible than the first.

This was the world situation that existed when the founding congress of the Fourth International was held in September 1938. The programmatic document that Trotsky had written for the congress defined the epoch as the "death agony of capitalism." Permit me to quote just two paragraphs from this extraordinary document:

> The economic prerequisite for the proletarian revolution has already in general achieved the highest point of fruition that can be reached under capitalism. Mankind's productive forces stagnate. Already new inventions and improvements fail to raise the level of material wealth. Conjunctural crises under the conditions of the social crisis of the whole capitalist system inflict ever heavier deprivations and sufferings upon the masses. Growing unemployment, in its turn, deepens the financial crisis of the state and undermines the unstable monetary systems. Democratic regimes, as well as fascist, stagger on from one bankruptcy to another.
>
> The bourgeoisie itself sees no way out. In countries where it has already been forced to stake its last upon the card of fascism, it now toboggans with closed eyes toward an economic and military catastrophe. In the historically privileged countries, i.e., in those where the bourgeoisie can still for a certain period permit itself the luxury of democracy at the expense of national accumulations (Great Britain, France, United States, etc.), all of capital's traditional parties are in a state of perplexity bordering on a paralysis of will.[1]

Without changing too many words, Trotsky's description of the capitalist world in 1938 could serve very well as a description of the conditions that exist in 2018. Were he alive today, I do not think that Trotsky would find the contemporary world so hard to understand. Of course, he would have to learn how to use computers, cell phones, and social media. But he would have no reason to change his historical and political prognosis. The contemporary epoch is still that of capitalism's "death agony." Indeed, there are many indications that we are rapidly approaching a convulsive and violent stage in that historical death agony.

Nearly thirty years ago, following the dissolution of the Stalinist regimes in Eastern Europe and within the Soviet Union, the ideologists of the capitalist ruling elites proclaimed the "End of History." Capitalism had proved, once and for all, its unchallengeable superiority over socialism; it had shown that mankind would henceforth dally happily, beneath the warm glow of

---

1. Leon Trotsky, *The Death Agony of Capitalism and the Tasks of the Fourth International: The Transitional Program* (New York: Labor Publications, 1981), p. 1.

global financial markets, in the luxuriant garden of rising prosperity, universal democracy, and eternal peace.

As we now know, these boastful predictions were not realized. The global capitalist system is beset by mounting economic, social, and political crises. No less than the crash of 1929, the crash of 2008 exposed the fragility of the entire economic system. Its legacy is mountainous levels of debt and massive social inequality. Capitalist governments, first of all in the United States, bailed out the rich at the expense of the overwhelming mass of the population. In the process, they discredited capitalist democracy as a political fraud, a cover for the rule of billionaire oligarchs who rule the world economy. This accounts for the rise of right-wing demagogues and fascistic movements. In the United States, the White House is occupied by an out-and-out gangster by the name of Donald Trump. In Germany, fascism is once again on the rise.

Throughout the world, desperate refugees—the victims of economic crises and the brutal military operations launched by the imperialists under the banner of the "war on terror"—are being blamed and victimized for the conditions created by capitalism.

And as in the 1930s, the relentless intensification of geopolitical conflicts is leading inexorably to a third world war, a war which will be fought with nuclear weapons, with horrific consequences. The words written by Trotsky in the founding document of the Fourth International acquire an intensely contemporary relevance:

> The bourgeoisie, of course, is aware of the mortal danger to its domination represented by a new war. But that class is now immeasurably less capable of averting war than on the eve of 1914. ...
>
> Without a socialist revolution, in the next historical period at that, a catastrophe threatens the whole culture of mankind.[2]

The "next historical period" of which Trotsky wrote is now the one in which we live. Humanity is searching for a progressive answer to the prevailing capitalist chaos. It wants a future without poverty, exploitation, and war. The working people want a world based not on religious, ethnic, and national hatreds, but on human solidarity. That is why, all over the world—and even in the United States, the citadel of capitalist greed and reaction—there is a

---

2. Ibid., pp. 1–2.

growing interest in and support for socialism. But the fight for socialism today must be informed by historical knowledge. And that is why an examination of the founding of the Fourth International in 1938, and the struggles through which it has passed in the course of its eighty-year history, is of immense contemporary relevance.

8

Eighty Years of the Fourth International: The Lessons of History and the Struggle for Socialism Today

It is a pleasure and an honor to have the opportunity to lecture in Sri Lanka on the history of the Fourth International. The heroic role played by Ceylonese revolutionary socialists in the early years of the Fourth International is well known by Trotskyists throughout the world. In the face of immense difficulties, the pioneer Trotskyists who founded the Lanka Sama Samaja Party (LSSP) in 1935, and later, in 1942, the Bolshevik-Leninist Party of India (BLPI), opposed the political agents of imperialism in the Indian and Ceylonese national bourgeoisie. Their political perspective was based on the theory of permanent revolution, which had been elaborated by Leon Trotsky in the first decade of the twentieth century, and which provided the political strategy that guided the Russian working class to victory in 1917.

In 1939, Trotsky addressed a letter to the workers of India. With his characteristic grasp of history and the dynamic of the class struggle, Trotsky summed up the essential strategic issues that confronted the masses of the Indian subcontinent:

Lecture given October 7, 2018 in Colombo. Published on the World Socialist Web Site, October 9, 2018.

> The Indian bourgeoisie is incapable of leading a revolutionary struggle. They are closely bound up with and dependent upon British capitalism. They tremble for their own property. They stand in fear of the masses. They seek compromises with British imperialism no matter what the price and lull the Indian masses with hopes of reforms from above. The leader and prophet of this bourgeoisie is Gandhi. A fake leader and a false prophet![1]

Trotsky denounced the treacherous role played by the Stalinist regime in the Soviet Union, which demanded, under the banner of the "People's Front," the subordination of the working class to the national bourgeoisie. He wrote:

> What a mockery of the people! "People's Front" is only a new name for that old policy, the gist of which lies in class collaboration, in a coalition between the proletariat and the bourgeoisie. In every such coalition, the leadership invariably turns out to be in the hands of the right wing, that is, in the hands of the propertied class. The Indian bourgeoisie, as has already been stated, wants a peaceful horse trade and not a struggle. Coalition with the bourgeoisie leads to the proletariat's abnegating the revolutionary struggle against imperialism. The policy of coalition implies marking time on one spot, temporizing, cherishing false hopes, engaging in hollow maneuvers and intrigues. As a result of this policy disillusionment inevitably sets in among the working masses, while the peasants turn their backs on the proletariat and fall into apathy.[2]

The founders of the LSSP heeded this warning, opposed the national bourgeoisie, and created a powerful revolutionary party of the working class in Ceylon. But in 1964, with tragic consequences, the LSSP turned its back on its founding principles, and entered into a coalition with the Sri Lanka Freedom Party (SLFP) government of Madam Bandaranaike.[3] It was in struggle against this "Great Betrayal" that the Revolutionary Communist League

---

1. Leon Trotsky, "India faced with imperialist war," *Writings of Leon Trotsky [1939-40]* (New York: Pathfinder Press, 1973, second edition, eighth printing, 2019), p. 32.
2. pp. 35–36.
3. Sri Lanka Freedom Party (SLFP) was formed in 1951 by S.W.R.D. Bandaranaike as a Sinhala chauvinist party, in opposition to the LSSP. After Bandaranaike was assassinated in

(RCL)—the predecessor of Socialist Equality Party (SEP), the Sri Lankan section of the International Committee of the Fourth International—was founded in 1968. For a half century, the Sri Lankan section of the International Committee has waged an uncompromising struggle to overcome the legacy of the betrayal of 1964. But in waging this fight, it has never forgotten the great contribution that the founders of the BLPI and LSSP originally made to the cause of revolutionary socialism, not only in Sri Lanka, but throughout the world.

The importance of studying history

My lectures in Sri Lanka are part of an international celebration of the eightieth anniversary of the founding of the Fourth International. The Trotskyist movement is, of necessity, conscious of history. In the absence of a historically-grounded perspective, political analysis is degraded to the level of eclectically selected impressions. Serious politics—and revolutionary activity is politics at its most serious—requires a scientific method. In navigation, there is an instrument called the sextant. Its invention enabled a captain to precisely establish his ship's position by measuring the angular distance between the visible horizon and an astronomical object. In the process of political navigation, the revolutionary party must correlate the visible political horizon with a critical historical reference point.

A political opponent of the International Committee by the name of Said Gafurov—who is also a supporter of the Putin government in Russia—has recently protested against our harping on the crimes and betrayals carried out by the Stalinists. Why can we not just let bygones be bygones, and find ways to work together with the political heirs of Stalin? Why should we let past crimes and betrayals get in the way of collaborating today? After all, our opponent complains, Trotsky was assassinated in 1940, seventy-eight years ago; and Stalin died in 1953, sixty-five years ago. The Soviet Union was dissolved in 1991, twenty-seven years ago. Why is it still necessary to recall Trotsky's references to the "river of blood" that divided the Fourth International from the Stalinists, who, during the late 1930s, carried out a campaign of political genocide against the finest representatives of revolutionary Marxism in the Soviet Union?

September 1959 by an extremist Buddhist monk, his widow Madam Bandaranaike was elected in 1960. The LSSP joined her coalition government in 1964.

This opponent declared that "today the differences and contradictions between Trotskyism and Stalinism have only a historical, not a political character," no more relevant to the present than the differences "between Robespierre and Hébert or Danton which are only of interest to historians." These differences, our opponent asserts, "are important to study, but only for the sake of historical lessons (and history, to be honest and slightly cynical, never teaches anyone anything.)"[4]

The argument being made by our opponent is that history and politics exist in different and unrelated spheres. The study of history may be of some abstract intellectual interest. But it teaches us nothing that is of any particular value for our present day practical political activity. Those who argue in this way have absolutely nothing in common with Marxist politics. The revolutionary movement develops its program and activity through the continuous critical reworking of historical experience. Without a historical reference point, it is impossible to navigate through the turbulent currents of the class struggle. Moreover, how can a revolutionary party train its young cadres, and the working class as a whole, without studying the monumental revolutionary events of the past century?

The twentieth century was the most revolutionary in history. On every continent, the oppressed masses were drawn into the vortex of struggle against capitalism and imperialism. The century witnessed, in 1917, for the first time in history, the conquest of political power by the working class, under the leadership of the Bolshevik Party. Mass communist parties emerged throughout the world, reflecting the desire and determination of the working class to put an end to capitalism and establish a socialist society.

And yet, by the end of the twentieth century, despite all the struggles and sacrifices, the capitalist class held power throughout the world. The Soviet Union, which arose out of the 1917 revolution, had been dissolved by its own government. In China, the ruling Communist Party became the most ferocious advocate of capitalist economics. We now live in a world of staggering levels of social inequality. How is this process of political regression to be explained?

All over the world, outrage over existing conditions is mounting. "Capitalism" is once again becoming a dirty word. There is a renewal of interest in socialism as an alternative to the existing social order. But, it must be

---

4. Gafurov's statement was posted on the June 27, 2018 blog of his wife, Darya Mitina, secretary of international relations of the United Communist Party of Russia (OKP).

stated bluntly, what is clearly absent amidst this progressive striving is knowledge of the great political experiences and revolutionary struggles of the past century. The very word "revolution" lacks substantial content, in terms of an understanding of its social foundations, class dynamics, and political strategy.

Young people, born in the aftermath of the dissolution of the Soviet Union and the restoration of capitalism in China, have little knowledge of how these events came about, let alone a detailed knowledge of the histories of the Russian and Chinese revolutions. They are not familiar with the actual theoretical and political content of terms such as Stalinism, Maoism, or, for that matter, Castroism. Of course, young people all over the world are familiar with the romantic and evocative image of Che Guevara, but they know nothing of his political strategy and program—which were, if I may speak frankly, utterly bankrupt.

The impact of academic attacks on Marxism

Of course, young people cannot be blamed for their limited knowledge of the revolutionary upheavals of the past century. From whom and from where are they to acquire the necessary knowledge? The capitalist media certainly will not dispense knowledge that may contribute to the overthrow of the existing social order. But what about the universities, with their many learned professors? Unfortunately, for many decades the intellectual environment has been deeply hostile to genuine socialist theory and politics. Marxist theory—rooted in philosophical materialism—was long ago banished from the major universities.

Academic discourse is dominated by the Freudian pseudo-science and idealist subjectivism of the Frankfurt School and the irrationalist gibberish of post-modernism. Professors inform their students that the "Grand Narrative" of Marxism is without relevance in the modern world. What they actually mean is that the materialist conception of history, which established the central and decisive revolutionary role of the working class in capitalist society, cannot and should not be the basis of left-wing politics.

For the theoreticians and practitioners of middle-class pseudo-left politics, there is no need to study the history of the revolutionary struggles of the past. Its lessons contradict all their politically opportunist and reactionary nostrums. Indeed, Trotsky is anathema in these intellectual circles. But it is impossible to fight for socialism in the twenty-first century without studying and assimilating the lessons of Trotsky's struggle against Stalinism in the twentieth century. This remains the fundamental theoretical and political struggle of the last century, of the most profound and immediate significance to every critical issue of political strategy that confronts workers and all those seeking seriously the correct path of struggle against capitalism in the contemporary world. That is why it is necessary to give a brief summary of the historical and political origins of the Fourth International.

The significance of Trotsky's struggle against Stalinism

The founding of the Fourth International in September 1938 is a critical milestone in the history of the Trotskyist movement, the political culmination of the struggle that Leon Trotsky had waged over the previous fifteen years—beginning with the formation of the Left Opposition in the Soviet Union in October 1923—against the bureaucratic degeneration of the Russian Communist Party under the leadership of Stalin.

The far-reaching international implications of Trotsky's struggle against the Stalinist regime emerged in late 1924, when Stalin advanced the claim that it was possible to build socialism in the Soviet Union apart from the international struggle against the world capitalist system, and without the successful revolutionary overthrow of the capitalist ruling class in the major imperialist centers of Western Europe and North America.

The program of "socialism in one country"—a fundamental break with the internationalist strategy that underlay the Bolshevik Party's conquest of power and the subsequent founding of the Communist International in 1919—gave political expression to the interests of the growing bureaucracy within the Soviet Union, whose privileges were derived from its usurpation of political power and the exploitation, in its own interests, of the resources of the nationalized economy created in the aftermath of 1917. The totalitarian dictatorship established by Stalin was the political means—murderously suppressing Marxist revolutionaries and employing police terror as its basic instrument—by which the bureaucracy defended its privileges and enforced social inequality within the Soviet Union.

The nationalist degeneration of the Soviet regime found its most devastating impact in the transformation of the Communist International into an instrument of Soviet foreign policy. In seeking to defend the nationalist orientation implicit in the theory of socialism in one country, the Stalinist bureaucracy claimed that socialism could be built in the USSR, as long as military intervention by the imperialist powers was forestalled. Thus, the aim of the Communist International was redirected toward the search for and cultivation of foreign allies, even if the forging of these alliances came at the expense of the revolutionary struggles of the working class in the countries where the Stalinist regime was seeking alliances with bourgeois and petty-bourgeois forces.

The tragedy of the Chinese revolution

The political consequences of the subordination of the Communist International to the national opportunism of the Soviet bureaucracy found tragic expression in China, where Stalin had insisted that the Chinese Communist Party accept the political authority of the bourgeois Kuomintang and its leader, Chiang Kai-shek. Stalin had come to view Chiang as a potential ally, and portrayed him as a trusted leader of the anti-imperialist struggle in China. The working class, Stalin argued, was obligated to support the progressive sections of the national bourgeoisie. Trotsky rejected Stalin's efforts to portray the national bourgeoisie, in countries with a belated capitalist development, as more revolutionary than the capitalist class in the advanced countries. Trotsky stressed that this view—in essence, a revival of the position of the Russian Mensheviks prior to 1917—was based on a false assessment of the class dynamics in the colonial and semi-colonial countries. He wrote:

> The powerful role of foreign capital in the life of China has caused very strong sections of the Chinese bourgeoisie, the bureaucracy, and the military to join their destiny with that of imperialism. Without this tie, the enormous role of the so-called militarists in the life of modern China would be inconceivable.
>
> It would further be profound naiveté to believe that an abyss lies between the so-called comprador bourgeoisie, that is, the economic and political agency of foreign capital in China, and the so-called national bourgeoisie. No, these two sections stand incomparably closer to each other than the bourgeoisie and the masses of workers and peasants.[5]

Trotsky's analysis was vindicated by events. Chiang Kai-shek proceeded in April 1927 to carry out the slaughter of the Communists in Shanghai and

---

5. Leon Trotsky, *Leon Trotsky on China* (New York: Pathfinder Press, 1976), p. 177.

Canton, delivering a blow from which the Chinese Communist Party never recovered. In the aftermath of this catastrophe, the Chinese Communist Party, under the leadership of Mao Zedong, retreated from the cities and moved into the countryside. This shift profoundly changed the class composition and orientation of the Chinese Communist Party, which, from 1927 on, based itself primarily on the rural peasantry, rather than the urban working class. The Maoist orientation would prove, in subsequent decades, to be a source of grave political disorientation and strategic errors by those organizations, including the JVP (Janatha Vimukthi Peramuna) here in Sri Lanka, that adopted the peasant orientation of the Chinese CP.

Despite the political disaster in China, Trotsky continued to fight for the reform of the Soviet Communist Party. In 1928, Trotsky—who had been expelled in 1927 from the Russian Communist Party and from the Communist International—was living in exile in Alma Ata, a town in Soviet Central Asia, near the border of China. But even in remote exile, thousands of miles from Moscow, Trotsky remained a master of revolutionary strategy. He obtained a copy of the program that had been drafted by Nikolai Bukharin— who was then allied with Stalin—as the main document of the upcoming Sixth Congress of the Communist International. Trotsky subjected this document, which was based on the theory of socialism in one country, to a devastating critique, and upheld revolutionary internationalism, the foundation of the theory of permanent revolution, as the basic strategic orientation of the Marxist movement. He wrote:

> In our epoch, which is the epoch of imperialism, i.e., of *world* economy and *world* politics under the hegemony of finance capital, not a single communist party can establish its programme by proceeding solely or mainly from conditions and tendencies of developments in its own country. This also holds entirely for the party that wields the state power within the boundaries of the USSR. On August 4, 1914, [the beginning of World War I], the death knell sounded for national programmes for all time. The revolutionary party of the proletariat can base itself only upon an international programme corresponding to the character of the present epoch, the epoch of the highest development and collapse of capitalism. An international communist program is in no case the sum total of national programmes or an amalgam of their common features.... The international programme must

proceed directly from an analysis of the conditions and tendencies of world economy and of the world political system taken as a whole in all its connections and contradictions, that is, with the mutually antagonistic interdependence of its separate parts. In the present epoch, to a much larger extent than in the past, the national orientation of the proletariat must and can flow only from a world orientation and not *vice versa*. Herein lies the basic and primary difference between communist internationalism and all varieties of national socialism.[6]

Even after the passage of ninety years, Trotsky's analysis of the dynamic of socialist revolution, of the primacy of international over national conditions, remains the essential strategic principle of the struggle for socialism.

As the fortuitous result of a bureaucratic error, Trotsky's *Critique of the Draft Program* was translated into English, and it came accidentally into the possession of an American and a Canadian delegate to the Sixth Congress, James P. Cannon and Maurice Spector. They smuggled Trotsky's document out of the USSR. This led to the formation of the International Left Opposition. The fight against the Stalinist national degeneration of the Soviet Communist Party was expanded into a struggle against the degeneration of the Communist International.

Germany: "The key to the international situation"

Between 1928 and 1933, the International Left Opposition considered itself a faction of the Communist International. Its activities were directed toward the revolutionary reorientation of the Stalinist-dominated International and parties. Trotsky was not willing to abandon the Communist International, as long as there remained the possibility of bringing about a change in its policies. A major factor in Trotsky's political calculations was the crisis in Germany, which he described as "the key to the international situation."

In January 1929, Trotsky was deported from the Soviet Union to the Turkish island of Prinkipo. He now lived as a stateless exile on what he referred to as "a planet without a visa." But despite his isolation on an island

---

6. Leon Trotsky, "The Draft Programme of the Communist International-A Criticism of Fundamentals," *The Third International after Lenin* (London: New Park Publications, 1974), pp. 3–4.

off the coast of Istanbul, Trotsky developed an analysis of the situation in Germany that was extraordinarily prescient. He called for the formation of a united front of the German Communist Party and the Social Democratic Party against the fascist menace.

The Nazi party had become a mass movement. Were it to come to power, Trotsky warned, the results would be a political catastrophe for the international working class. Everything had to be done to block the Nazis' march to power. But this required a change in the reckless, utterly disoriented, and unbelievably stupid policies of the German Communist Party. Following blindly the line set in Moscow, the German Communist Party not only refused to form a united front with the other mass workers party, the Social Democratic Party, it claimed that the SPD—which still commanded the support of millions of workers—was a "social-fascist" organization, all but identical to the Nazis. As there was, it claimed, no difference between the SPD and the Nazis, no common defensive actions between the two mass workers' parties against Hitler's forces were permissible.

As Trotsky had warned, the policies of the Communist Party cleared Hitler's path to power. With the critical support of high-placed bourgeois politicians, Hitler became chancellor of Germany on January 30, 1933. The Nazi regime moved quickly to destroy—without any organized resistance—the mass organizations of the working class. Despite this historically unprecedented political disaster, the Communist Party—without any opposition within the Communist International—continued to insist that its policies had been correct. The German catastrophe compelled Trotsky to alter his approach to the struggle against Stalinism. He concluded that the reform of the Communist International was impossible. The Third International was dead as a revolutionary organization. It was necessary to build the Fourth International.

Trotsky's founding of the Fourth International

Trotsky's call for the creation of a Fourth International was linked to his assessment of the Soviet regime. He concluded that the reform of the bureaucratic regime was impossible. The bureaucracy had become a counter-revolutionary social force, ruthlessly defending its privileges through the suppression of the working class within the Soviet Union, and cynically betraying the struggles of the working class beyond the borders of the USSR. The evolution of the Soviet Union toward socialism required the overthrow of the

Stalinist regime in a political revolution. Only through a revolutionary uprising of the Soviet working class and the overthrow of the bureaucracy would it be possible to re-establish Soviet democracy and prevent the destruction of the Soviet Union and the reintroduction of capitalism.

The five years between Trotsky's call for the formation of the Fourth International in 1933 and the founding congress in 1938 were among the most tragic in the history of the socialist movement. Despite the unprecedented crisis of the world capitalist system, the working class suffered a series of disastrous defeats. The cause of the defeats was not an absence of the will to struggle. Rather, the years between 1933 and 1938 witnessed an immense upsurge in the class struggle. In 1936, France was convulsed by strikes of an incipiently revolutionary character. In May and June, there were more than 12,000 strikes involving more than two million workers, affecting virtually every section of industry. The most militant actions involved the seizure of factories by revolutionary-minded workers. In July 1936, Spanish and Catalan workers responded to an attempted coup d'état by fascist-minded generals, led by Francisco Franco, with a mighty uprising.

But in both France and Spain, the initial victories of the working class ended in demoralization and defeat. The political instrument of the defeats was the "Popular Front," that is, the alliance of the Stalinist and social democratic parties and trade unions with the bourgeoisie. The explicit basis of this alliance was the defense of capitalist property against the revolutionary aspirations of the working class. The Stalinists insisted that the fight against fascism consisted of nothing more than the defense of bourgeois democracy. The working class, the Stalinists insisted, could only fight fascism in an alliance with the liberal democratic sections of the capitalist class. It was, therefore, impermissible to advance and fight for a socialist program, for it would alienate the democratic capitalists and drive them into the camp of the fascists.

The counterrevolutionary significance of the Popular Front found its fullest expression in Spain, where the Stalinist party, controlled by agents of the Soviet secret police, the GPU, hunted down and murdered those who insisted that the defeat of Franco required the mobilization of the working class and the peasantry on the basis of a revolutionary program. The Stalinists ensured the victory of Franco.

As Stalin was carrying out the betrayal of the working class beyond the borders of the USSR, his "Great Terror" within the Soviet Union—epitomized by three public trials in Moscow between 1936 and 1938—involved the physical extermination of an entire generation of Marxist revolutionaries.

These were the conditions under which Trotsky founded the Fourth International. His insistence on the necessity of a new International encountered opposition from those who claimed that his condemnation of the Stalinist regime was too uncompromising and absolute. Another criticism was that the Trotskyist movement was too small to establish a new International, and that, moreover, an International could only be founded on the basis of "great events."

Trotsky answered his critics by insisting that the founding of the Fourth International was, indeed, based on "great events"—the greatest defeats of the working class in history. These defeats had exposed the treachery and political worthlessness of the old organizations. Moreover, the critical issue was not the size of a party, but the quality of its program—that is, whether or not the program advanced by the Fourth International was based on a correct appraisal of the nature of the historical epoch and the correct formulation of the political tasks of the working class.

Of course, the question of size is not unimportant. The overthrow of capitalism cannot be accomplished through a conspiracy of a handful of people. The socialist revolution requires the conscious participation of great masses of people. But it is an axiom of Marxism that theory can only become a material force, in a historically progressive and revolutionary sense, if the program of the party identifies and articulates objective necessity. Those parties that are based on a false appraisal of objective conditions, whose program does not correspond to the demands of the historical epoch, must eventually suffer, whatever their ephemeral successes, political shipwreck.

The persistence of the Fourth International

What, then, accounts for the historical *persistence* of the Fourth International? Above all, it is the correspondence of the analysis and program of the Fourth International with the objective character of the epoch. The founding document of the Fourth International defined the present historical epoch as that of the death agony of capitalism. Trotsky wrote:

> The economic prerequisite for the proletarian revolution has already in general achieved the highest point of fruition that can be reached under capitalism. Mankind's productive forces stagnate. Already new inventions and improvements fail to raise the level of material wealth. Conjunctural crises under

the conditions of the social crisis of the whole capitalist system inflict ever heavier deprivations and sufferings upon the masses. Growing unemployment, in its turn, deepens the financial crisis of the state and undermines the unstable monetary systems. Democratic regimes, as well as fascist, stagger on from one bankruptcy to another.[7]

Trotsky's warnings of a catastrophe were realized. The Second World War, which erupted exactly one year after the founding of the Fourth International, claimed more than sixty million lives.

With the indispensable assistance of the Stalinist parties, the capitalist class was able to survive—through a combination of political compromises, tactical concessions, and, when absolutely necessary, ruthless repression—the upheavals that swept the globe in the aftermath of the war. For several decades, rebuilding upon the ruins of war, capitalism experienced a substantial economic growth. But the fundamental contradictions—between social production and private ownership of the productive forces, between the integrated character of the world economy and the nation-state system—persisted.

The dissolution of the Stalinist regimes in Eastern Europe and the Soviet Union was universally hailed by the ruling elites and their media propagandists and academic apologists as the triumph of capitalism over socialism. The triumphalism of the 1990s was based on two lies: that the Stalinist regimes had been socialist, and that the contradictions of capitalism had been somehow overcome. But, in light of the experiences of the past thirty years, it is evident that the celebrations of capitalism's triumph were, to say the least, premature. The ruling elites had proclaimed that, in the aftermath of the dissolution of the Stalinist regimes, capitalism would bestow upon humanity peace, prosperity, and universal democracy.

The reality has proved very different. Beginning with the American invasion of Iraq in 1991 and the civil war in Yugoslavia, there has been endless military conflict. The "War on Terror"—launched after the events of 9/11—is now in its eighteenth year, with no end in sight. Rather, the intensification of geopolitical rivalries and conflicts is leading, inexorably, to the outbreak of a Third World War. The United States has made it clear that it will not allow China to replace it as the principal world power, even if it must use military

---

7. Leon Trotsky, *The Death Agony of Capitalism and the Tasks of the Fourth International: The Transitional Program* (New York: Labor Publications, 1981), p. 1.

force to counter the rise of China. At the same time, the United States is on a collision course with Russia, which Washington views as an obstacle to its plans to dominate Eurasia and the Middle East. Only last week, the US ambassador to NATO declared that the United States was prepared to carry out a preemptive strike against Russia to counter what it claims to be the illegal development of offensive weapons. Such an open threat is a dangerous escalation of the conflict between the two most heavily nuclear-armed powers. The world is moving to the very brink of a nuclear war, whose lethal consequences defy description.

Against the backdrop of escalating international violence, social tensions are mounting in every country—and especially in the advanced capitalist countries, including the United States. The underlying causes of the tensions are persistent economic crisis and staggering levels of social inequality. Less than a dozen billionaires possess more wealth than half the world's population. Jeff Bezos, the owner of Amazon, has a personal fortune estimated at $150 billion. In the course of just one hour, the millions that are added to his fortune constitute a substantial multiple of the total amount of money that will be earned by the average worker in the course of a lifetime.

Social inequality and the breakdown of democracy

Social inequality inevitably generates social and class conflict. At a certain point, the social tension becomes so extreme that the mechanisms of democracy begin to break down. This is the situation that is now emerging throughout the world. The election of Donald Trump as president of the United States is the symptom of a systemic breakdown of the long-established democratic political structures through which the capitalist class has ruled. There is widespread discussion of the danger of fascism returning to power.

In *How Democracies Die*, authors Steven Levitsky and Daniel Ziblatt write forlornly:

> Is our democracy in danger? It is a question we never thought we'd be asking... Over the past two years, we have watched politicians say and do things that are unprecedented in the United States—but that we recognize as having been the precursors of democratic crisis in other places. We feel dread, as do so many other Americans, even though we try to reassure ourselves that things can't really be that bad here...

> Yet, we worry. ... Are we living through the decline and fall of one of the world's oldest and most successful democracies?[8]

Madeleine Albright, the former US secretary of state, has written a book, titled *Fascism: A Warning,* in which she provides the following simplistic explanation for the resurgence of the extreme right in the United States:

> If we think of fascism as a wound from the past that had almost healed, putting Trump in the White House was like ripping off the bandage and picking at the scab.[9]

But this political diagnosis ignores the fact that the resurgence of authoritarianism is a worldwide phenomenon. In *The People Versus Democracy*, Yascha Mounk calls attention to the global scale of the revival of fascist movements:

> It is tempting, for example, to see Donald Trump as a uniquely American phenomenon. ... And yet, the real nature of the threat Trump poses can only be understood in a much wider context: that of the far-right populists who have been gaining strength in every major democracy, from Athens to Ankara, from Sydney to Stockholm, and from Warsaw to Wellington. Despite the obvious differences between the populists who are on the rise in all these countries, their commonalities go deep—and render each of them a danger to the political system in surprisingly similar ways.[10]

Another recently published book, *How Fascism Works*, by Jason Stanley, calls attention to the global character of the growth of right-wing extremism:

> In recent years, multiple countries across the world have been overtaken by a certain kind of far-right nationalism; the list includes Russia, Hungary, Poland, India, Turkey, and the United States ... I have chosen the label "fascism" for ultranationalism of some

---

8. Steven Levitsky and Daniel Ziblatt, *How Democracies Die* (New York: Broadway Books, 2018), pp. 1–2.
9. Madeleine Albright, *Fascism: A Warning* (New York: Harper Collins, 2018), pp. 4–5.
10. Yascha Mounk, *The People Versus Democracy* (Cambridge MA: Harvard University Press, 2018), pp. 6–7.

variety (ethnic, religious, cultural), with the nation represented in the person of an authoritarian leader who speaks on its behalf.[11]

The most dangerous manifestation of the fascist resurgence is provided by recent developments in Germany, where the Nazis—more than seventy years after the collapse of the Third Reich and end of World War II—are once again emerging as a serious political force. Nazi demonstrators, chanting racist and antisemitic slogans, have marched through the streets of Chemnitz and Dortmund. What makes these demonstrations particularly significant is not their size. The Nazis are still a relatively small political force, and are despised within Germany. But the Nazis enjoy powerful patrons at the highest levels of the German state. Following the September 1, 2018 demonstration in Chemnitz, the interior minister of the ruling coalition government, Horst Seehofer, expressed his warm sympathy for the Nazi mob. The head of the Ministry for the Protection of the Constitution, Hans Georg Maassen, denied—despite video evidence to the contrary—that the mob had threatened foreign bystanders who were witnessing the demonstration.

What is to account for the revival of Nazism in Germany, the very country which experienced the full horrors of the Third Reich? All over the country there are countless memorials that pay tribute to the memory of the victims of Hitlerism. But, like a disease that has been in remission but not cured, the old symptoms are once again manifesting themselves. Trotsky, who produced the greatest analysis of fascism, insisted that this political scourge was rooted in the contradictions of capitalism, and that the breakdown of bourgeois democracy—beneath the pressure of global economic crisis, international geopolitical tensions, and domestic social conflict—was an irreversible process.

Democracy cannot be rescued and restored to health on the basis of capitalism. All the warnings made by Trotsky in the 1930s, when he denounced the treacherous politics of Popular Frontism—which subordinated the working class to the "liberal" and "progressive" bourgeois parties and, thereby, assured the victory of fascism—acquire immense contemporary relevance. In 1936, Trotsky wrote:

> By lulling the workers and peasants with parliamentary illusions, by paralyzing their will to struggle, the People's Front

---

11. Jason Stanley, *How Fascism Works: The Politics of Us and Them* (New York: Random House, 2018), p. xxviii.

creates favorable conditions for the victory of fascism. The policy of coalition with the bourgeoisie must be paid for by the proletariat with years of new torments and sacrifices, if not by decades of fascist terror.[12]

All of Trotsky's warnings were realized. The "People's Front" (or "Popular Front") ended in disasters that cost the lives of tens of millions of people between 1939 and 1945. And yet, the enemies of Trotskyism—i.e., the pseudo-left political frauds who dismiss the lessons of history—today advocate the same policies that were responsible for the catastrophes of the 1930s and 1940s.

Professor Chantal Mouffe, who is among the most celebrated of contemporary pseudo-left theorists, advocates a "Left Populism," which is nothing more than the latest version of neo-Stalinist popular front class collaboration. Calling openly for the rejection of "essentialist" left politics, based on the revolutionary role of the working class and the centrality of its struggle against capitalist exploitation, Mouffe asserts that Left Populism "does not require a 'revolutionary' break with the liberal-democratic regime."[13]

She writes that "it is possible to bring about a transformation of the existing hegemonic order without destroying liberal-democratic institutions."[14] The capitalist-imperialist state—the brutal and massively armed guardian of exploitation, oppression, and inequality—should be left intact. And, so, what is Professor Mouffe's alternative to the Marxist program for the revolutionary overthrow by the working class of the capitalist state, the expropriation of the capitalist oligarchs, and the abolition of private ownership of the means of production and finance? She writes: "A left populist approach should try to provide a different vocabulary" and a "different language" that might appeal to supporters of right-wing parties!ial[15] Is it possible to imagine a more blatant expression of political bankruptcy? Professor Mouffe would have us believe that the danger of fascism can be combated without mobilizing the working class on the basis of a revolutionary program. It is merely necessary to decorate reformism with a new vocabulary.

---

12. Leon Trotsky, "The New Revolutionary Upsurge and the Tasks of the Fourth International", *Writings of Leon Trotsky [1935–36]* (New York: Pathfinder Press, 1977), pp. 339–40.
13. Chantal Mouffe, *For a Left Populism* (London: Verso Books, 2018), p. 36.
14. Ibid.
15. Ibid., p. 22.

The crisis of revolutionary leadership

The political alternatives that present themselves in the epoch of the death agony of capitalism are either fascist barbarism or socialist revolution. The triumph of one or the other will determine the future of mankind. The victory of fascism means the death of human civilization. The victory of the socialist revolution opens up the possibility of a revival and flowering of human civilization on a new and glorious level. That is the choice before us.

Surveying the vicissitudes of the revolutionary struggles of the first decades of the twentieth century, and seeking to explain the cause of the many defeats that had followed the great victory of October 1917, Trotsky identified the "crisis of the revolutionary leadership" as the basic problem of the epoch. The objective conditions existed for the victory of socialism. But what remained was the unresolved problem of subjective leadership. This remains the fundamental task of our epoch.

The opponents of Trotskyism—particularly among the representatives of the countless varieties of petty-bourgeois pseudo-left politics—habitually attack the Fourth International as "sectarian." They cannot abide the refusal of the International Committee to tie itself, as the petty-bourgeois pseudo-left has, to the apron strings of the ruling class.

Incensed by our adherence to principles, our opponents point to the fact that the Trotskyist movement has not recruited millions to its ranks. A refrain popular among our enemies is that "The Fourth International was proclaimed by Trotsky, but never built." With this sentence they separate the evolution of the Fourth International from the entire history of the class struggle over the last eighty years. They prefer to forget that the parties and organizations favored by the pseudo-left—the Stalinists, the Maoists, the bourgeois nationalists, the labor bureaucracies—sought to block the development of the Fourth International by slandering, imprisoning, and murdering Trotskyists.

And what do our opponents offer as an alternative to the Fourth International? If they attempted to commemorate the last eighty, forty, or even twenty years of their political activities, to what political achievements could they proudly point? The Stalinists can point to the ruins of the Soviet Union and the subsequent economic rape of Russia. The Maoists can point to the transformation of China into a focal point of global capitalism, the home of dozens of newly minted billionaires. The Castroites can point to how Cuba is again a haven for American tourists, whose dollars are essential for the survival of the local economy. The Social Democratic parties are virtually indistinguishable from the traditional right-wing parties of the bourgeoisie. The example of Corbyn in Britain only proves again that the social democratic organizations cannot be transformed into instruments of the struggle for socialism. Indeed, they cannot any longer even be transformed into instruments of mild social reforms. What all these organizations have in common, to recall the phrase employed by Trotsky, is that they are rotten through and through.

The Fourth International was founded by Trotsky to resolve the crisis of revolutionary leadership in the working class. He understood that the political tasks posed in the epoch of capitalism's death agony would not be easily accomplished. In May 1940, just three months before his assassination by an agent of the Stalinist regime, Trotsky wrote:

> The capitalist world has no way out, unless a prolonged death agony is so considered. It is necessary to prepare for long years, if not decades, of war, uprisings, brief interludes of truce, new wars, and new uprisings. A young revolutionary party must base itself on this perspective.[16]

Mankind has passed, as Trotsky anticipated, through "decades of war, uprisings, brief interludes of truce, new wars, and new uprisings." Defending the heritage of Marxism as a politically persecuted minority under the most unfavorable conditions, the Fourth International, under the leadership of the International Committee, has accumulated immense experience. Events have vindicated its historical perspective. Now, at this late and very advanced stage of the death agony of capitalism, the conditions exist to build the Fourth International as the mass World Party of Socialist Revolution.

---

16. Leon Trotsky, "Manifesto of the Fourth International on the Imperialist War and the Proletarian World Revolution," *Writings of Leon Trotsky [1939–1940]*), p. 290.

9

Leon Trotsky's Four Fateful Years in Prinkipo: 1929–1933

There is a certain historical justice at work, however belated, in the publication of a Turkish-language edition of *In Defense of Leon Trotsky*. Just over ninety years ago, in February 1929, Trotsky, accompanied by his wife Natalia Sedova, arrived in Turkey as a political exile from the Soviet Union. He had already spent a year in internal exile in Alma Ata in Kazakhstan, where he had been consigned following his expulsion from the Soviet Communist Party on November 14, 1927. But despite the remoteness of Alma Ata, Trotsky was able to give political direction to the Left Opposition, which he had led since 1923. His withering critiques of the domestic and international policies of the Stalinist bureaucracy continued to circulate throughout the Soviet Union.

Unable to answer Trotsky with principled arguments, Stalin was determined to silence him. The Politburo sent a representative of the GPU, the Soviet secret police, to demand that Trotsky end his oppositional activity and sever contact with his supporters. If he refused to accept this ultimatum, the GPU warned Trotsky that it would "be obliged to alter the conditions of your existence to the extent of completely isolating you from political life. In this

---

Author's preface to the 2019 Turkish edition of *In Defense of Leon Trotsky*. Published in English on the World Socialist Web Site, September 23, 2019.

connection, the question of changing your place of residence will arise."[1] In a letter to the Central Committee of the Communist Party, dated December 16, 1928, Trotsky replied defiantly to the ultimatum:

> To demand that I renounce my political activity is to demand that I renounce the struggle for the interests of the international proletariat, a struggle that I have been conducting without interruption for thirty-two years, that is, throughout my whole conscious life. The attempt to represent this activity as "counterrevolutionary" comes from those whom I accuse before the international proletariat of trampling underfoot the basic teachings of Marx and Lenin, of infringing upon the historical interests of the world revolution, of breaking with the traditions and heritage of October, and of unconsciously—but therefore the more dangerously—preparing the way for Thermidor.
>
> To renounce political activity would mean to give up the struggle against the blindness of the present leadership, which heaps upon the objective difficulties of socialist construction ever greater political difficulties that arise out of its opportunist inability to conduct a proletarian policy on a large historical scale.
>
> It would mean renouncing the struggle against the stifling party regime, which reflects the growing pressure of the enemy classes upon the proletarian vanguard.
>
> It would mean passively acquiescing in the economic policy of opportunism, a policy which is undermining and destroying the foundations of the proletarian dictatorship, hampering the material and cultural growth of this dictatorship, and at the same time dealing heavy blows to the alliance of workers and working peasants, the basis of Soviet power.[2]

Trotsky contrasted the stature and role of the ruling bureaucracy to that of the Left Opposition:

---

1. Leon Trotsky, *My Life* (New York: Charles Scribner's Sons, 1931), pp. 558–59.
2. Leon Trotsky, "Reply to Stalin," *The Challenge of the Left Opposition [1928–29]* (New York: Pathfinder Press, 1981), pp. 458–59.

> The incurable weakness of the reaction headed by the party apparatus, despite all its apparent power, lies in the fact that it does not know what it is doing. It is carrying out the command of the enemy classes. There can be no greater historical curse on a faction that arose out of the revolution and is now undermining it.
>
> The great historical strength of the Opposition, despite its apparent weakness, lies in the fact that it keeps its fingers on the pulse of the world historical process, that it clearly perceives the dynamics of class forces, that it foresees the future and consciously prepares for it. To renounce political activity would be to renounce the preparations for tomorrow.[3]

Political conditions then existing in the Soviet Union had not yet reached the point where Stalin could murder Trotsky. Several more years of the bureaucratic regime's political degeneration and unrelenting resort to repression were required before Stalin could stage the Moscow Trials and carry out the physical annihilation of the Trotskyist opposition and hundreds of thousands of Marxist revolutionaries. In 1929, Stalin had to limit his political vengeance to the physical expulsion of Trotsky from the Soviet Union. He calculated that Trotsky, once deported from the Soviet Union and isolated from his network of supporters, would be effectively silenced.

Deriving his own power from the resources of the party and state bureaucracy, Stalin underestimated Trotsky's capacity to exert political influence, even under conditions of extreme isolation, through the power of his ideas.

The formal decision to deport Trotsky was taken by the GPU, on January 18, 1929. Two days later, when he was asked to sign an official document confirming that he had been informed of the deportation order, Trotsky wrote: "The decision of the GPU, criminal in substance and illegal in form, has been announced to me, January 20, 1929." A lengthy journey by train from Central Asia to the port city of Odessa commenced. Then he and Natalia Sedova were placed on the steamer *Ilyich* for the voyage into the Bosphorus. On February 12, Trotsky and Natalia arrived in Turkey. Before disembarking, Trotsky gave to the police who had boarded the ship the following message for transmission to President Kemal Ataturk:

---

3. Ibid., p. 461.

Dear Sir: At the gate of Constantinople, I have the honor to inform you that I have arrived at the Turkish frontier not of my own choice, and that I cross this frontier only by submitting to force. I request you, Mr. President, to accept my appropriate sentiments. L. Trotsky[4]

Thus began Trotsky's final period of exile, which was to last eleven and a half years, until his assassination in Mexico, in August 1940.

Following his arrival in Turkey, two months were to pass until Trotsky and Natalia were transferred to the island of Prinkipo. Except for a period of approximately nine months, between March 1931 and January 1932, when they temporarily relocated to the coastal town of Kadiköy, they lived on the island. The four and a half years in Turkey, from his arrival in February 1929 until his departure for France in July 1933, must be considered among the most significant of Trotsky's life.

In lines that he wrote just before his exile in Turkey came to an end, Trotsky described Prinkipo as "an island of peace and forgetfulness."[5] But the exiled revolutionary had little peace, nor was he inclined to forget the lessons that he had learned in the course of the tumultuous events in which he had played so brilliant a role. During his years in Prinkipo, which he fondly referred to as "a fine place to work with a pen,"[6] Trotsky wrote two literary masterpieces, as they can be justly described, both from the standpoint of content and form: his autobiography *My Life*, and the three-volume *History of the Russian Revolution*.

But these great works do not encompass the scope of Trotsky's writings. Despite the remoteness of his island exile, to which newspapers and mail traveled at a glacial pace, Trotsky managed to follow and respond to world events with extraordinary acuity. The quality of his commentary leaves no doubt that Trotsky's grasp of international geopolitics was unequaled by any of his contemporaries. He remained the greatest strategist of world socialist revolution.

The years between 1929 and 1933 were among the most consequential of the twentieth century. During these four years, the capitalist system was overtaken by an economic catastrophe. The crash on Wall Street in October

---

4. Trotsky, *My Life*, pp. 565–66.
5. Leon Trotsky, "Farewell to Prinkipo," *Writings of Leon Trotsky [1932–33]* (New York: Pathfinder Press, 1972), p. 361.
6. Ibid.

1929 set into motion a global crisis that placed the survival of the capitalist system in question. The collapse of industrial production and the massive rise in unemployment throughout North America and Europe led to a political radicalization of the working class. Confronted with the growing threat of socialist revolution, powerful sections of the capitalist elites looked to fascism for political salvation. It is among the greatest tragedies in history that, at precisely the point when the world capitalist system was confronted with a massive systemic breakdown, the revolutionary potential of the working class was fatally undermined by the treachery, disorientation, and sheer incompetence of its mass organizations.

The political epicenter of the crisis of world capitalism was located in Germany, 2,000 kilometers from Prinkipo. The brutal impact of the world depression transformed Hitler's Nazi Party into a mass organization. Despite the danger posed by the rapid growth of fascism, the German working class was paralyzed by the policies of the Social Democratic and Communist parties.

The Social Democratic Party (SPD) remained hopelessly tied to the discredited Weimar regime, ruling out any politically independent struggle by the working class against the Nazi threat. The challenge that confronted the German Communist Party (KPD), as Trotsky insisted, was to fight for the broadest social and political mobilization of the working class against Hitler by calling for a united front with the SPD. Instead, the KPD, applying the directives of the Stalinized Third International (Comintern), categorically rejected all proposals for a United Front against fascism.[7] The KPD labeled the SPD "social-fascist," thereby claiming that there existed no fundamental difference between the Nazi party and the Social Democracy.

Trotsky's analysis of the counterrevolutionary dynamic of fascism and his critique of the disastrous trajectory of the Stalinist "Third Period" ultra-leftism testify to his extraordinary political foresight. "Trotsky maintained during Hitler's rise to power," the late British historian E. H. Carr has written, "so persistent and, for the most part, so prescient a commentary on the course of events in Germany as to deserve record."[8] As early as September

---

7. A "united front" is a principled political agreement between mass working-class parties and organizations to collaborate in a struggle against fascism and other counterrevolutionary forces. It is not to be confused with a "popular front," which is an unprincipled subordination of working-class parties and organizations to parties of the capitalist class, in the name of defending bourgeois democracy. Trotsky vehemently opposed such alliances, which entail the renunciation of socialist revolution.

8. E. H. Carr, *The Twilight of the Comintern 1930–1935* (New York: Pantheon Books, 1982), p. 433.

26, 1930, nearly two and a half years before Hitler was lifted into power by a clique of bourgeois political conspirators, Trotsky warned: "*Fascism in Germany has become a real danger*, as an acute expression of the helpless position of the bourgeois regime, and the accumulated powerlessness of the Communist Party to abolish it. Whoever denies this is either blind or a braggart."[9]

One year later, Trotsky completed an essay, dated November 26, 1931, with the title: "Germany, the key to the international situation."

> The economic and political contradictions have here reached unprecedented acuteness. The solution is approaching. The moment has come when the prerevolutionary situation must be transformed into the revolutionary or—the counterrevolutionary. On the direction in which the solution of the German crisis develops will depend not only the fate of Germany herself (and that is already a great deal), but also the fate of Europe, the destiny of the entire world, for many years to come."[10]

Trotsky foresaw with chilling precision the consequences of a Nazi victory:

> The coming to power of the National Socialists would mean first of all the extermination of the flower of the German proletariat, the destruction of its organizations, the eradication of its belief in itself and in its future. Considering the far greater maturity and acuteness of the social contradictions in Germany, the hellish work of Italian fascism would probably appear as a pale and almost humane experiment in comparison with the work of the German National Socialists.[11]

To read these words today, knowing how fully and tragically they were to be confirmed by events in virtually every detail, is a painful experience. One cannot help but reflect on how many tens of millions of lives would have been saved, how much human suffering would have been averted, and how

---

9. Leon Trotsky, "The turn in the Communist International," *The Struggle Against Fascism in Germany* (New York: Pathfinder Press, 1971), p. 78.
10. "Germany, the key to the international situation," ibid., p. 156.
11. Ibid, p. 160.

different the future course of twentieth century history would have been had the warnings of Trotsky been heeded!

There remain to this day countless petty-bourgeois academics, pretending to be historians, who claim that the conflict between Stalin and Trotsky was merely a struggle for individual power; and that the victory of Trotsky and the Left Opposition over the Stalinist faction would not have had a significant impact on the development of the Soviet Union, world politics, and the fate of socialism. But such claims are clearly refuted by the consequences of the Stalinist policies, opposed by Trotsky, which cleared the path for the victory of Nazism in 1933. Even if all other political issues are set aside and ignored—which, of course, they cannot be—the German catastrophe reveals the world historical implications of the struggle waged by Trotsky against Stalinism.

The Nazi victory in January 1933 marked a critical turning point in the history of the Trotskyist movement. Since the founding of the Left Opposition, Trotsky's political objective had been to bring about the reform of the Russian Communist Party and the Communist International (Comintern). This was the principled strategy that guided the International Left Opposition following Trotsky's deportation from the Soviet Union and the first four years of his exile in Prinkipo. But the defeat in Germany demanded a reconsideration of the International Left Opposition's policy of reforming the Communist International and its national sections.

In the months that followed Hitler's victory, Trotsky waited to see if any criticism of the policies pursued by Stalin would emerge from any of the parties of the Comintern. On April 7, 1933, the Communist International unequivocally endorsed the policy of the KPD, which, it declared, "was completely correct up to and during Hitler's coup d'état."[12] Trotsky concluded that a new course was necessary. In the last major political statement written before he left Prinkipo, dated July 15, 1933, Trotsky called for a break with the Comintern and the building of a new International. Two days later, having finally received visas to enter France, Trotsky and Natalia boarded a ship bound for Marseilles. "For better or worse," Trotsky noted in his diary, "the chapter called 'Prinkipo' is ended."[13]

* * * * *

---

12. Editors' note, *The Struggle Against Fascism in Germany*, p. 487.
13. "Farewell to Prinkipo," *Writings of Leon Trotsky [1932–33]*, p. 368.

The essays in *In Defense of Leon Trotsky* were written between 2001 and 2012. They are divided into four parts. The first part consists of two lectures that review Trotsky's extraordinary role in the history of the twentieth century and the undiminished relevance of his life struggles and ideas.

The last three parts are extended replies to three biographies by English historians, published between 2003 and 2009, that set out to discredit Trotsky. The methods employed by these academics consisted of distortions, falsifications, and cynically constructed half-truths. As Professors Swain, Thatcher, and Service never attempted to reply to my exposure of their intellectual charlatanry, there are no new arguments that need to be examined and refuted.

Nearly a decade has passed since the publication of the first English-language edition of this book. The second edition, upon which this translation is based, was published in 2013. We are now approaching the end of the second decade of the twenty-first century, whose shoulders are already sagging beneath the weight of intractable global crises. The same maladies that afflicted capitalism in the last century—social inequality, militarism, and the breakdown of democracy— are the dominant features of the contemporary world. In Germany, fascism is making a comeback. And eighty years after the outbreak of World War II, imperialist and interstate conflicts are leading inexorably to another global conflagration.

The words with which Trotsky defined the great challenge of modern history resonate as if they were written today:

> All talk to the effect that historical conditions have not yet "ripened" for socialism is the product of ignorance or conscious deception. The objective prerequisites for the proletarian revolution have not only "ripened"; they have begun to get somewhat rotten. Without a socialist revolution, in the next historical period at that, a catastrophe threatens the whole culture of mankind.[14]

When the essays in this book were being written, I was convinced that objective events would lead inevitably to a resurgence of interest in the life and ideas of Trotsky. This unstoppable process finds particularly gratifying

---

14. Leon Trotsky, *The Death Agony of Capitalism and the Tasks of the Fourth International: The Transitional Program* (New York: Labor Publications, 1981), pp. 1–2.

expression in the fact that this volume has been translated into the Turkish language by the comrades of *Sosyalist Eşitlik*, who are working in political solidarity with the International Committee of the Fourth International. Thanks to their efforts, *In Defense of Leon Trotsky* will now be available in the country that gave shelter to the great Marxist revolutionary.

Detroit
September 21, 2019

10

Trotsky's Last Year: 1939–1940

I. The outbreak of World War II and Trotsky's defense of Marxism

Eighty years ago, on August 20, 1940, Leon Trotsky—the exiled co-leader of the 1917 October Revolution and founder of the Fourth International—was mortally wounded by an agent of the Soviet Union's secret police, the GPU. The revolutionary leader died in a Mexico City hospital twenty-six hours later, in the early evening of August 21.

The murder of Trotsky was the outcome of a massive political conspiracy organized by the totalitarian bureaucratic regime headed by Stalin, whose name will for all of history be synonymous with counterrevolutionary treachery, betrayal, and limitless criminality. Trotsky's assassination was the climax of the campaign of political genocide, directed by the Kremlin, whose aim was the physical extirpation of the entire generation of Marxist revolutionaries and advanced socialist workers who had played a central role in the preparation and leadership of the Bolshevik revolution and the establishment of the first workers state in history. The three show trials held in Moscow between 1936 and 1938—judicial frame-ups that provided a pseudo-legal cover for the murder of virtually all the principal leaders of the October

---

The six parts of this essay were published on the World Socialist Web Site between August 20, 2020 and September 7, 2020.

Revolution—were only the public manifestation of a campaign of terror that consumed hundreds of thousands of lives and dealt a shattering blow to the intellectual and cultural development of the Soviet Union and the worldwide struggle for socialism.

Driven into exile, deprived of citizenship by the Soviet Union, and living on "a planet without a visa," lacking all access to conventional attributes of power, armed only with a pen, and dependent on the support of a relatively small number of persecuted comrades throughout the world, there was no man more feared by the powers that ruled the earth than Leon Trotsky. The founder and leader of the Fourth International, "the party of irreconcilable opposition, not only in capitalist countries, but also in the USSR," exerted a political and intellectual influence that was unequalled by any of his contemporaries. He towered above them all. In an essay titled "Trotsky's Place in History," C.L.R. James, the Caribbean socialist intellectual and historian, wrote:

> During his last decade he [Trotsky] was an exile, apparently powerless. During those same ten years, Stalin, his rival, assumed power such as no man in Europe since Napoleon has wielded. Hitler has shaken the world and bids fair to bestride it like a colossus while he lasts. Roosevelt is the most powerful president who has ever ruled America, and America today is the most powerful nation in the world. Yet the Marxist judgment of Trotsky is as confident as Engels's judgment of Marx. Before his period of power, during it, and after his fall, Trotsky stood second only to Lenin among contemporary men, and after Lenin died in 1924, was the greatest head of our times. That judgment we leave to history.[1]

Trotsky's stature was determined not only by the fact that he analyzed, with incomparable brilliance, the world as it was. He also personified the revolutionary process that would determine its future. As he had stated during a session of the Dewey Commission that held hearings in April 1937 to investigate the Kremlin's allegations against Trotsky—and which subsequently found the Moscow Trials to be a frameup—"My politics are established not

---

1. "Trotsky's place in History," *C. L. R. James and Revolutionary Marxism: Selected Writings of C.L.R. James 1939–1949*, Scott McLemee and Paul Le Blanc, eds. (Chicago: Haymarket Books, 2018), p. 93.

for the purpose of diplomatic conventions, but for the development of the international revolutionary movement of the working class."[2]

Trotsky despised every form of political charlatanry, which pretends that there are easy—i.e., non-revolutionary—solutions to the immense historic problems arising out of the death agony of the capitalist system. Revolutionary politics did not achieve its aims by promising miracles. Great social advances can be achieved, he insisted, "exclusively through the education of the masses through agitation, through explaining to the workers what they must defend and what they should overthrow." This profoundly principled approach to revolutionary politics also formed the basis of Trotsky's conception of morality. "Only those methods are permissible," he wrote, "which do not conflict with the interests of the revolution." Adherence to this principle placed Trotsky, even if considered only from a moral standpoint, in absolute opposition to Stalinism, whose methods were utterly destructive of the needs of social revolution and, therefore, the progress of humanity.[3]

The premature death of Lenin in January 1924, when he was only fifty-three years old, was a political tragedy. The assassination of Trotsky at the age of sixty was a catastrophe. His murder deprived the working class of the last surviving representative of Bolshevism and the greatest strategist of world socialist revolution. However, the theoretical and political work that Trotsky carried out in the final year of his life—a year dominated by the outbreak of World War II—was decisive in ensuring the survival of the Fourth International, in the face of what might have proved to be insurmountable difficulties.

Trotsky was murdered at the height of his intellectual powers. Despite his sense that his health was declining, there was no sign of a waning of his political energies. Even as he was producing on a daily basis political analysis and polemical essays, Trotsky was hard at work on a biography of Stalin which, even as an uncompleted work, may be justly described as a literary masterpiece.

Trotsky's writings during the final year of his life were not only as brilliant as those of earlier periods; the scope of his analysis of the events of 1939–40 extended, in terms of enduring relevance, far into the future. No other figure of his time exhibited a comparable grasp of the state of the world and where it was headed.

---

2. *The Case of Leon Trotsky* (New York: Merit Publishers, 1968), p. 291.
3. Leon Trotsky, "The USSR in War," *In Defence of Marxism* (London: New Park Publications, 1971), p. 21.

For example, Trotsky was interviewed by a group of American journalists on July 23, 1939, just six weeks before the outbreak of World War II. They were anxious to know his assessment of the world situation. For the benefit of the journalists, Trotsky spoke in English. He began by recalling that he had promised a visiting American professor that he would improve his English if the American government would grant him a visa to enter the United States. Regrettably, Trotsky observed, "it seems that they are not interested in my English."

Though Trotsky was not satisfied with his command of English, the transcript of his remarks leaves no doubt of his mastery of the complexity of the world situation. "The capitalist system," he stated, "is in a state of impasse." Trotsky continued:

> From my side, I do not see any normal, legal, peaceful outcome from this impasse. The outcome can only be created by a tremendous historic explosion. Historic explosions are of two kinds—wars and revolutions. I believe we will have both. The programs of the present governments, the good ones as well as the bad ones—if we suppose that there are good governments also—the programs of different parties, pacifist programs and reformist programs, seem now, at least to a man who observes them from the side, as child's play on the sloping side of a volcano before an eruption. This is the general picture of the world today.[4]

Trotsky then referenced the ongoing New York World's Fair, whose theme was the "World of Tomorrow."

> You created a World's Fair. I can judge it only from the outside for the same reason which my English is so bad, but from what I have learned about the Fair from the papers, it is a tremendous human creation from the point of view of the "World of Tomorrow." I believe this characterization is a bit one-sided. Only from a technical point of view can your World's Fair be named "World of Tomorrow," because if you wish to consider the real world of tomorrow we should see a hundred military

---

4. Leon Trotsky, "On the Eve of World War II," *Writings of Leon Trotsky [1939–40]* (New York: Pathfinder Press, 1973, second edition, eighth printing, 2019), pp. 17–18.

airplanes over the World's Fair, with bombs, some hundreds of bombs, and the result of this activity would be the world of tomorrow. This grandiose human creative power from the one side, and this terrible backwardness in the field which is most important for us, the social field—technical genius, and, permit me the word, social idiocy—this is the world of today.[5]

As a description of the *contemporary* "World of Today" and a prediction of the "World of Tomorrow"—that is, the world that will emerge from the crises of the present decade—it would hardly be necessary to change a single word. All over the world, with governments—combining limitless greed with limitless stupidity—incapable of responding with either competence or humanity, the question is being asked: How will this crisis be solved? Our answer is the same given by Trotsky: The solution will come in the form of a "tremendous historic explosion." And, as Trotsky explained in 1939, such explosions are of two kinds: wars and revolutions. Both are on the agenda.

The journalists who questioned Trotsky in July 1939 were also anxious to know whether he had any advice to give the American government as to its conduct of foreign policy. Not without a trace of humor, Trotsky replied:

> I must say that I do not feel competent to give advice to the Washington government because of the same political reason for which the Washington government finds it is not necessary to give me a visa. We are in a different social position from the Washington government. I could give advice to a government which had the same objectives as my own, not to a capitalist government, and the government of the United States, in spite of the New Deal, is, in my opinion, an imperialistic and capitalistic government. I can only say what a revolutionary government should do—a genuine workers' government in the United States.
>
> I believe the first thing would be to expropriate the Sixty Families. It would be a very good measure, not only from the national point of view, but from the point of view of settling world affairs—it would be a good example to the other nations.[6]

---

5. Ibid., p. 18.
6. Ibid., p. 27.

Trotsky recognized that this would not be accomplished in the immediate future. The defeats of the working class in Europe and the imminence of war would delay revolution in the United States. The entry of the United States into the coming war was only a matter of time. "If American capitalism survives, and it will survive for some time, we will have in the United States the most powerful imperialism and militarism in the world."[7]

Trotsky made one other prediction in the July interview. In fact, it was a restatement of a political analysis of Soviet foreign policy that he had been advancing for the previous five years. Referring to the removal of the old Soviet diplomat, Maxim Litvinov, from the post of foreign minister, and his replacement by Stalin's closest accomplice in crime, Molotov, Trotsky stated that the change was "a hint from the Kremlin to Hitler that we [Stalin] are ready to change our politics, to realize our objective, our aim, that we presented to you and Hitler some years ago, because the objective of Stalin in international politics is a settlement with Hitler."[8]

Even at that late date, the idea that the Soviet Union would ally itself with Nazi Germany was considered preposterous by virtually all "expert" opinion. But as was the case so often in the past, events confirmed Trotsky's analysis. Exactly one month after Trotsky's interview, on August 23, 1939, the Stalin-Hitler Non-Aggression Pact was signed in Moscow. The final obstacle to Hitler's war plans was removed by Stalin. On September 1, 1939 the Nazi regime invaded Poland. Two days later Britain and France declared war on Germany. Twenty-five years after the outbreak of the First World War, the Second World War had begun.

Having repeatedly predicted the Kremlin's turn to Hitler, Trotsky was not in the least surprised by Stalin's treachery. The Soviet Union, he warned, would pay a terrible price for Stalin's shortsightedness and incompetence. The dictator's belief that he had spared the Soviet bureaucracy from the perils of war with Nazi Germany would prove to be yet another disastrous miscalculation.

* * * * *

The outbreak of war triggered a political crisis within the Fourth International that became the central focus of Trotsky's work during the

---

7. Ibid., pp. 28–29.
8. Ibid., p. 20.

final year of his life. The concentration was not misplaced: his response to the minority faction in the American Socialist Workers Party (SWP) led by James Burnham, Max Shachtman, and Martin Abern was of fundamental significance not only in its defense of the theoretical foundations of Marxism and the historical advance, notwithstanding the crimes of the Soviet bureaucracy, represented by the October Revolution. Trotsky's polemics anticipated many of the most difficult questions of revolutionary strategy, program, and perspective that were to arise during and in the aftermath of World War II.

The signing of the Stalin-Hitler Pact, followed by the Soviet invasion of Poland in mid-September 1939 and Finland (the Winter War of 1939–40), provoked outrage among broad sections of petty-bourgeois radical intellectuals and artists in the United States. Many members of this large and influential social milieu had managed to come to terms with, and even support, Stalin's annihilation of the Old Bolsheviks during the Terror and the strangling of the Spanish Revolution. The crimes of 1936–39 occurred while the Stalinist regime was still advocating an international alliance between the Soviet Union and the "Western Democracies." The domestic application of this orientation was the promotion by Stalinist parties of an alliance, on the basis of a capitalist program, between working-class organizations and the capitalist political parties (the "Popular Front"). Stalin's signing of the Pact with Germany, in an utterly cynical and opportunist manner, dealt a blow to this particular form of class collaboration. The mood of the democratic petty bourgeoisie turned against the Soviet Union. To the extent that the democratic intelligentsia had uncritically and falsely identified Stalinism with socialism, the turn against the Soviet Union assumed an openly anti-communist character.

This political shift was reflected in the development of an oppositional tendency within the Socialist Workers Party and other sections of the Fourth International. The most important leaders of this tendency within the SWP were Max Shachtman—a founding member of the American Trotskyist movement and, next to James P. Cannon, the most influential figure in the SWP— and James Burnham, a professor of philosophy at New York University. They insisted that as a consequence of the Stalin-Hitler Pact and the invasion of Poland by the USSR, the definition of the Soviet Union as a degenerated workers state was no longer acceptable. The Soviet Union, they claimed, had evolved into a new form of exploitative society, with the bureaucracy functioning as a new type of ruling class unforeseen in Marxist theory. One of the terms employed by the minority to describe Soviet society was "bureaucratic collectivism." A corollary of this new appraisal was the rejection of the defense of the Soviet Union in the event of war with an imperialist state, even if the adversary was Nazi Germany.

For Trotsky, the demand of Shachtman and Burnham that the Fourth International revoke its definition of the Soviet Union as a degenerated workers state was not merely a matter of terminology. What were, Trotsky asked, the practical political consequences of the demand that the Soviet Union no longer be defined as a workers state?

> Let us concede for the moment that the bureaucracy is a new "class" and that the present regime in the USSR is a special system of class exploitation. What new political conclusions flow from these definitions? The Fourth International long ago recognized the necessity of overthrowing the bureaucracy by means of a revolutionary uprising of the toilers. Nothing else is proposed or can be proposed by those who proclaim the bureaucracy to be an exploiting "class."[9]

But the change in the definition of the Soviet Union demanded by the SWP minority had implications that went far beyond a clarification of terminology. The established definition of the USSR as a degenerated workers state was connected to the demand for a *political* rather than *social* revolution. Underlying this distinction was the conviction that the overthrow of the Stalinist bureaucracy would not involve a change in the property relations established on the basis of the October Revolution. The working class, having destroyed the bureaucratic regime and reestablished Soviet democracy, would preserve the economic system based on the nationalization of property achieved through the overthrow of the Russian bourgeoisie and the expropriation of capitalist property. This fundamental conquest of the October Revolution, the critical economic foundation for the subsequent economic and cultural development of the Soviet Union, would not be abandoned.

The position of the minority proceeded from the assumption that there was nothing left from the October Revolution that was worth saving. Therefore, there was no reason to retain the defense of the Soviet Union in the program of the Fourth International.

Trotsky raised another critical issue. If the bureaucracy represented a new class, which had established in the USSR a new form of exploitative

---

9. Trotsky, "The USSR in War," *In Defence of Marxism*, p. 4.

society, what were the new forms of property relations uniquely identified with this new class? Of what new stage of economic development, beyond capitalism and socialism, was "bureaucratic collectivism" a historically legitimate and even necessary expression? The Fourth International maintained that the bureaucracy had usurped political power, which it utilized to acquire privileges based on the nationalization of property achieved through the workers' revolution of 1917. The dictatorial power wielded by the bureaucracy under Stalin's leadership was the product of the degeneration of the Soviet state under specific political conditions. These were, principally, the historical backwardness of the pre-1917 Russian capitalist economy, which the Bolsheviks inherited, and the protracted political isolation of the Soviet Union as a consequence of the defeat of revolutionary movements in Europe and Asia in the aftermath of the Bolshevik conquest of power in Russia.

Were these conditions to persist—that is, if the isolation of the Soviet Union were to persist as a consequence of defeats of the working class and the long-term survival of capitalism in the major centers of imperialism—the workers state would cease to exist. But the outcome of this process, Trotsky insisted, would take the form of the liquidation of nationalized property and the re-establishment of capitalist property relations. This outcome would involve the transformation of a powerful section of bureaucrats, exploiting their political power to steal state assets, into a reconstituted capitalist class. Trotsky had warned that this outcome was a real possibility, which could be prevented only through the political revolution—in conjunction with the socialist revolution in the advanced capitalist countries.

This careful examination of the argument over the appropriate terminological definition of the Soviet Union enabled Trotsky to identify the far-reaching historical and political implications of the changes in program raised by the SWP opposition:

> The historic alternative, carried to the end, is as follows: either the Stalin regime is an abhorrent relapse in the process of transforming bourgeois society into a socialist society, or the Stalin regime is the first stage of a new exploiting society. If the second prognosis proves to be correct, then, of course, the bureaucracy will become a new exploiting class. However onerous the second perspective may be, if the world proletariat should actually prove incapable of fulfilling the mission placed upon it by the course of development, nothing else would remain except

only to recognize that the socialist programme, based on the internal contradictions of capitalist society, ended as a Utopia. It is self-evident that a new "minimum" programme would be required—for the defence of the interests of the slaves of the totalitarian bureaucratic society.

But are there such incontrovertible or even impressive objective data as would compel us today to renounce the prospect of the socialist revolution? That is the whole question.[10]

Therefore, what was at stake was the historical legitimacy of the entire socialist project. Was Stalin's alliance with Hitler, combined with the outbreak of the Second World War, incontrovertible proof that the working class was incapable of fulfilling the historical task assigned to it in Marxist theory? Thus, the entire dispute with Burnham and Shachtman—and, indeed, with all the many layers of demoralized petty-bourgeois intellectuals for whom they were speaking—hinged on whether the working class was, as established by Marx and Engels in their development and elaboration of the materialist conception of history, a revolutionary class. The response given by Trotsky to this historical issue, which has dominated political and intellectual life for the last eighty years, is sufficient, almost by itself, to establish his stature as the most profound and far-sighted political thinker, equaled only by Lenin, of the twentieth century. It is, therefore, appropriate, to quote this passage in full:

> The crisis of capitalist society which assumed an open character in July 1914, from the very first day of the war produced a sharp crisis in the proletarian leadership. During the 25 years that have elapsed since that time, the proletariat of the advanced capitalist countries has not yet created a leadership that could rise to the level of the tasks of our epoch. The experience of Russia testifies, however, that such a leadership can be created. (This does not mean, of course, that it will be immune to degeneration.) The question consequently stands as follows: Will objective historical necessity in the long run cut a path for itself in the consciousness of the vanguard of the working class; that is, in the process of this war and those profound shocks which it must engender,

---

10. Ibid., p. 11.

will a genuine revolutionary leadership be formed capable of leading the proletariat to the conquest of power?

The Fourth International has replied in the affirmative to this question, not only through the text of its programme, but also through the very fact of its existence. All the various types of disillusioned and frightened representatives of pseudo-Marxism proceed *on the contrary* from the assumption that the bankruptcy of the leadership only "reflects" the incapacity of the proletariat to fulfill its revolutionary mission. Not all our opponents express this thought clearly, but all of them—ultralefts, centrists, anarchists, not to mention Stalinists and social-democrats—shift the responsibility for the defeats from themselves to the shoulders of the proletariat. None of them indicate under precisely what conditions the proletariat will be capable of accomplishing the socialist overturn.

If we grant as true that the cause of the defeats is rooted in the social qualities of the proletariat itself then the position of modern society will have to be acknowledged as hopeless. Under conditions of decaying capitalism, the proletariat grows neither numerically nor culturally. There are no grounds, therefore, for expecting that it will sometime rise to the level of the revolutionary tasks. Altogether differently does the case present itself to him who has clarified in his mind the profound antagonism between the organic, deep-going, insurmountable urge of the toiling masses to tear themselves free from the bloody capitalist chaos, and the conservative, patriotic, utterly bourgeois character of the outlived labour leadership. We must choose one of these two irreconcilable conceptions.[11]

Neither Shachtman nor Burnham had attempted to work through the consequences of their perspectives. They were not even capable of predicting their own right-wing and pro-imperialist political trajectory, let alone foreseeing the course of world history. Their political thinking was guided by the most vulgar pragmatism, which consisted of improvising political responses on the basis of day-to-day impressions of "the reality of living events," without attempting to place the events to which they were reacting within the

---

11. Ibid., pp. 14–15.

essential world historical context. Trotsky called attention to their political eclecticism.

> The opposition leaders split sociology from dialectic materialism. They split politics from sociology. In the sphere of politics they split our tasks in Poland from our experience in Spain—our tasks in Finland from our position on Poland. History becomes transformed into a series of exceptional incidents; politics becomes transformed into a series of improvisations. We have here, in the full sense of the term, the disintegration of Marxism, the disintegration of theoretical thought, the disintegration of politics into its constituent elements. Empiricism and its foster-brother, impressionism, dominate from top to bottom.[12]

In the course of this polemic, Trotsky, in a manner which certainly caught Burnham and Shachtman by surprise, introduced the question of dialectical logic into the discussion. Trotsky was, of course, aware of the fact that Burnham dismissed dialectics as meaningless, and that he despised Hegel, whom the pompous professor stupidly described as "the century-dead arch-muddler of human thought."[13] As for Max Shachtman, he had no particular interest in matters relating to philosophy and declared himself to be an agnostic on the relation of dialectical materialism to revolutionary politics. In this situation, there was nothing contrived or capricious about Trotsky's "philosophical turn."

In a manner that exemplified its pragmatic cynicism, not to mention ignorance, the opposition asked sarcastically when Trotsky had become an expert in philosophy. How could the old revolutionary politician, who had never received a doctorate degree from an appropriately accredited academic institution, presume to lecture Professor James Burnham of New York University on matters pertaining to philosophy? To anyone familiar with the revolutionary intellectual milieu within which Trotsky's theoretical conceptions developed and matured, the opposition's question appears both insufferably arrogant and downright stupid.

As Trotsky acknowledged, the greatest influences on his own development as a Marxist were, in addition to Marx and Engels, such champions of

---

12. "An Open Letter to Comrade Burnham," ibid., pp. 114–15.
13. James Burnham, "Science and Style," appendix, ibid., p. 236.

dialectical and historical materialism as Franz Mehring, Antonio Labriola, and Georgi Plekhanov. Moreover, the seminal years of Trotsky's political and theoretical education coincided with the intense struggle being waged by orthodox Marxists against opportunism, which was rooted theoretically in various forms of neo-Kantianism and the even more extreme forms of subjective idealist irrationalism associated with Nietzscheanism. He had witnessed the right-wing political evolution of Russian opponents of philosophical materialism such as Berdaiev, Struve, and Chernov.

In the course of the first decade of his political activity (1897–1907), Trotsky—through intensive study, personal experience, and political struggle—had acquired a mastery of the dialectical method that was clearly expressed in his analysis of the dynamic of the Russian Revolution of 1905 and his formulation of the theory of permanent revolution.

An essential element of his refutation of Burnham's empiricist-pragmatic outlook was Trotsky's insistence that the dialectic of thought developed out of and reflected the dialectic of nature. In his Open Letter to Burnham, Trotsky explained "that our methods of thought, both formal logic and the dialectic, are not arbitrary constructions of our reason but rather expressions of the actual inter-relationships within nature itself. In this sense, the universe throughout is permeated with 'unconscious' dialectics."[14]

Many of the arguments that Trotsky made in his demolition of Burnham and Shachtman had been anticipated in several remarkable essays and lectures that he wrote in the 1920s. Almost exactly eighteen years earlier, Trotsky had placed particular emphasis on the dialectic of nature—in full conformity with the views of Marx and Engels—in a letter that was published as the introduction to the first issue of the militantly materialist Soviet journal, *Pod Znamenem Marxizma* [*Under the Banner of Marxism*]:

> Human society itself, both by its historical roots and by its contemporary economy, extends into the world of natural history. We must see contemporary man as a link in the whole development that starts from the first tiny organic cell, which came in its turn from the laboratory of nature, where the physical and chemical properties of matter act. The person who has learned to look with a clear eye on the past of the whole world, including human society, the animal and vegetable kingdoms, the solar

---

14. "An Open Letter to Comrade Burnham," ibid., pp. 106–07.

system, and the endless systems around it, will not start to hunt for keys to the secrets of the universe in ancient "holy books," those philosophical fairy tales of primitive infantilism.[15]

Trotsky restated with exceptional clarity and beauty this Marxist conception of the dialectic of nature in his December 1939 analysis of the petty-bourgeois opposition in the SWP:

> We call our dialectic, materialist, since its roots are neither in heaven nor in the depths of our "free will", but in objective reality, in nature. Consciousness grew out of the unconscious, psychology out of physiology, the organic world out of the inorganic, the solar system out of the nebulae. On all the rungs of the ladder of development, the quantitative changes were transformed into qualitative. Our thought, including dialectical thought, is only one of the forms of the expression of changing matter. There is place within this system for neither God, nor Devil, nor immortal soul, nor eternal norms of laws and morals. The dialectic of thinking, having grown out of the dialectic of nature, possesses consequently a thoroughly materialist character.[16]

Trotsky belonged to that rare category of truly great writers who sought and was able to express the most profound ideas in accessible language. But he did not achieve clarity at the expense of intellectual depth. Rather, the clarity is a manifestation of his mastery of the essential theoretical issues. Moreover, Trotsky's defense of Marxism was not motivated by any sort of abstract and dogmatic pedantry. He was all too familiar with pseudo-radical poseurs who — in the doleful tradition of the Left Hegelians of the 1840s—habitually invoked "the dialectic" to cover up their insufficient empirical knowledge of the disputed subject and simply did not know what they were talking about. Rather, Trotsky insisted on the significance of dialectical thought as a method of analyzing and understanding, for the purpose of revolutionary action, objective reality.

The development of a scientific perspective, necessary for the political orientation of the working class, required a level of analysis of a complex,

---

15. Leon Trotsky, "Attention to Theory," *Problems of Everyday Life* (New York: Pathfinder, 1973), p. 357.
16. Trotsky, "A Petty-bourgeois opposition in the Socialist Workers Party," *In Defence of Marxism*, p. 66.

contradictory, and, therefore, rapidly changing socio-economic and political situation that could not be acquired on the basis of formal logic, diluted with pragmatic impressionism. The absence of scientific method, for all his pretensions to philosophical expertise, found crude expression in the manner in which Burnham's analysis of Soviet society and policies was devoid of historical content and based largely on impressionistic descriptions of phenomena visible on the surface of society. Burnham's pragmatic commonsense approach to complex socio-economic and political processes was theoretically worthless. He contrasted the existing Soviet Union to what he thought, in ideal terms, a genuine workers state should be. He did not seek to explain the historical process and conflict of social and political forces, on a national and international scale, which underlay the degeneration.

He was appropriately chastised by Trotsky:

> Vulgar thought operates with such concepts as capitalism, morals, freedom, workers' state, etc. as fixed abstractions, presuming that capitalism is equal to capitalism, morals are equal to morals, etc. Dialectical thinking analyzes all things and phenomena in their continuous change, while determining in the material conditions of those changes that critical limit beyond which "A" ceases to be "A", a workers' state ceases to be a workers' state.
>
> The fundamental flaw of vulgar thought lies in the fact that it wishes to content itself with motionless imprints of a reality which consists of eternal motion. Dialectical thinking gives to concepts, by means of closer approximations, corrections, concretisation, a richness of content and flexibility; I would even say a succulence which to a certain extent brings them close to living phenomena. Not capitalism in general, but a given capitalism at a given stage of development. Not a workers' state in general, but a given workers' state in a backward country in an imperialist encirclement, etc.
>
> Dialectical thinking is related to vulgar thinking in the same way that a motion picture is related to a still photograph. The motion picture does not outlaw the still photograph but combines a series of them according to the laws of motion. Dialectics does not deny the syllogism, but teaches us to combine syllogisms in such a way as to bring our understanding closer to the

eternally changing reality. Hegel in his *Logic* established a series of laws: change of quantity into quality, development through contradictions, conflict of content and form, interruption of continuity, change of possibility into inevitability, etc., which are just as important for theoretical thought as is the simple syllogism for more elementary tasks.[17]

It is worth noting that this passage reveals a striking confluence of Trotsky and Lenin's conception of dialectical logic. In his *Conspectus of Hegel's Science of Logic* (which comprises a portion of Lenin's notebooks on philosophy published in Volume 38 of the Bolshevik leader's *Collected Works*), Lenin, commenting on Hegel, wrote:

> Logic is the science of cognition. It is the theory of knowledge. Knowledge is the reflection of nature by man. But this is not a simple, not an immediate, not a complete reflection, but the process of a series of abstractions, the formation and development of concepts, laws, etc., and these concepts, laws, etc. (thought, science = "the logical Idea") *embrace* conditionally, approximately, the universal law-governed character of eternally moving and developing nature. Here there are *actually*, objectively, three members: 1) nature; 2) human cognition = the human **brain** (as the highest product of this same nature), and 3) the form of reflection of nature in human cognition, and this form consists precisely of concepts, laws, categories, etc. Man cannot comprehend = reflect = mirror nature *as a whole*, in its completeness, its "immediate totality," he can only *eternally* come closer to this, creating abstractions, concepts, laws, a scientific picture of the world, etc., etc. [emphasis in the original][18]

In April 1940, the minority broke with the SWP and created its "Workers Party." Burnham remained in its ranks for little more than one month. On May 21, he sent a letter of resignation to the organization that

---

17. Ibid, pp. 65–66.
18. V.I. Lenin, "Conspectus of Hegel's Science of Logic," *Collected Works*, Volume 38 (Moscow: Progress Publishers, 1961), p. 182.

he had co-founded with Shachtman, in which he announced his total and absolute repudiation of socialism. Drawing the final conclusions from his rejection of dialectical materialism, Burnham wrote: "Of the most important beliefs, which have been associated with the Marxist movement, whether in its reformist, Leninist, Stalinist, or Trotskyist variants, there is virtually none which I accept in its traditional form."[19] Upon learning of the desertion of the theoretician of the opposition, Trotsky wrote to his attorney (and SWP member) Albert Goldman, "Burnham doesn't recognise dialectics but dialectics does not permit him to escape from its net. He is caught as a fly in a web."[20]

Following his abandonment of the Workers Party, Burnham moved rapidly to the extreme right of bourgeois politics, became an advocate of preventive nuclear war against the Soviet Union, and was, not long before his death in 1987, awarded the Medal of Freedom by President Ronald Reagan. Shachtman's evolution was more protracted. His "Third Camp" was defined by the slogan "Neither Washington nor Moscow." Eventually, Shachtman abandoned his ban on support for Washington and became an advocate of the Cold War waged by the United States, which eventually entailed full support for the Bay of Pigs invasion in 1961 and, later in the decade, the bombing of North Vietnam.

II. War and the perspective of socialist revolution

In the aftermath of the split with the Socialist Workers Party minority, Trotsky was able to turn his attention to the writing of a Manifesto for the Emergency Conference of the Fourth International, which had been called to respond to the sudden expansion of the war in Western Europe. The rapid conquest of Poland by Nazi Germany in the autumn of 1939 had been followed by a protracted lull in military conflict, the so-called "Sitzkrieg." But in April 1940 Hitler initiated a new stage in the war. The Wehrmacht moved westward, first seizing Norway and Denmark and, in May, sweeping into the Netherlands, Belgium, and France.

Trotsky's Manifesto began with a stirring appeal to all the victims of capitalist-imperialist oppression.

---

19. "Letter of resignation of James Burnham from the Workers Party," *In Defence of Marxism*, p. 257.
20. Trotsky, "A Letter to Albert Goldman," ibid, p. 224.

> The Fourth International turns not to the governments who have dragooned the peoples into the slaughter, nor to the bourgeois politicians who bear the responsibility for these governments, nor to the labor bureaucracy which supports the warring bourgeoisie. The Fourth International turns to the working men and women, the soldiers and sailors, the ruined peasants and the enslaved colonial peoples. The Fourth International has no ties whatsoever with the oppressors, the exploiters, the imperialists. It is the world party of the toilers, the oppressed, and the exploited. This manifesto is addressed to them.[21]

The Manifesto rejected all the official explanations for the outbreak of war. "Contrary to the official fables designed to drug the people," Trotsky wrote, "the chief cause of war as of all other social evils—unemployment, the high cost of living, fascism, colonial oppression—is the private ownership of the means of production together with the bourgeois state which rests on this foundation."[22] As in the First World War, underlying the eruption of military conflict was the rivalry among imperialist powers.

For the time being, the principal protagonists in this global conflict were Britain, France, Germany, and Italy, with Japan pursuing its interests in Asia. But lurking in the background was the United States, which, Trotsky predicted, "will intervene in the tremendous clash in order to maintain its world domination. The order and the time of the struggle between American capitalism and its enemies is not yet known—perhaps even by Washington. War with Japan would be a struggle for 'living room' in the Pacific Ocean. War in the Atlantic, even if directed immediately against Germany, would be a struggle for the heritage of Great Britain."[23]

Trotsky brushed aside claims that the ruling elites were waging war in the "Defense of the 'Fatherland.'" The bourgeoisie, he wrote, "never defends the fatherland for the sake of the fatherland. They defend private property, privileges, profits. ... Official patriotism is a mask for the exploiting interests. Class conscious workers throw this mask contemptuously aside."[24] As for the pretentious invocation of democratic ideals, these were no less fraudulent than

---

21. Trotsky, "Manifesto of the Fourth International on the imperialist war and the proletarian revolution," *Writings of Leon Trotsky [1939–40]*, pp. 245–46.
22. Ibid., pp. 247–48.
23. Ibid., pp. 252.
24. Ibid., pp. 255–56.

the patriotic declarations. All the democracies, with Britain in the first rank, helped lift Hitler into power. And they all derived a substantial portion of their wealth from the brutal exploitation of the colonial peoples.

Hitler's regime was nothing other than "the chemically pure distillation of the culture of imperialism." The hypocritical claim that the democratic powers were fighting fascism was a blatant political distortion of history and reality.

> The democratic governments, who in their day hailed Hitler as a crusader against Bolshevism, now make him out to be some kind of Satan unexpectedly loosed from the depths of hell, who violates the sanctity of treaties, boundary lines, rules, and regulations. If it were not for Hitler the capitalist world would blossom like a garden. What a miserable lie! This German epileptic with a calculating machine in his skull and unlimited power in his hands did not fall from the sky or come up out of hell: he is nothing but the personification of all the destructive forces of imperialism.[25]

Trotsky then turned to an examination of the role played by the Stalinist regime in abetting the outbreak of war.

> Stalin's alliance with Hitler, which raised the curtain on the world war and led directly to the enslavement of the Polish people, resulted from the weakness of the USSR and the Kremlin's panic in face of Germany. Responsibility for this weakness rests with no one but this same Kremlin; its internal policy, which opened an abyss between the ruling caste and the people; its foreign policy, which sacrificed the interests of the world revolution to the interests of the Stalinist clique.[26]

Notwithstanding the crimes of Stalin, an invasion of the Soviet Union by the Nazis—which Trotsky believed to be inevitable—would call into question not merely the survival of the Kremlin dictatorship but that of the USSR. The conquests of the revolution, however distorted and disfigured by Stalinism, could not be surrendered to the invading armies of imperialism.

---

25. Ibid., p. 259.
26. Ibid., p. 263.

"While waging a tireless struggle against the Moscow oligarchy," Trotsky proclaimed, "the Fourth International decisively rejects any policy that would aid imperialism against the USSR." He continued:

> The defense of the USSR coincides in principle with the preparation of the world proletarian revolution. We flatly reject the theory of socialism in one country, that brain child of ignorant and reactionary Stalinism. Only the world revolution can save the USSR for socialism. But the world revolution carries with it the inescapable blotting out of the Kremlin oligarchy.[27]

Trotsky's analysis of the war encompassed the developments in the colonial possessions, which he was convinced would become a massive theater of global revolutionary struggles. "The entire present war," he wrote, "is a war over colonies. They are hunted by some; held by others who refuse to give them up. Neither side has the least intention of liberating them voluntarily. The declining metropolitan centers are impelled to drain away as much as possible from the colonies and to give them in return as little as possible. Only the direct and open revolutionary struggle of the enslaved peoples can clear the road for their emancipation."[28]

Trotsky surveyed the economic and political conditions in China, India, and Latin America. In each situation, taking into account the specific conditions, the victory of the struggle against the imperialist powers depended upon the establishment of the political independence of the working class from the corrupt and compromised national ruling elites. The theory of permanent revolution—which guided the Russian working class to power in 1917—retained full validity for the working class in all countries oppressed by imperialism. The overthrow of imperialist rule was inextricably connected to and inseparable from the struggle for workers power and socialism. Moreover, as the example of Russia had proved, there was no special order which determined a priori when one or another country would have conditions which allowed the working class to conquer power. Trotsky explained:

> The perspective of the permanent revolution in no case signifies that the backward countries must await the signal from the

---

27. Ibid., p. 267.
28. Ibid., p. 270.

advanced ones, or that the colonial peoples should patiently wait for the proletariat of the metropolitan centers to free them. Help comes to him who helps himself. Workers must develop the revolutionary struggle in every country, colonial or imperialist, where favorable conditions have been established, and through this set an example for the workers of other countries. Only initiative and activity, resoluteness and boldness can really materialize the slogan "Workers of the world, unite!"[29]

In the concluding sections of the Manifesto, Trotsky returned to the central theoretical and political issues that he had raised in the opening phase of the factional struggle against the petty-bourgeois minority and which would preoccupy him in the final weeks of his life. The outbreak of World War II was prepared by the betrayals of all the existing mass organizations of the working class, whether social democratic, Stalinist, anarchist, or some other variety of reformism. How, then, would the working class find the path to power?

Trotsky reviewed the essential conditions for the conquest of power by the working class: a crisis that creates a political impasse which disorients the ruling class; intense dissatisfaction with existing conditions among large sections of the middle class that deprives the big capitalists of their support; the conviction within the working class that the situation is intolerable and a willingness to take radical action; and, finally, a program and decisive leadership within the advanced sections of the working class. But each of these conditions may develop at a different tempo. While the bourgeoisie finds itself in a political impasse and the middle class looks for alternatives to the existing conditions, the working class—under the influence of past defeats—may display a reluctance to enter into decisive struggles. Trotsky acknowledged that the betrayals during the years leading up to the outbreak of war had created a mood of discouragement among the workers. "One should not, however, overestimate the stability or durability of such moods," Trotsky advised. "Events created them; events will dispel them."[30]

In the final analysis, taking into consideration the complex interaction of the contradictory elements of a fundamental societal crisis, the fate of the revolution depends upon the resolution of the problem of leadership. In confronting this problem, Trotsky posed hypothetically two questions:

---

29. Ibid., p. 275.
30. Ibid., p. 289.

"Will not the revolution be betrayed this time too, inasmuch as there are two Internationals [the Social Democratic Second International and Stalinist Communist International, also known as the Comintern] in the service of imperialism while the genuine revolutionary elements constitute a tiny minority? In other words: shall we succeed in preparing in time a party capable of leading the proletarian revolution?"[31]

In his essay, "The USSR and War," written eight months earlier in September 1939, Trotsky had indicated that the outcome of the Second World War could prove decisive in determining the viability of the perspective of socialist revolution. "The results of this test," he had written, "will undoubtedly have a decisive significance for our appraisal of the modern epoch as the epoch of proletarian revolution."[32] But this statement was in the character of an *obiter dictum*, an incidental remark intended, legitimately, to stress the gravity of the world situation and the dangers it posed to the working class. It was not intended to be read as an unalterable historical timetable. In an ensuing document, written in April 1940, Trotsky made a critical point about the methodology of Marxist analysis:

> Every historical prognosis is always conditional, and the more concrete the prognosis, the more conditional it is. A prognosis is not a promissory note which can be cashed on a given date. Prognosis outlines only the definite trends of the development. But along with these trends a different order of forces and tendencies operate, which at a certain moment begin to predominate. All those who seek exact predictions of concrete events should consult the astrologers. Marxist prognosis aids only in orientation.[33]

By May, 1940, it is clear that Trotsky was seeking to orient the Fourth International on the basis of a perspective whose analysis extended beyond the war and its immediate outcome. The war was not only the culmination of the crisis of the post-World War I era; it was also the beginning of a new stage in the crisis of the capitalist system and world revolution. The cadre of the Fourth International had to prepare for an extended period of struggle.

---

31. Ibid.
32. Trotsky, "The USSR in War," *In Defence of Marxism*, p. 17.
33. "Balance sheet of the Finnish events," ibid., pp. 218–19.

"Naturally," he candidly acknowledged, "this or that uprising may end and surely will end in defeat, owing to the immaturity of the revolutionary leadership. But it is not a question of a single uprising. It is a question of an entire revolutionary epoch."

What conclusion flowed from this appraisal of the war as a turning point in world history?

> The capitalist world has no way out, unless a prolonged death agony is so considered. It is necessary to prepare for long years, if not decades, of war, uprisings, brief interludes of truce, new wars and new uprisings. A young revolutionary party must base itself on this perspective. History will provide it with enough opportunities and possibilities to test itself, to accumulate experience, and to mature. The swifter the ranks of the vanguard are fused the more the epoch of bloody convulsions will be shortened, the less destruction will our planet suffer. But the great historical problem will not be solved in any case until a revolutionary party stands at the head of the proletariat. The question of tempos and time intervals is of enormous importance; but it alters neither the general historical perspective nor the direction of our policy. The conclusion is a simple one: it is necessary to carry on the work of educating and organizing the proletarian vanguard with tenfold energy. Precisely in this lies the task of the Fourth International.[34]

III. May 24, 1940: the first attempt on Trotsky's life

Following the completion of his Manifesto for the Emergency Conference of the Fourth International, Trotsky's relentless and punishing schedule of writing projects was interrupted by an event he had long foreseen, though its exact date could not have been predicted. In the early morning hours of May 24, 1940, the Mexican painter and fanatical Stalinist David Alfaro Siqueiros led a squad of assassins, armed with 45-caliber Thompson submachine guns, 30-caliber automatic rifles and incendiary bombs, in an assault against the leader of the Fourth International.

---

34. Trotsky, "Manifesto of the Fourth International," *Writings of Leon Trotsky [1939–40]*, p. 290.

The assassins did not have to storm the villa on the Avenida Viena. The guard on duty, Robert Sheldon Harte, unlocked the iron gate and allowed the assassins to enter. The gunmen clearly were familiar with the entire layout of the compound. One group moved toward the section of the villa that housed the bedroom of Trotsky and his wife Natalia and that of their grandson Seva. Another group moved rapidly to the opposite end of the courtyard, outside the section of the compound where Trotsky's guards were quartered. While the second group of gunmen laid down fire in the direction of the guards' rooms, effectively pinning them down and rendering them totally ineffective, the main team of assassins entered Trotsky's bedroom.

The room was dark, and the assassins fired wildly in all directions. Trotsky had taken a sleeping pill upon retiring for the night and was groggy as he was awakened by the gunfire. Natalia responded more quickly and saved Trotsky's life. As he recalled in "Stalin Seeks My Death," an account of the assault written in the first week of June 1940:

> My wife had already jumped from her bed. The shooting continued incessantly. My wife later told me that she helped me to the floor, pushing me into the space between the bed and the wall. This was quite true. She had remained hovering over me, beside the wall, as if to shield me with her body. But by means of whispers and gestures I convinced her to lie flat on the floor. The shots came from all sides, it was difficult to tell just from where. At a certain time my wife, as she later told me, was able clearly to distinguish spurts of fire from a gun: consequently, the shooting was being done right here in the room although we could not see anybody. My impression is that altogether some two hundred shots were fired, of which about one hundred fell right here, near us. Splinters of glass from windowpanes and chips from walls flew in all directions. A little later I felt that my right leg had been slightly wounded in two places.[35]

As the gunmen withdrew from the room, Trotsky heard his fourteen-year-old grandson, Seva, cry out. Trotsky recalled this terrible moment:

---

35. "Stalin seeks my death," ibid., pp. 311–12.

> The voice of the child in the darkness under the gunfire remains the most tragic recollection of that night. The boy—after the first shot had cut his bed diagonally as evidenced by marks left on the door and wall—threw himself under the bed. One of the assailants, apparently in a panic, fired into the bed, the bullet passed through the mattress, struck our grandson in the big toe and imbedded itself in the floor. The assailants threw two incendiary bombs and left our grandson's bedroom. Crying, "Grandfather!" he ran after them into the patio, leaving a trail of blood behind him and, under gunfire, rushed into the room of one of the guards.[36]

Trotsky credited his survival to "a fortunate accident."

> The beds were under a cross-fire. Perhaps the assailants were afraid to hit each other and instinctively fired either higher or lower than they should have. But that is only a psychological conjecture. It is also possible that my wife and I came to the aid of the happy accident by not losing our heads, not flying around the room, not crying out or calling for help when it was hopeless to do so, not shooting when it was senseless, but remained quietly on the floor pretending to be dead.[37]

The assassination squad made its escape, not realizing that its mission had ended in failure. Trotsky left his room and entered the courtyard, from which the smoke from gunfire was still rising. He was searching for members of the guard, who were still in their rooms. None of them had been trained to react to an assault of this character. Their efforts to return fire had been sporadic and ineffective. Harold Robins' machine gun jammed on the first round. He learned later that the wrong ammunition had been loaded into the weapon. Robins recalled that Trotsky's demeanor was remarkably calm. Having experienced numerous battles during the savage Russian Civil War of 1918–21, the former supreme commander of the Red Army was not unfamiliar with gun fire. But Robins also sensed that Trotsky was disappointed with the utterly ineffective response of his guards.[38]

---

36. Ibid., p. 312.
37. Ibid., p. 314.
38. The author of this essay engaged in numerous discussions with Harold Robins (1908–1987) during our collaboration in the 1970s and 1980s on the International Committee's

The guards discovered that a detail of Mexican police, who had been assigned to man a post outside the villa, had been tied up. On Trotsky's instructions, they were immediately unbound. A more disturbing discovery was that Robert Sheldon Harte had departed with the assailants, which immediately aroused suspicions that he was involved in the conspiracy. In the absence of definite evidence of Harte's involvement, Trotsky upheld his innocence—a position that seemed to be vindicated when the guard's body was discovered several weeks later.

For reasons that can be well understood, Trotsky was reluctant, in the immediate aftermath of the assault, to level an accusation against Harte. But he did not exclude the possibility that Harte had acted in collusion with the GPU. "Despite all precautions," Trotsky wrote, "it is, of course, impossible to consider as absolutely excluded the possibility that an isolated agent of the GPU could worm his way into the guard."[39] He noted that Harte, due to his disappearance, had come under suspicion. But based on the evidence then available, Trotsky was not prepared to conclude that Harte was guilty. He accepted the possibility that new information might require a reevaluation of Harte's role. Whatever the final verdict, he continued, "If contrary to all my suppositions such a participation should be confirmed, then it would change nothing essential in the character of the assault. With the aid of one of the members of the guard or without this aid the GPU organized a conspiracy to kill me and to burn my archives."[40]

Trotsky expressed confidence in the SWP's choice of guards. "They were all sent here after special selection by my experienced and old friends."[41] What Trotsky did not know was that the Socialist Workers Party did not seriously vet the individuals it dispatched from the United States to Coyoacán. In the case of Harte, the twenty-five-year-old New Yorker had virtually no political history in the SWP. After his son's disappearance, his father, Jesse Harte, a wealthy businessman and friend of J. Edgar Hoover, flew to Mexico. In the course of meetings with the Mexican police, the elder Harte informed them that a photo of Stalin had been found in his son's New York apartment. When this information was leaked to the press somewhat later, Trotsky sent Jesse Harte a telegram, asking for

---

investigation into the assassination of Trotsky.
39. Trotsky, "Stalin seeks my death," *Writings of Leon Trotsky [1939–40]*, p. 330.
40. Ibid.
41. Ibid.

confirmation of this report. Harte replied with an unequivocal and dishonest denial: "DEFINITELY DETERMINED STALINS PICTURE NOT IN SHELDONS ROOM."[42]

As part of the investigation into the assassination of Trotsky, which it initiated in 1975, the International Committee of the Fourth International reviewed all the evidence relating to Sheldon Harte's role in the May 24 raid. The ICFI concluded that Harte was, indeed, a participant in the conspiracy. This finding was denounced by the Socialist Workers Party (SWP), led by Joseph Hansen, and its allies in anti-Trotskyist Pabloite organizations all over the world, who were bitterly opposed to the exposure of Stalinist and other police agents inside the Fourth International. They denounced the investigation into Trotsky's assassination as "agent baiting." The ICFI was accused in a public statement issued by the SWP and its international allies of "desecrating the grave of Robert Sheldon Harte."[43]

The release of GPU archives following the dissolution of the Soviet Union in 1991 established definitively that Harte was a Stalinist agent, who played a critical role in the May 24 attempt on Trotsky's life. Several days after the assassination attempt, the GPU rewarded Harte for his treachery by murdering him. Contemptuous of the young traitor, Siqueiros and his accomplices viewed Harte as an unreliable individual who might talk if he were eventually questioned by police. While Harte slept, they fired a bullet into his brain, threw his body into a dirt pit and covered it with lime. Harte's decomposed remains were discovered several weeks later.

Despite the obvious fact that the attempt on Trotsky's life had been carried out on Stalin's orders, the hirelings of the GPU operating in the Mexican Communist Party, the trade unions, and newspapers initiated a campaign to disorient public opinion by claiming that the May 24 raid was actually a "self-assault," initiated by Trotsky himself. In two major articles, "Stalin Seeks My Death" and "The Comintern and the GPU"—the latter was completed on August 17, 1940, only three days before the second, and successful, attack, carried out by Ramon Mercader—Trotsky subjected the Stalinist lies to a devastating refutation.

In "The Comintern and the GPU," Trotsky exposed the absurdity of the claim that he would have or could have orchestrated the May 24 attack.

---

42. Bertrand M. Patenaude, *Trotsky: Downfall of a Revolutionary* (Harper Perennial, 2009), p. 256.
43. Socialist Workers Party, "Healy's Big Lie," *Education for Socialists*, December 1976, p. 36.

What aim could I pursue in venturing on so monstrous, repugnant, and dangerous an enterprise? No one has explained it to this day. It is hinted that I wanted to blacken Stalin and his GPU. But would another assault add anything at all to the reputation of a man who has destroyed an entire old generation of the Bolshevik Party? It is said that I wish to prove the existence of the "Fifth Column." Why? What for? Besides, GPU agents are quite sufficient for the perpetration of an assault; there is no need of the mysterious "Fifth Column." It is said that I wanted to create difficulties for the Mexican government. What possible motives could I have for creating difficulties for the only government that has been hospitable to me? It is said that I wanted to provoke a war between the United States and Mexico. But this explanation completely belongs to the domain of delirium. In order to provoke such a war it would have been in any case much more expedient to have organized an assault on an American ambassador or on oil magnates and not a revolutionist-Bolshevik, alien and hateful to imperialist circles.

When Stalin organizes an attempt to assassinate me, the meaning of his actions is clear: he wants to destroy his enemy number one. Stalin incurs no risks thereby; he acts at long distance. On the contrary, by organizing "self-assault" I have to assume responsibility for such an enterprise myself; I risk my own fate, the fate of my family, my political reputation, and the reputation of the movement which I serve. What do I stand to gain from it?

But even if one were to allow the impossible, namely, that after renouncing the cause of my whole life, and trampling underfoot common sense and my own vital interests, I did decide to organize "self-assault" for the sake of some unknown goal, then there still remains the following question: Where and how did I obtain twenty executors? How did I supply them with police uniforms? How did I arm them? How did I equip them with all the necessary things? etc., etc. In other words, how did a man, who lives almost completely isolated from the outside world, contrive to fulfill an enterprise conceivable only for a powerful apparatus? Let me confess that I feel awkward in subjecting to criticism an idea that is beneath all criticism.[44]

---

44. "The Comintern and the GPU," *Writings of Leon Trotsky 1939–40*, pp. 486–87.

In his analysis of the GPU's political preparation of the assault, Trotsky provided fresh evidence of his extraordinary perspicacity. He called attention to the Extraordinary Congress of the Mexican Communist Party, which had been held in March of 1940. The main theme that dominated the congress was the need to exterminate Trotskyism. Trotsky surmised that the congress' decision to expel Hernán Laborde, the secretary general of the Mexican Communist Party, and Valentín Campa, a leading figure in the trade unions, was bound up with the need to remove from positions of authority individual leaders who were reluctant to involve the party in a politically dangerous and unpopular assassination plot. Trotsky emphasized that the initiative for this purge clearly came from outside the organization, that is, from the GPU acting on the directives of the Kremlin regime. Explaining that the implementation of the brutal organizational changes at the congress would have required several months to prepare, Trotsky argued that the order for the assassination attempt had arrived from Moscow in November or December 1939.

Trotsky's analysis of the protracted preparations for the May 24 assault and the significance of the Mexican CP's Extraordinary Congress has been substantiated by recent scholarship, which has demonstrated that planning for Trotsky's murder began in the spring of 1939. Laborde was approached by an agent of the GPU who was operating under the cover of the Comintern. The agent's mission "was to seek the cooperation of the PCM Secretariat in plans to eliminate Trotsky. Laborde allegedly consulted with Campa and Rafael Carrillo [another leading member of the Mexican CP] and reached the conclusion that not only would such a move endanger the PCM's relations with the Cárdenas government, but that it was in any case unnecessary since Trotsky was a spent force."[45]

The GPU did not agree with Laborde and Campa's assessment of Trotsky's political influence. Laborde, Campa, and Carrillo traveled to New York in May 1939 to seek support from Earl Browder, leader of the Communist Party of the United States (CPUSA), for opposition to an attack on Trotsky. They were not successful. The decision to convene an extraordinary congress was taken at the September 1939 plenum of the Mexican CP's National Committee. According to scholar Barry Carr, the CPUSA and the Comintern were concerned "over the inadequacies of the Mexican party's anti-Trotsky campaign and over its supposedly shallow defense of Soviet

---

45. Barry Carr, "Crisis in Mexican Communism: The Extraordinary Congress of the Mexican Communist Party," *Science & Society*, Spring, 1987, Vol. 51, No. 1, p. 50.

foreign policy, particularly the decision to intervene militarily in Finland in November 1939."[46]

The first public call for the Extraordinary Congress was issued in November. Comintern delegates from Europe, actually agents of the GPU, began arriving in Mexico from Europe. Among them was Vittorio Codovilla, who had been stationed in Spain. Carr writes that the Comintern envoys were dissatisfied with the preparations and agenda of the planned congress.

> Codovilla suggested a complete rewriting of the agenda and a concentration on one essential point "so as not to distract the attention of delegates." He went on to outline the structure of the revised agenda, including a new item on the struggle against the enemies of the people (with the main theme being the struggle against Trotskyism). ...
>
> The envoys did not limit their activities to suggestions about the format of the Extraordinary Congress' preliminary documents. They also urged the party to conduct a "house cleaning" prior to the Congress, expelling Trotskyites ... The services of exiled Spanish communists was offered [sic] for this latter task.[47]

Stalin viewed Trotsky as the most serious political threat to his regime. He had come to view the decision to deport Trotsky from the Soviet Union in 1929 as his greatest political mistake. Stalin had assumed that Trotsky, isolated in a foreign country, would be incapable of mounting serious opposition to the Kremlin. Stalin was mistaken. As Trotsky noted, "Events have shown, however, that it is possible to participate in political life without possessing either an apparatus or material resources."[48] Stalin's biographer, Dmitri Volkogonov, who had access to his subject's private papers, wrote that the dictator was obsessed by "Trotsky's ghost."

> He [Stalin] thought of Trotsky when he had to sit and listen to Molotov, Kaganovich, Khrushchev and Zhdanov [members of the Stalinist Politburo]. Trotsky was of a different calibre intellectually, with his grasp of organization and his talents as a

---

46. Ibid., p. 51.
47. Ibid., p. 54.
48. "Stalin seeks my death," *Writings of Leon Trotsky [1939–40]*, p. 315.

speaker and writer. In every way he was far superior to this bunch of bureaucrats, but he was also superior to Stalin and Stalin knew it. "How could I have let such an enemy slip through my fingers?" he almost wailed. On one occasion he confessed to his small circle that this had been one of the biggest mistakes of his life...

The thought that Trotsky was speaking not only for himself, but for all his silent supporters and the oppositionists inside the USSR, was particularly painful to Stalin. When he read Trotsky's works, such as *The Stalinist School of Falsification*, *An Open Letter to Members of the Bolshevik Party*, or *The Stalinist Thermidor*, the Leader almost lost his self-control.[49]

Stalin's hatred of Trotsky was not of a purely, or even predominately, personal character. The homicidal dimensions of his rage were the concentrated expression of the hostility that the ruling bureaucracy, as a privileged caste, felt toward its most implacable opponent. As Trotsky explained in "The Comintern and the GPU":

> The Moscow oligarchy's hatred of me is engendered by its deeprooted conviction that I "betrayed" it. This accusation has a historical meaning of its own. The Soviet bureaucracy did not elevate Stalin to leadership at once and without vacillation. Until 1924 Stalin was unknown even among the broader party circles, let alone the population, and as I have already said he did not enjoy popularity in the ranks of the bureaucracy itself. The new ruling stratum had hopes that I would undertake to defend its privileges. No few efforts were expended in this direction. Only after the bureaucracy became convinced that I did not intend to defend its interests against the toilers, but on the contrary the interests of the toilers against the new aristocracy, was the complete turn toward Stalin made, and I was proclaimed "traitor." This epithet on the lips of the privileged caste constitutes evidence of my loyalty to the cause of the working class. It is not accidental that 90 percent of those revolutionists

---

49. Dmitri Volkogonov, *Stalin: Triumph & Tragedy*, tr. Harold Shukman (New York, 1988), pp. 254, 256.

who built the Bolshevik Party, made the October Revolution, created the Soviet state and the Red Army, and led the civil war were destroyed as "traitors" in the course of the past twelve years. On the other hand, the Stalinist apparatus has taken into its ranks during this period people the overwhelming majority of whom stood on the other side of the barricades in the years of the revolution.[50]

The political degeneration and moral decay were not confined to the Soviet Communist Party. The same insidious process was to be observed throughout the Comintern, whose leading personnel in every country had been changed in line with the political and ideological requirements of the Kremlin. National leaders were not chosen on the basis of their revolutionary intransigence, political intelligence, and personal integrity. What the Kremlin sought in the individuals it selected as leaders of national parties was spinelessness, opportunism, and willingness to take orders. Trotsky was very familiar with the type favored by Stalin:

> Lacking independent stature, independent ideas, independent influence, the leaders of the sections of the Comintern are only too well aware that their positions and reputations stand and fall with the position and reputation of the Kremlin. In the material sense, as will be later shown, they live on the handouts of the GPU. Their struggle for existence resolves itself therefore into a rabid defense of the Kremlin against any and all opposition. They cannot fail to sense the correctness and therefore the danger of the criticism which comes from the so-called Trotskyists. But this only redoubles their hatred of me and my co-thinkers. Like their Kremlin masters, the leaders of the Communist parties are unable to criticize the real ideas of the Fourth International and are forced to resort to falsifications and frame-ups which are exported from Moscow in unlimited quantities. There is thus nothing "national" in the conduct of the Mexican Stalinists: they merely translate into Spanish the policies of Stalin and the orders of the GPU.[51]

---

50. "The Comintern and the GPU," *Writings of Leon Trotsky [1939–40]*, pp. 468–69.
51. Ibid., p. 470.

Trotsky documented the systematic corruption of the Comintern sections fostered by the GPU. Bribes, backed by threats, replaced political argument as a means of ensuring the implementation of policies desired by the Kremlin.

The outbreak of World War II intensified Stalin's fear of Trotsky. Despite Stalin's desperate hope that Hitler would adhere to the Non-Aggression Pact and refrain from invading the Soviet Union, he certainly realized that, notwithstanding all the concessions he had made to Hitler, the danger of a German invasion was very real. If and when that occurred, the disastrous consequences of Stalin's policies—which included the launching of a bloody purge of the military in 1937–38 that involved the physical annihilation of the Red Army's most experienced and capable generals and approximately three-quarters of its officer corps—would leave the regime totally discredited. The defeats suffered by the tsarist armies during World War I had been a major factor in the eruption of the Russian Revolution only a little more than twenty years earlier. The tsar, who had assumed supreme command of the military, was swept from power. Did there not exist, therefore, the possibility that a new war would result in an uprising within the Soviet Union, especially if the outbreak of war were followed by defeats caused by the incompetence of the regime? Stalin was certainly familiar with the essay written in 1937 by the celebrated writer and revolutionary Victor Serge. Despite all the persecutions, Serge wrote, the "Old Man"—as Trotsky was affectionately called by so many of his followers—had not been forgotten by the Soviet people.

> As long as the Old Man lives, there will be no security for the triumphant bureaucracy. One mind of the October revolution remains, and that is the mind of a true leader. At the first shock, the masses will turn towards him. In the third month of a war, when the difficulties begin, nothing will prevent the entire nation from turning to the "organizer of victory."[52]

There was yet another reason why Stalin sought Trotsky's death. The Kremlin dictator knew that Trotsky was hard at work on a biography of Stalin. One of the aims of the May 24 raid had been to destroy Trotsky's archives. Stalin certainly assumed that among Trotsky's papers was the

---

52. Victor Serge, *From Lenin to Stalin* (New York: Pioneer Publishers, 1937), p. 104.

manuscript of the biography, which the May 24 raid failed to locate and destroy. The only way the completion of the biography could be prevented was to murder its author. Stalin feared the consequences of Trotsky's exposure of his background, his political mediocrity, his minor role in the history of the Bolshevik party prior to 1917 and during the Revolution, his incompetence during the Civil War, and, above all, the pattern of disloyalty and treachery that led Lenin to conclude in early 1923 that Stalin had to be removed from his post as general secretary. Stalin's determination to stop the completion and publication of the biography was certainly a major factor in the very short period of time—less than three months—that elapsed between the unsuccessful assault of May 24 and the assassination carried out by Ramon Mercader on August 20, 1940.

The assassination did, in fact, prevent the completion of the biography. But Trotsky left behind a large manuscript that provided an extraordinary insight into Stalin's personality and political evolution. It was not until 1946 that Trotsky's biography was published; but this version was incompetently organized, mixing together completed chapters with fragments of notes and passages that had not been clearly integrated by Trotsky into the biographical narrative. The translator, Charles Malamuth, was incompetent. As early as 1939, based on what he had seen of Malamuth's initial efforts to translate sections of the manuscript, Trotsky complained: "Malamuth seems to have at least three qualities: he does not know Russian; he does not know English; and he is tremendously pretentious."[53]

Still worse, following the assassination, Malamuth took extraordinary liberties with Trotsky's text, arbitrarily inserting his own words and phrases, intentionally imposing on the biography opinions that directly contradicted those of the author. Malamuth's interpolations frequently extended for several pages, thus diluting and distorting the narrative as written by Trotsky. This was the only version of the biography to which the general public had access for approximately seventy years. In 2016, a new version of the biography was published, with a far more conscientious approach to the translation and organization of the manuscript and previously unassimilated fragments.[54]

---

53. Leon Trotsky, *Writings of Leon Trotsky: Supplement [1934–40]* (New York: Pathfinder Press, 1979), p. 354.
54. The translator and editor of this new edition is Alan Woods. Though he is associated with a left-wing political tendency with which the International Committee has well-known and fundamental political differences, Woods' efforts in producing this edition of Trotsky's *Stalin* deserve appreciative recognition and commendation.

In the final volume of his Trotsky trilogy, Isaac Deutscher wrote that the biography of Stalin—even if the author had lived to complete it—"would probably have remained his weakest work." This criticism, which arose from Deutscher's political objections to Trotsky's unequivocal appraisal of Stalinism as counterrevolutionary, is profoundly wrong. Despite the fact that the biography was left incomplete, both in terms of its content and the evident absence of a final editing process that would have enabled the great writer to impart the full scope of his artistry to the manuscript, Trotsky's *Stalin* is a masterpiece. Countless biographies of Stalin have been written, including one by Deutscher that presented Stalin as a political giant. None of these works comes close to matching Trotsky's biography in terms of political depth, psychological insight, and literary brilliance.

Trotsky's biography is informed by an unequaled knowledge of the economic, social, cultural, and political environment in which the revolutionary workers movement developed throughout the vast Russian Empire. Trotsky's recreation of Stalin's personality is not a caricature. The persona of Djughashvili-Stalin, as Trotsky demonstrates, was shaped by the backward conditions of his family upbringing and the cultural and political environment within which his early political activities unfolded.

This is not the place for a comprehensive and detailed review of this extraordinary work. But the one critical element of the biography to which attention must be called is Trotsky's preoccupation with the objective conditions, and the reflective subjective processes, which made possible Stalin's rise to supreme power. Trotsky calls attention repeatedly to the change in the social culture of the Bolshevik Party in the aftermath of the Civil War. The party that led the revolution provided a heroic example "of such solidarity, such idealistic resurgence, such devotion, such selflessness" as to be almost beyond comparison with any other movement in history.[55]

> Within the Bolshevik Party there were internal debates, conflicts, in a word, all those things that are a natural part of human existence. As for members of the Central Committee, they too were only human, but a special epoch lifted them above themselves. Without idealising anything, and without closing one's eyes to human weaknesses, we can nevertheless say that in those

---

55. Leon Trotsky, *Stalin*, ed. and tr., Alan Woods (London: Wellred Books, 2016), p. 545.

years, the air that one breathed in the Party was that of the mountain peaks.[56]

But the atmosphere changed in the aftermath of the Civil War, as new, untested, and socially alien elements poured into the party. There were episodic efforts to protect the party against the influx of careerists. But objective conditions were moving in an unfavorable direction.

> After the Civil War, and especially after the defeat of the revolution in Germany, the Bolsheviks no longer felt like warriors on the march. At the same time, the Party passed from a revolutionary period to a sedentary one. Not a few marriages took place during the years of the Civil War. Towards its end, couples produced children. The question of apartments, of furnishings, of the family began to assume an ever greater importance. The ties of revolutionary solidarity which had overcome difficulties on the whole were replaced to a considerable degree with ties of bureaucratic and material dependants. Before, it was possible to win by means of revolutionary ideals alone. Now, many began to learn to win with material positions and privileges.[57]

Trotsky was not arguing for a perpetual and unattainable asceticism remote from all personal and material concerns. He himself had four children. He was, rather, explaining how a conservative social environment gradually developed within the party and interacted with far-reaching socioeconomic processes within the country, associated with the New Economic Policy's revival of a capitalist market. The renewed importance of private enterprise in the countryside created a sudden acceptance and even encouragement of social inequality. The emphasis placed by Trotsky and his supporters in the Left Opposition on equality came under attack. Stalin adapted to and exploited this mood. Equality "was proclaimed by the bureaucracy as a petty-bourgeois prejudice." The animus to equality was accompanied by a growing hostility to the perspective of permanent revolution:

---

56. Ibid.
57. Ibid.

> The theory of "socialism in one country" was championed in that period by a bloc of the bureaucracy with the agrarian and urban petty-bourgeoisie. The struggle against equality welded the bureaucracy more strongly than ever, not only to the agrarian and urban petty-bourgeoisie, but to the labour aristocracy as well. Inequality became the common social basis, the source and the *raison d'être* of these allies. Thus economic and political bonds united the bureaucracy and the petty-bourgeoisie from 1923 to 1928.[58]

Stalin's rise to power was bound up with the crystallization of the bureaucratic apparatus and its growing awareness of its specific interests. "In this respect Stalin presents a completely exceptional phenomenon. He is neither a thinker, nor a writer, nor an orator. He assumed power before the masses had learned to discern his figure from others at the celebratory marches on the Red Square. Stalin rose to power not thanks to personal qualities, but to an impersonal apparatus. And it was not he who created the apparatus, but the apparatus that created him."[59]

Trotsky shattered the "myth of Stalin" by revealing the socioeconomic and class relations from which it emerged. This myth, Trotsky wrote, "is devoid of any artistic qualities. It is only capable of astonishing the imagination through the grandiose sweep of shamelessness that corresponds completely with the character of the greedy caste of upstarts, which wishes to hasten the day when it has become master of the house."[60]

Trotsky's description of Stalin's relationship to his entourage of corrupt satraps brings to mind the satires of Juvenal:

> Caligula made his favourite horse a Senator. Stalin has no favourite horse and so far there is no equine deputy sitting in the Supreme Soviet. However, the members of the Supreme Soviet have as little influence on the course of affairs in the Soviet Union as did Caligula's horse, or for that matter even the influence his Senators had on the affairs of Rome. The Praetorian Guard stood above the people and in a certain sense even above the State. It had to have an Emperor as final arbiter. The Stalinist

---

58. Ibid., p. 565.
59. Ibid., p. 676.
60. Ibid., p. 672.

bureaucracy is a modern counterpart of the Praetorian Guard with Stalin as its Supreme Leader. Stalin's power is a modern form of Caesarism. It is a monarchy without a crown, and so far, without an heir apparent.[61]

In the realm of politics, Trotsky was the greatest mind of his age. He posed an intolerable threat to the Stalinist regime, which functioned in the final analysis as an agency of world imperialism. It could not allow him to live. Trotsky understood very well the forces arrayed against him: "I can therefore state that I live on this earth not in accordance with the rule, but as an exception to the rule."[62] But even in the face of such extreme danger, Trotsky maintained an extraordinary degree of personal objectivity:

> In a reactionary epoch such as ours, a revolutionist is compelled to swim against the stream. I am doing this to the best of my ability. The pressure of world reaction has expressed itself perhaps most implacably in my personal fate and the fate of those close to me. I do not at all see in this any merit of mine: this is the result of the interlacing of historical circumstances.[63]

IV. June 1940: Critical discussions with the US Socialist Workers Party

Trotsky's miraculous survival of the assassination attempt of May 24, 1940 proved to be only a reprieve. The GPU immediately set into motion an alternate plan for the murder of Trotsky. The next attempt would be carried out, not by a heavily armed squad of killers, but by a lone assassin. Ramon Mercader, the Spanish agent chosen for the assignment by the GPU, had been introduced as early as 1938 into the milieu of the Fourth International by his girlfriend Sylvia Ageloff. Her specific relationship to the Socialist Workers Party remains unclear, though she seems to have functioned as a courier for the Fourth International and SWP.

---

61. Ibid.
62. "Stalin seeks my death," *Writings of Leon Trotsky [1939–40]*, p. 333.
63. Ibid., pp. 333–34.

It is hard to reconcile Ageloff's high-level connections to the Fourth International with her personal and political naïveté. In the course of an intimate relationship that spanned nearly two years, she either did not notice or suppressed concerns over the glaring anomalies, contradictions, and mysteries that swirled around her very strange companion: his multiple identities (Frank Jacson, Jacques Mornard, Vandendresched), highly dubious business activities and unlimited supply of ready cash. It never occurred to Ageloff—or so she claimed in the aftermath of the assassination to suspicious and unbelieving Mexican prosecutors—that there was something very wrong about her boyfriend, and that he was definitely not the sort of person who should be allowed anywhere near Trotsky.

In the spring of 1940, Jacson-Mornard utilized the opportunity provided by Ageloff to make himself a familiar presence to Trotsky's guards, even though he evinced no interest in meeting the revolutionary leader. Frequently driving Ageloff to the villa on the Avenida Viena, Jacson-Mornard appeared content to wait outside until she had completed her work. But he chatted with the guards and carefully cultivated a relationship with Trotsky's close friends, Alfred and Marguerite Rosmer. Despite decades in the revolutionary movement, they found nothing peculiar about Jacson-Mornard, the supposedly apolitical businessman with plenty of money and a great deal of free time. The French-born couple failed to detect an accent in the Spanish-born agent who claimed to be Belgian.

It was not until four days after the May 24 assault that Jacson-Mornard entered the compound for the first time and briefly met Trotsky. On one of his trips to Coyoacán, Jacson-Mornard approached the guards, who were strengthening the external walls of the villa. They told him that they were preparing for another assault by the GPU. Jacson-Mornard remarked, with studied casualness, that the GPU's next attempt on Trotsky's life would use a different method.

Trotsky's work continued at his customarily grueling pace. Though intensely occupied with the exposure of the May 24 conspiracy and the refutation of the brazen claims by the Mexican Communist Party and the Stalinist-controlled trade unions and press that the attack was a "self-assault" planned by Trotsky and executed by his supporters, he carefully followed the unfolding of World War II. By mid-June, France had surrendered and Hitler's armies ruled over Western Europe. A tragedy of unprecedented dimensions had befallen the working class. In a brief note written on June 17, 1940, two days after France's defeat, Trotsky wrote:

> The capitulation of France is not a simple military episode. It is part of the catastrophe of Europe. Mankind can no longer live under the regime of imperialism. Hitler is not an accident; he is only the most consistent and the most bestial expression of imperialism, which threatens to crush our whole civilization.[64]

The monstrous crimes of Hitler arose out of capitalism and the noxious global politics of imperialism. But Hitler's conquest of Western Europe was made possible by the assistance he received from Stalin. The dictator's betrayals of the working class—first through his "popular front" alliances with the democratic imperialists, then followed suddenly by his agreement with Hitler—disoriented the working class and strengthened Nazi Germany's military position. "By demoralizing the popular masses in Europe, and not solely in Europe, Stalin played the role of an agent provocateur in the service of Hitler. The capitulation of France is one of the results of such politics," Trotsky wrote. Stalin has taken the USSR "to the very brink of the abyss." Trotsky warned that Hitler's "victories in the West are only preparation for a gigantic move toward the East."[65] Almost exactly one year later, on June 22, 1941, Hitler launched Operation Barbarossa, the invasion of the Soviet Union.

The political and security issues arising from the May 24 raid and the epochal events in Europe necessitated a visit to Mexico by a delegation of SWP leaders, headed by party founder and leader James P. Cannon. Between Wednesday, June 12, and Saturday, June 15, Trotsky participated in a comprehensive discussion of the SWP's political work under conditions of war. Participants in this discussion included, in addition to Trotsky and Cannon, Charles Cornell, Farrell Dobbs, Sam Gordon, Antoinette Konikow, Harold Robins and Joseph Hansen. Long suppressed documents obtained in the 1970s and 1980s by the International Committee of the Fourth International were to establish that Hansen was a GPU plant inside Trotsky's secretariat.

An unedited stenographic report of this discussion was circulated to the SWP membership. The discussion on the first item on the agenda, which was a report on the Fourth International's Emergency Conference, was not transcribed. The verbatim record of the discussions begins with the second item on the agenda, "War and Perspectives." Trotsky's contributions to this

---

64. "The Kremlin's role in the European catastrophe," ibid., p. 383.
65. Ibid., pp. 384–85.

discussion emphasized that the party's principled opposition to the imperialist war should not be confused or in any way associated with petty-bourgeois pacifism.

The entry of the United States into the war was inevitable. Trotsky insisted that the SWP had to translate principled opposition to the war into effective revolutionary agitation that intersected with the consciousness of the workers, without adapting to national chauvinism.

> Militarization now goes on on a tremendous scale. We cannot oppose it with pacifist phrases. This militarization has wide support among the workers. They bear a sentimental hatred against Hitler mixed with confused class sentiments. They have a hatred against the victorious brigands. The bureaucracy utilizes this to say help the defeated gangster. Our conclusions are completely different. But this sentiment is the inevitable base for the last period of preparation.[66]

The challenge confronting the SWP was to develop an approach to the young workers which, even as they were being drawn into the military, developed their class consciousness. The party had to place its agitation "on a class basis."[67] Trotsky provided examples of the approach the party should take:

> We are against the bourgeois officers who treat you like cattle, who use you for cannon-fodder. We are concerned about the deaths of the workers, unlike the bourgeois officers. We want workers' officers.
>
> We can say to the workers: We are ready for revolution. But you aren't ready. But both of us want our own workers' officers in this situation. We want special workers' schools which will train us to be officers...
>
> We reject the control of the Sixty Families. We want an improvement of conditions for the worker-soldier. We want to safeguard his life. Not waste it.[68]

---

66. "Discussions with Trotsky," ibid., p. 338.
67. Ibid., p. 339.
68. Ibid., pp. 339–40.

The discussion turned on Thursday, June 13, to the SWP's policy for the 1940 presidential election. The Democratic incumbent, Franklin Roosevelt, was running for a third term. The party had not nominated a candidate of its own. "What do we tell the workers when they ask which president they should vote for?" Cannon replied, "They shouldn't ask such embarrassing questions."[69]

Trotsky asked why the SWP had not called for a congress of trade unions to nominate a candidate in opposition to Roosevelt. "We cannot remain completely indifferent," he argued. "We can very well insist in unions where we have influence that Roosevelt is not our candidate and the workers must have their own candidate. We should demand a nationwide congress connected with the [demand for an] independent labor party."[70]

Trotsky raised the question of the presidential candidacy of the American Communist Party. Since the signing of the Non-Aggression Pact, the Communist Party had adopted a position of opposition to the entry of the United States into the war. No doubt, this maneuver by the Stalinist leadership was determined entirely by the foreign policy of the Kremlin. But it was taken seriously by sections of the Communist Party membership. Did this not provide an opportunity for the SWP to intervene among the Stalinist workers? Trotsky proposed that the SWP, having no candidate of its own, consider giving critical support to the presidential campaign of Communist Party leader Earl Browder. However disoriented by the Stalinist leadership, the membership of the party included a significant layer of class-conscious workers. A timely political maneuver by the SWP—extending critical support to the Communist Party campaign on the basis of its present opposition to American entry into the war—would open up the possibility of approaching the Stalinist workers.

Trotsky's proposal was vehemently opposed by Cannon and virtually all the other participants in the discussion. In the course of years of bitter struggle against the Stalinists, the SWP's influence within the trade unions had required the development of alliances with "progressive" sections of the trade union bureaucracy. The maneuver proposed by Trotsky would undermine these relations.

Trotsky was critical of the SWP's approach to the "progressive bureaucrats," who were aligned politically with Roosevelt and the Democratic Party.

---

69. Ibid., p. 347.
70. Ibid.

"These progressive bureaucrats," Trotsky noted, "can lean on us for advisors in the fight against the Stalinists. But the role of an advisor to a progressive bureaucrat doesn't promise much in the long run."[71]

Countering Trotsky, Antoinette Konikow—who had been one of the first American supporters of the Left Opposition back in the 1920s—stated that unlike the Stalinists, American AFL leaders like Dan Tobin (leader of the Teamsters) and John L. Lewis (leader of the United Mine Workers) would not try to kill Trotskyists.

"I am not so sure," Trotsky replied. "Lewis would kill us very efficiently if he were elected and war came."[72]

Trotsky did not insist that the SWP adopt the policy he proposed. But as the discussion continued on Friday, June 14, he made a trenchant criticism of the party's orientation to the progressives.

> I believe we have the critical point very clear. We are in a bloc with so-called progressives—not only fakers but honest rank and file. Yes, they are honest and progressive but from time to time they vote for Roosevelt—once in four years. This is decisive. You propose a trade union policy, not a Bolshevik policy. Bolshevik policies begin outside the trade unions. The worker is an honest trade unionist but far from Bolshevik politics. The honest militant can develop but it is not identical with being a Bolshevik. You are afraid to become compromised in the eyes of the Rooseveltian trade unionists. They on the other hand are not worried in the slightest about being compromised by voting for Roosevelt against you. We are afraid of being compromised. If you are afraid, you lose your independence and become half-Rooseveltian. In peacetimes this is not catastrophic. In wartimes it will compromise us. They can smash us. Our policy is too much for pro-Rooseveltian trade unionists. I notice that in the *Northwest Organizer* [the newspaper of Teamsters Local 544 in Minneapolis, edited and controlled by the SWP] this is true. We discussed it before, but not a word was changed; not a single word. The danger—a terrible danger—is adaptation to the pro-Rooseveltian trade unionists. You don't give any answer to the

---

71. Ibid., p. 354.
72. Ibid., p. 355.

elections, not even the beginning of an answer. But we must have a policy.[73]

Trotsky continued his criticism of the SWP's adaptation to the trade union progressives on Saturday, June 15, the final day of the discussion.

> It seems to me that a kind of passive adaptation to our trade union work can be recognized. There is not an immediate danger, but a serious warning indicating a change in direction is necessary. Many comrades are more interested in trade union work than in party work. More party cohesion is needed, more sharp maneuvering, a more serious systematic theoretical training; otherwise the trade unions can absorb our comrades.[74]

As the discussion on the SWP's policy in the 1940 election drew to a conclusion, one final issue arose: could the Communist Party be considered a legitimate part of the workers movement? Trotsky replied emphatically:

> Of course the Stalinists are a legitimate part of the workers' movement. That it is abused by its leaders for specific GPU ends is one thing, for Kremlin ends another. It is not at all different from other opposition labor bureaucracies. The powerful interests of Moscow influence the Third International, but it is not different in principle. Of course we consider the terror of the GPU control differently; we fight with all means, even bourgeois police. But the political current of Stalinism is a current in the workers' movement.[75]

Despite the crimes committed by the Stalinists—and only three weeks had passed since the attempt on his life—Trotsky insisted upon an objective appraisal of Stalinism. "We must consider them from the objective Marxist viewpoint," Trotsky insisted. "They are a very contradictory phenomenon. They began with October as the base, they have become deformed, but they

---

73. Ibid., pp. 361–62.
74. Ibid., p. 371.
75. Ibid., p. 373.

have great courage."[76] The purpose of the maneuver proposed by Trotsky was to exploit this contradiction in the loyalties of the Stalinist rank and file:

> I think that we can hope to win these workers who began as a crystallization of October. We see them negatively; how to break through this obstacle. We must set the base against the top. The Moscow gang we consider gangsters but the rank and file don't feel themselves to be gangsters, but revolutionists. ... If we show that we understand, that we have a common language, we can turn them against their leaders. If we win five percent, the party will be doomed.[77]

Trotsky and the SWP delegation did not come to an agreement on the proposal for the extension of critical support to the Communist Party candidate, which he did not insist on. The difference did not undermine Trotsky's relationship with the Socialist Workers Party, and the discussions ended amicably. In any event, to the extent that the SWP had evinced a detectable level of adaptation to the progressive bureaucrats, Trotsky's criticism had a salutary impact on the party. Within weeks, Trotsky noticed and commented favorably on the political strengthening of the *Northwest Organizer*.

One of the participants in the discussion later recalled a remarkable incident that cast light on Trotsky's pedagogical approach to political discussions. Harold Robins, a New York-born worker who had traveled to Mexico in 1939 and become the captain of Trotsky's guard, took part in the morning discussion on June 13, during which Trotsky raised the question of critical support for the CP's presidential candidate. In an obituary that I wrote following Robins' death in 1987 at the age of seventy-nine, I included an account of his personal experience that he had relayed to me.

> When his turn to speak came, Harold launched into a vitriolic denunciation of the Stalinists, enumerating their many betrayals of the working class, and their slavish collaboration with the bourgeois politicians. Harold proclaimed that there wasn't "any god-damn difference between the Stalinists and the Democrats."

---

76. Ibid., pp. 373–74.
77. Ibid., p. 374.

Trotsky raised his hand and broke into Harold's speech. "Permit me a question, Comrade Robins. If there exist no differences between the Stalinists and the Democrats, why do they retain an independent existence and call themselves Communists? Why do they not simply join the Democratic Party?"

Harold was taken aback by these simple questions. This elementary lesson in dialectics immediately made it clear to Harold that his own position was wrong. But the story did not end there.

With the issue still undecided, the meeting broke for lunch. Trotsky approached Harold and asked him what his position was.

"Well, I now think you're right, Comrade Trotsky."

The "Old Man" beamed with satisfaction. "Then, Comrade Robins, I propose we form a bloc and conduct the struggle together when the meeting resumes."

Harold remembered thinking that he could not believe the "Old Man" was serious.

"Why the hell would Trotsky want or need a bloc with Harold Robins?"

At any rate, he accepted Trotsky's offer and looked forward to the start of the afternoon session. However, as the lunch break was coming to a close, Robins was approached by another guard, Charles Cornell, who was bitterly disappointed that he was to remain on duty during the afternoon and would not be able to participate in the discussion with Trotsky. Cornell pleaded with Robins to change places with him, and Robins relented. And so Cornell went into the discussion while Robins patrolled the premises.

Late in the afternoon, soon after the meeting ended, Harold found himself suddenly confronted by an obviously angry Trotsky. "Where were you, Comrade Robins?" Trotsky demanded.

Harold sought to explain the circumstances which had intervened during the lunch break. Trotsky brushed his arguments aside. "We had a bloc, Comrade Robins, and you betrayed it."

Harold recounted such incidents without the slightest sense of embarrassment, even though they hardly placed him in the best light. But for Harold, these events were precious examples of Trotsky's utter completeness as a revolutionary, inflexibly devoted to principles in all aspects of his life and under all conditions.

Here was a man, Harold seemed to be saying, who had led the greatest revolution in history, organized an army of millions, and participated in epochal political struggles alongside of the legendary figures of the international Marxist movement. And yet the same man, Trotsky, could propose a bloc with an unknown rank-and-file "Jimmy Higgins" and view it as seriously as he once viewed an alliance with Lenin! Harold was more than happy to "diminish himself" and recount his own youthful mistakes in order to convey the moral grandeur of Trotsky.[78]

In the course of their trip to Coyoacán, the SWP leaders inspected the villa and approved construction work that would fortify the compound against attack. Despite their sincere commitment to Trotsky's defense, their efforts were undermined by a disturbing level of personal carelessness. Even though there remained unanswered questions about the role of Sheldon Harte in the May 24 assault, there is no indication that SWP leaders were taking a more cautious attitude toward their personal associations. Given the continuing campaign against Trotsky in the Stalinist press, it should have been clear to the SWP leaders that the political environment in Mexico City was dangerous, and that the capital was crawling with GPU agents intent on eliminating Trotsky.

Nevertheless, on the evening of June 11, James P. Cannon and Farrell Dobbs accepted an invitation to dinner at the Hotel Geneva, followed by drinks at another locale. The host of the two SWP leaders was Jacson-Mornard.[79] This encounter was reported by Cannon in the course of a brief internal investigation conducted by the SWP leadership following the assassination. This information was, however, concealed from the rank and file party membership.

---

78. David North, *A Tribute to Harold Robins, Captain of Trotsky's Guard* (Detroit: Labor Publications, 1987), pp. 8–10.
79. Patenaude, *Trotsky: Downfall of a Revolutionary*, p. 270.

V. Trotsky's analysis of the trade unions in the epoch of imperialism

In his discussions with James P. Cannon and Farrell Dobbs during the visit of the Socialist Workers Party delegation to Coyoacán in June 1940, Trotsky had expressed concern over the SWP's excessively syndicalist approach to its work in the trade unions. There was insufficient attention to politics, that is, to revolutionary socialist strategy. This found expression in the SWP's adaptation to the pro-Roosevelt trade unionists, which Trotsky described as "a terrible danger."[80] He felt it necessary to remind the leaders that "Bolshevik policies begin outside the trade unions."[81]

It is evident that Trotsky intended to continue and deepen the discussion of the issues that had arisen during the SWP leaders' visit. Following their departure from Mexico, Trotsky began working on an article devoted to an analysis of the trade unions. The draft was found on Trotsky's desk after his assassination and was published posthumously in the February 1941 issue of the theoretical journal, *Fourth International*. It was titled "Trade Unions in the Epoch of Imperialist Decay."

As is characteristic of Trotsky's writings, he sought to situate his analysis of the trade unions in the appropriate historical and international context, and to identify the essential processes that determined, apart from the personal motivations and rationalizations of individual leaders, the policies of these organizations. Only on this objective basis was it possible to develop a Marxist, i.e., genuinely revolutionary approach to work in the trade unions. Trotsky's article began with a concise identification of the place of the trade unions in the world capitalist order:

> There is one common feature in the development, or more correctly the degeneration, of modern trade union organizations in the entire world: it is their drawing closely to and growing together with the state power. This process is equally characteristic of the neutral, the Social-Democratic, the Communist and "anarchist" trade unions. This fact alone shows that the tendency towards "growing together" is intrinsic not in this or that

---

80. "Discussions with Trotsky," *Writings of Leon Trotsky [1939–40]*, p. 362.
81. Ibid., p. 361.

doctrine as such but derives from social conditions common for all unions.

Monopoly capitalism does not rest on competition and free private initiative but on centralized command. The capitalist cliques at the head of mighty trusts, syndicates, banking consortiums, etcetera, view economic life from the very same heights as does state power; and they require at every step the collaboration of the latter. In their turn the trade unions in the most important branches of industry find themselves deprived of the possibility of profiting by the competition between the different enterprises. They have to confront a centralized capitalist adversary, intimately bound up with state power.[82]

Arising from this universal feature of modern capitalist development, Trotsky argued that the trade unions—to the extent that they accept the capitalist framework—could not maintain an independent position. The rulers of the trade unions—the bureaucracy— sought to pull the state over to their side, a goal which could only be achieved by demonstrating that they had no interests independent of, let alone hostile to, the capitalist state. So as to make clear the extent and implications of this subordination, Trotsky wrote: "By transforming the trade unions into organs of the state, fascism invents nothing new; it merely draws to their ultimate conclusion the tendencies inherent in imperialism."[83] Trotsky emphasized that the development of modern imperialism required the stamping out of any semblance of democracy within the old unions. In Mexico, he noted, the trade unions "have, in the nature of things, assumed a semi-totalitarian character."[84]

Trotsky insisted that it was necessary for revolutionists to continue to conduct work within the trade unions because masses of workers remained organized within them. For that same reason, and that reason only, revolutionists could not, Trotsky insisted, "renounce the struggle within the compulsory labor organizations created by fascism."[85] Clearly, Trotsky did not believe that fascist unions were "workers organizations," in the sense that they represented the interests of the working class. Work within the unions,

---

82. Leon Trotsky, "Trade unions in the epoch of imperialist decay," *Marxism and the Trade Unions* (New York: Labor Publications, 1973), pp. 9–10.
83. Ibid., p. 10.
84. Ibid., p. 11.
85. Ibid.

a tactical necessity, did not signify reconciliation with the bureaucracy, let alone a vote of confidence in this reactionary social stratum. The aim of the Marxists' interventions within the trade unions under all conditions was "to mobilize the masses not only against the bourgeoisie but also against the totalitarian regime within the trade unions themselves and against the leaders enforcing this regime."[86]

Trotsky proposed two slogans upon which the struggle against the bureaucratic agents of imperialism should be based. The first was the "*complete and unconditional independence of the trade unions in relation to the capitalist state.*" [Emphasis in the original] This slogan implied "a struggle to turn the trade unions into the organs of the broad exploited masses and not the organs of a labor aristocracy."[87] But the achievement of this was inseparably linked to the winning of masses of workers to the revolutionary party and the program of socialism.

Commenting on the situation in the United States, Trotsky viewed the sudden emergence of industrial unions as a major development. The CIO [Congress of Industrial Organizations], he wrote, "is incontrovertible evidence of the revolutionary tendencies within the working masses."[88] But the weakness of the new unions was already evident.

> Indicative and noteworthy in the highest degree, however, is the fact that the new "leftist" trade union organization was no sooner founded than it fell into the steel embrace of the imperialist state. The struggle among the tops between the old federation and the new is reducible in large measure to the struggle for the sympathy and support of Roosevelt and his cabinet.[89]

The intensification of the global crisis of capitalism and the extreme exacerbation of social tensions produced within the trade unions, in the United States and internationally, a sharp turn to the right, i.e., toward an even more extreme suppression by the trade unions of working-class resistance to capitalism. "The leaders of the trade union movement," Trotsky explained, "sensed or understood, or were given to understand, that now was no time to play the

---

86. Ibid., p. 12.
87. Ibid.
88. Ibid., p. 16.
89. Ibid.

game of opposition." The trade union officialdom were not innocent bystanders in the consolidation of the most repressive forms of bourgeois rule. "The basic feature, the swing towards the totalitarian regime," Trotsky bluntly stated, "passes through the labor movement of the whole world."[90]

To the extent that the Socialist Workers Party harbored even the slightest illusions in the possibility of amicable relations with the "progressive" trade unionist leaders, it failed to recognize the historical role of the labor bureaucracies in the epoch of imperialism. As Trotsky had warned the very courageous but surprisingly naive comrade Antoinette Konikow of the SWP delegation: "Lewis [the famed leader of the United Mine Workers] would kill us very efficiently…"[91]

The last paragraph of his essay summed up the historical situation that confronted the trade unions:

> Democratic unions in the old sense of the term, bodies where in the framework of one and the same mass organization different tendencies struggled more or less freely, can no longer exist. Just as it is impossible to bring back the bourgeois-democratic state, so it is impossible to bring back the old workers' democracy. The fate of the one reflects the fate of the other. As a matter of fact, the independence of trade unions in the class sense, in their relations to the bourgeois state can, in the present conditions, be assured only by a completely revolutionary leadership, that is, the leadership of the Fourth International. This leadership, naturally, must and can be rational and assure the unions the maximum of democracy conceivable under the present concrete conditions. But without the political leadership of the Fourth International the independence of the trade unions is impossible.[92]

These words were written eighty years ago. The analysis Trotsky made of the degeneration of the unions—their integration into the state power and corporate management—was extraordinarily prescient. The tendency toward the "growing together" of the unions, the state, and capitalist corporations continued throughout the post-World War II period. Moreover, the process of global

---

90. Ibid., pp. 16–17.
91. "Discussions with Trotsky," *Writings of Leon Trotsky [1939–40]*, p. 355.
92. Trotsky, *Marxism and the Trade Unions*, p. 18.

economic integration and transnational production deprived the trade unions of a national framework within which they could apply pressure for limited social reforms. No room was left for even the most moderate resort to the methods of class struggle to achieve minimal gains. The unions, rather than extracting concessions from the corporations, were transformed into adjuncts of the state and corporations that serve to extract concessions from the workers.

Consequently, not a trace of "workers democracy" remains in the bureaucratic-corporatist structures that are called unions. The old terminology survives. Corporatist organizations like the AFL-CIO and its affiliates are still called "unions." But the actual practice of these organizations bears no relationship to the socio-economic function traditionally associated with the word "union." The practice of the revolutionary party cannot be based on the uncritical use of terminology that does not reflect the evolution of the phenomenon it ostensibly described. The degeneration of the old organizations cannot be overcome simply by calling them "unions." As Trotsky had insisted in September 1939, in the early stages of the fight against Shachtman and Burnham, "We must take the facts as they are. We must build our policy by taking as our starting point the real relations and contradictions."[93]

The fight for workers democracy and the complete independence of the organizations of the working class remain critical elements of the contemporary revolutionary program. But this perspective will not be realized through the renewal of the old organizations. The process of corporatist degeneration over a period of eighty years precludes, in all but the most exceptional circumstances, the resuscitation of the old unions. The alternative strategical course, raised by Trotsky in *The Transitional Program* in 1938, is the policy that conforms to present-day conditions; that is, "to create in all possible instances independent militant organizations corresponding more closely to the tasks of mass struggle against bourgeois society; and, if necessary, not flinching even in the face of a direct break with the conservative apparatus of the trade unions."[94]

* * * * *

On August 7, 1940, exactly two weeks before his death, Trotsky participated in a discussion on "American Problems." Responding to a question

---

93. "The USSR in War," *In Defence of Marxism*, p. 24.
94. Leon Trotsky, *The Death Agony of Capitalism and the Tasks of the Fourth International: The Transitional Program* (New York: Labor Publications, 1981), p. 8.

about the draft, Trotsky insisted that party members should not evade conscription. To keep them out of the army, under conditions in which their generation was being mobilized, would be a mistake. The SWP could not avoid the reality of war:

> We should understand that the life of this society, politics, everything, will be based upon war, therefore the revolutionary program must also be based on war. We cannot oppose the fact of the war with wishful thinking; with pious pacifism. We must place ourselves upon the arena created by this society. The arena is terrible—it is war—but inasmuch as we are weak and incapable of taking the fate of society into our hands; inasmuch as the ruling class is strong enough to impose upon us this war, we are obliged to accept this basis for our activity.[95]

Trotsky recognized that there existed a profound and legitimate hatred of Hitler and Nazism among masses of workers. The party had to adapt its agitation and political formulations to the politically confused patriotic moods without making any concessions to national chauvinism.

> We cannot escape from the militarization but inside the machine we can observe the class line. The American workers do not want to be conquered by Hitler, and to those who say, "Let us have a peace program," the worker will reply, "But Hitler does not want a peace program." Therefore *we* say: We will defend the United States with a workers' army, with workers' officers, with a workers' government, etc. If we are not pacifists, who wait for a better future, and if we are active revolutionists, our job is to penetrate into the whole military machine. ...
>
> We must use the example of France to the very end. We must say, "I warn you, workers, that they (the bourgeoisie) will betray you! Look at Petain [the French general who led the Vichy regime and ruled the country on Hitler's behalf], who is a friend of Hitler. Shall we have the same thing happen in this country? We must create our own machine, under workers' control." We must be careful not to identify ourselves with the chauvinists,

---

95. "American problems," *Writings of Leon Trotsky 1939–40*, p. 445.

nor with the confused sentiments of self-preservation, but we must understand their feelings and adapt ourselves to these feelings critically, and prepare the masses for a better understanding of the situation, otherwise we will remain a sect, of which the pacifist variety is the most miserable.[96]

Trotsky was asked how the political backwardness of the American worker would affect the ability to resist the spread of fascism. His reply cautioned against a simplistic and one-sided evaluation of the working class. "The backwardness of the United States working class is only a relative term. In many very important respects it is the most progressive working class of the world: technically, and in its standard of living."[97] In any event, objective developments would provide a powerful impetus for the development of class consciousness. Trotsky emphasized the contradictions in the development of the American working class:

> The American worker is very combative—as we have seen during the strikes. They have had the most rebellious strikes in the world. What the American worker misses is a spirit of generalization, or analysis, of his class position in society as a whole. This lack of social thinking has its origin in the country's whole history—the Far West with the perspective of unlimited possibilities for everyone to become rich, etc. Now all that is gone, but the mind remains in the past. Idealists think the human mentality is progressive, but in reality it is the most conservative element of society. Your technique is progressive but the mentality of the worker lags far behind. Their backwardness consists of their inability to generalize their problem; they consider everything on a personal basis.[98]

Nevertheless, despite all the objective difficulties and problems in the development of mass consciousness, Trotsky rejected the view that the United States stood on the brink of fascism. "The next historic waves in the United States," he predicted, "will be waves of radicalism of the masses; not fascism."

---

96. Ibid., pp. 446–48.
97. Ibid., p. 450.
98. Ibid., p. 451.

An essential condition for the victory of fascism was the political demoralization of the working class. That condition did not exist in the United States. Therefore, Trotsky stated confidently to the interviewers, "I am sure you will have many possibilities to win the power in the United States before the fascists can become a dominant force."[99]

Trotsky's analysis of fascism was dialectical and active, not mechanical and passive. The danger posed by fascism could not be determined merely on the basis of quantitative measurements. The victory of fascism was not merely the outcome of the numerical growth of its adherents, supplemented by the open and concealed sympathy and support of the capitalist elites and the bourgeois state apparatus. Following the August 7 discussion, Trotsky dictated another article, published posthumously, under the title "Bonapartism, Fascism, and War," in the October 1940 issue of *Fourth International*.

The motivation for this article was not only to clarify issues that had arisen in the August 7 discussion, but also to reply to an essay by Dwight Macdonald, a supporter of the Shachtman-Burnham minority. Published in the July-August 1940 issue of the left journal *Partisan Review*, Macdonald's essay expressed the demoralized skepticism of the petty-bourgeois intellectuals who were breaking with Marxism and shifting toward the right. Awed by Hitler's military successes, Macdonald proclaimed the Nazi regime "a new kind of society," whose durability had been underestimated by Trotsky.[100]

The same superficial impressionism that motivated the petty-bourgeois minority's theoretical improvisations in relation to the Soviet Union was applied by Macdonald to the Third Reich. He wildly declared that the German economy, under Hitler, "has come to be organized on the basis of production rather than profit," an empty phrase that explained nothing.[101] Macdonald stated that "these modern totalitarian regimes are not temporary affairs: they have already changed the underlying economic and social structure, not only manipulating the old forms but also destroying their inner vitality."[102]

Macdonald asserted that "the Nazis have won because they were fighting a new kind of war that, as clearly as Napoleon's military innovations, expressed a new kind of society," which surpassed the old capitalist systems of its

---

99. Ibid., p. 453.
100. Dwight Macdonald, "National Defense: The Case for Socialism," *Partisan Review*, July-August 1940, p. 252.
101. Ibid., p. 254.
102. Ibid., p. 256.

adversaries.¹⁰³ Macdonald's ignorant idealization of the Nazis' economic system had little to do with reality. By the late 1930s the state of the German capitalist economy was on the brink of disaster. Between 1933 and 1939, the national debt had tripled, and the regime was struggling to meet interest payments. It is widely recognized that Hitler's decision for war was to a great extent driven by fear of an economic collapse. As historian Tim Mason explained:

> The only 'solution' open to this regime of the structural tensions and crises produced by dictatorship and rearmament was more dictatorship and more rearmament, then expansion, then war and terror, then plunder and enslavement. The stark, ever-present alternative was collapse and chaos, and so all solutions were temporary, hectic, hand-to-mouth affairs, increasingly barbaric improvisations around a brutal theme. ... A war for the plunder of manpower and materials lay square in the dreadful logic of German economic development under National Socialist rule.¹⁰⁴

Trotsky described Macdonald's article as "very pretentious, very muddled, and stupid."¹⁰⁵ He saw no need to devote time to refuting Macdonald's analysis of Nazi society. But Trotsky did respond to Macdonald's failure, typical of demoralized intellectuals, to examine the political dynamic underlying the advance of fascism. Its victory was the outcome, above all, of a catastrophic failure of the leadership of the mass parties and organizations of the working class. Fascism is the political punishment meted out to the working class for the squandering of opportunities to overthrow the capitalist system. Why did fascism triumph? Trotsky explained:

> Both theoretical analysis as well as the rich historical experience of the last quarter of a century have demonstrated with equal force that fascism is each time the final link of a specific political cycle composed of the following: the gravest crisis of capitalist society; the growth of the radicalization of the working class; the growth of sympathy toward the working class and a yearning for change on the part of the rural and urban petty bourgeoisie;

---

103. Ibid., p. 252.
104. Tim Mason, *Nazism, Fascism, and the Working Class* (Cambridge: Cambridge University Press, 1995), p. 51.
105. "Bonapartism, fascism, and war," *Writings of Leon Trotsky [1939–40]*, p. 545.

the extreme confusion of the big bourgeoisie; its cowardly and treacherous maneuvers aimed at avoiding the revolutionary climax; the exhaustion of the proletariat; growing confusion and indifference; the aggravation of the social crisis; the despair of the petty bourgeoisie, its yearning for change; the collective neurosis of the petty bourgeoisie, its readiness to believe in miracles; its readiness for violent measures; the growth of hostility towards the proletariat which has deceived its expectations. These are the premises for a swift formation of a fascist party and its victory.[106]

In the cycle of American developments, Trotsky maintained, the situation was not yet propitious for the fascists. "It is quite self-evident that the radicalization of the working class in the United States has passed only through its initial phases, almost exclusively in the sphere of the trade union movement (the CIO)."[107] The fascists had assumed a defensive position. Countering the doubts of all those who wondered, while they sat on the sidelines, whether victory was possible, Trotsky wrote:

> No occupation is more completely unworthy than that of speculating whether or not we shall succeed in creating a powerful revolutionary leader-party. Ahead lies a favorable perspective, providing all the justification for revolutionary activism. It is necessary to utilize the opportunities which are opening up and to build the revolutionary party. ...
>
> Reaction wields today such power as perhaps never before in the modern history of mankind. But it would be an inexcusable blunder to see only reaction. The historical process is a contradictory one. Under the cover of official reaction profound processes are taking place among the masses who are accumulating experience and are becoming receptive to new political perspectives. The old conservative tradition of the democratic state which was so powerful even during the era of the last imperialist war exists today only as an extremely unstable survival. On the eve of the last war the European workers had numerically

---

106. Ibid., p. 548.
107. Ibid.

powerful parties. But on the order of the day were put reforms, partial conquests, and not at all the conquest of power.

The American working class is still without a mass labor party even today. But the objective situation and the experience accumulated by the American workers can pose within a very brief period of time on the order of the day the question of the conquest of power. This perspective must be made the basis of our agitation. It is not merely a question of a position on capitalist militarism and of renouncing the defense of the bourgeois state but of directly preparing for the conquest of power and the defense of the proletarian fatherland.[108]

Macdonald epitomized the rapidly growing stratum of demoralized petty-bourgeois intellectuals who saw in the victory of fascism the decisive refutation of Marxism and the entire socialist perspective. The situation was, for all intents and purposes, hopeless. He wrote:

Is not the working class everywhere in full retreat, where it has so far escaped the fascist yoke? And even if the workers later on show some signs of revolt, where will they find their leadership? From the corrupt and discredited Second and Third Internationals? From the tiny, isolated revolutionary groups, split by sectarian quarrels? And finally, has not the authority of Marxism itself, the very fountainhead of all revolutionary science, been shaken by the failure of its disciples to give adequate answers, in practice and in theoretical understanding, to the historical developments of the last two decades?

I must admit that these questions are, to say the least, justified. The sort of "revolutionary optimism" favored in certain quarters—an optimism which becomes more obstinate and irrational the worse things turn out—seems to me to do no service to the cause of socialism. We must face the fact that the revolutionary movement has suffered an unbroken series of major disasters in the last twenty years, and we must examine again, with a cold and sceptical eye, the most basic premises of Marxism.[109]

---

108. Ibid., pp. 549–50.
109. Macdonald, *Partisan Review*, p. 266.

Macdonald actually titled his funeral dirge "The Case for Socialism." It was, rather, as his own evolution soon proved, the case for the repudiation of socialism.

The demoralized skeptics, Trotsky observed, proclaimed the failure of Marxism because "fascism came instead of socialism." But the skeptics revealed in their criticism, aside from personal demoralization, a mechanical and passive conception of history. Marx did not promise the victory of socialism; he revealed only the objective contradictions in capitalist society that made socialism possible. But he never claimed that it would be achieved automatically. In fact, Marx, Engels, and Lenin waged a relentless struggle against all the political tendencies, opportunist and anarchistic, that undermined the struggle for socialism. They were aware that a bad leadership that succumbed to the influence of the ruling class "could obstruct, slow down, make more difficult, postpone the fulfillment of the revolutionary task of the proletariat."[110]

The existing situation was created to no small degree by the failures of working-class leadership.

> Fascism did not at all come "instead" of socialism. Fascism is the continuation of capitalism, an attempt to perpetuate its existence by means of the most bestial and monstrous measures. Capitalism obtained an opportunity to resort to fascism only because the proletariat did not accomplish the socialist revolution in time. The proletariat was paralyzed in the fulfillment of its task by the opportunist parties. The only thing that can be said is that there turned out to be more obstacles, more difficulties, more stages on the road of the revolutionary development of the proletariat than was foreseen by the founders of scientific socialism. Fascism and the series of imperialist wars constitute the terrible school in which the proletariat has to free itself of petty-bourgeois traditions and superstitions, has to rid itself of opportunist, democratic, and adventurist parties, has to hammer out and train the revolutionary vanguard, and in this way prepare for the solving of the task apart from which there is not and cannot be any salvation for the development of mankind.[111]

---

110. "Bonapartism, fascism, and war," *Writings of Leon Trotsky [1939–40]*, p. 553.
111. Ibid., pp. 553–54.

VI. August 1940: Trotsky's last writings, death, and his legacy

During the final year of his life, Trotsky grappled with critical questions of historical perspective raised by the outbreak of World War II. Why had the 1917 Revolution in Russia—which had been proclaimed by the Bolsheviks as the harbinger of world socialist revolution—been followed by the defeats of the working class in Italy, China, Germany, and Spain, to name only the most consequential of the political disasters? Why had the Great Depression—the greatest economic breakdown in the history of capitalism—led not to socialism, but, instead, to fascism and war? And, finally, why had the workers state founded on the basis of the October Revolution degenerated into a monstrous totalitarian regime?

The answer given by legions of petty-bourgeois intellectuals and erstwhile radicals was that the defeats proved the bankruptcy of Marxism and the entire perspective of socialist revolution. Trotsky, in an article written in March 1939, had described the political psychology and outlook of these layers:

> Force not only conquers but, in its own way, it "convinces." The onset of reaction not only wrecks parties physically, but also decomposes people morally. Many Radical gentlemen have their hearts in their shoes. Their fright in the face of reaction they translate into the language of immaterial and universal criticism. "Something must be wrong with old theories and methods!" "Marx was mistaken..." "Lenin failed to foresee..." Some even go further. "The revolutionary method has proved itself bankrupt."[112]

The greatest error of Marxism, the demoralized intellectuals concluded, was that it had attributed to the working class a revolutionary mission that it could not fulfill. The essential cause of all the disasters of the 1920s and 1930s was to be found in the nonrevolutionary character of the working class.

The founding document of the Fourth International began with an explicit repudiation of the defeatist and ahistorical perspective of the

---

112. Leon Trotsky, "Once again on the 'crisis of Marxism,'" *Writings of Leon Trotsky [1938–39]* (New York: Pathfinder Press, 1974, second edition, ninth printing, 2023), pp. 266-67.

anti-Marxists. The fundamental problem of the epoch of capitalism's death agony was not the absence of a revolutionary class, but, rather, the absence of revolutionary leadership capable of leading the working class to the conquest of power.

"The world political situation as a whole," Trotsky wrote, "is chiefly characterized by a historical crisis of the leadership of the proletariat."[113]

This well-known declaration is often read as merely an exhortation, intended to inspire the cadre of the Fourth International with a soaring rhetorical declaration of the party's political mission. Such an interpretation misses the real significance of the statement, which is a concise summation of the essential lesson that was to be drawn from the defeats of the working class.

In the second *Theses on Feuerbach*, Marx wrote in 1845: "The dispute over the reality or non-reality of thinking which is isolated from practice is a purely *scholastic* question."[114] Reworking this fundamental concept of philosophical materialism in the context of the fate of the socialist revolution, the formulation employed by Trotsky in the opening of the founding document of the Fourth International states, in essence, that all discussions of the revolutionary or non-revolutionary character of the working class, apart from the examination of the practice of its leading parties and organizations, are abstract, devoid of political content and false.

The essay upon which Trotsky was working at the time of his death was devoted to a substantiation of his concept of the crisis of leadership. It was titled "The Class, the Party and the Leadership: Why was the Spanish Proletariat Defeated? (Questions of Marxist Theory)." The article, which abruptly concludes midsentence, was published in the December 1940 issue of *Fourth International*, four months after Trotsky's death. Though incomplete, the essay—considered from both a philosophical-theoretical and political standpoint—ranks among the most profound expositions of the dialectical relationship between the objective and subjective factors of the revolutionary process in the epoch of capitalism's death agony.

Trotsky's essay was written in response to a hostile review, published in the French radical journal *Que Faire*, of a pamphlet titled *Spain Betrayed*. The pamphlet's author was Mieczyslaw Bortenstein, a member of the

---

113. Trotsky, *The Death Agony of Capitalism and the Tasks of the Fourth International: The Transitional Program*, p. 1.
114. Karl Marx, "Theses on Feuerbach," *Marx-Engels Collected Works* Vol. 5 (London: Lawrence & Wishart, 2010), p. 3.

Fourth International, who wrote under the pseudonym M. Casanova. Bortenstein had fought in Spain, where he witnessed the Stalinist sabotage of the revolution. The pamphlet, while fundamentally influenced by Trotsky's exposure of the Popular Front and his criticisms of the centrist politics of the POUM, drew upon the author's personal experiences in Spain. Apart from this one pamphlet, there is relatively little information available on Bortenstein's political activities. However, it is known that his life ended tragically at the age of thirty-five. Following the Nazi takeover of France, Bortenstein was arrested by the Vichy government and eventually deported to the extermination camp at Auschwitz, where he was murdered in 1942.

Bortenstein wrote his pamphlet following the surrender of Barcelona by the Stalinist-dominated Popular Front government, without resistance, to the fascist army led by Franco. The surrender of what had been the citadel of the workers' revolution was the culmination of Popular Front treachery. In the pamphlet's introduction, Casanova-Bortenstein wrote:

> I have to explain what has just happened on the basis of my own experience. I have to report the facts. I will describe how strategic positions of crucial importance were abandoned without a fight, how defence plans were handed over to the enemy by a treacherous general staff, how the war industry was sabotaged and the economy disorganised, how the finest working class militants were murdered, and how Fascist spies were protected by the "Republican" police, in order to explain how the revolutionary struggle of the proletariat against Fascism was betrayed and Spain was surrendered to Franco.
>
> My analysis and the facts I shall describe all go back to one and the same theme: the criminal policy of the Popular Front. Only the workers' revolution could have defeated Fascism. The whole policy of the Republican, Socialist, Communist and Anarchist leaders worked to destroy the revolutionary energy of the working class. "First win the war and make the revolution afterwards!"—this reactionary slogan was to kill the revolution only to lose the war afterwards.[115]

---

115. Mieczyslaw Bortenstein (M. Casanova), *Spain Betrayed: How the Popular Front Opened the Gate to Franco*, available: https://marxists.architexturez.net/history/etol/document/spain2/intro.htm

It was critical that the lessons of the Spanish catastrophe be learned, Casanova-Bortenstein declared. "Neither Socialism nor Marxism failed in Spain, but those who so criminally betrayed it."[116]

The hostile review of Bortenstein's pamphlet published in *Que Faire*, a journal produced by dissident former members of the Communist Party in France, exemplified the cynical attitude of petty-bourgeois centrists. It attacked Bortenstein for concentrating on the parties and policies responsible for defeat, rather than focusing on the attributes of the Spanish working class—above all, its "immaturity"—which rendered it incapable of defeating fascism. "We are ushered," claimed *Que Faire*, "into the domain of pure demonology; the criminal responsible for the defeat is the chief Devil, Stalin, abetted by the anarchists and all the other little devils; the God of revolutionists unfortunately did not send a Lenin or a Trotsky to Spain as He did in Russia in 1917."[117]

Trotsky subjected *Que Faire*'s attack on Bortenstein's pamphlet to a scathing criticism. The "theoretical haughtiness" of *Que Faire*'s review, he wrote, "is made all the more magnificent by the fact that it is hard to imagine how so great a number of banalities, vulgarisms, and mistakes quite specifically of conservative philistine type could be compressed into so few lines."[118]

The central purpose of *Que Faire*'s review was to absolve the parties, organizations, and individuals in the leadership of the working class of all responsibility for the debacle in Spain. Blame for the "false policy of the masses" was to be placed not on its political authors, but on the working class, which as a consequence of its "immaturity" was inclined to follow an incorrect political line. This argument devised by the author of the *Que Faire* review was a contemptible apology for the architects of defeat. Trotsky wrote:

> Anyone searching for tautologies couldn't find in general a flatter one. A "false policy of the masses" is explained by the "immaturity" of the masses. But what is "immaturity" of the masses? Obviously, their predisposition to false policies. Just what the false policy consisted of, and who were its initiators, the masses or the leaders—that is passed over in silence by our author. By means of a tautology, he unloads the responsibility on the

---

116. Ibid.
117. Citation by Trotsky from *Que Faire* article in "The Class, the Party, and the Leadership," *The Spanish Revolution [1931–39]* (New York: Pathfinder Press, 1973), p. 355.
118. Ibid.

masses. This classical trick of all traitors, deserters, and their attorneys is especially revolting in connection with the Spanish proletariat.[119]

But even if the leaders of the Spanish working class were bad, argued the apologists, was it not the fault of the masses that they followed the bad leaders? In response to such pernicious sophistry, Trotsky—substantiating Bortenstein's eyewitness account—pointed out that the working class sought again and again to break through the political barricades erected by the Stalinists, Social Democrats, and anarchists; and that whenever the working class was on the verge of taking the offensive, their treacherous leaders deployed force in support of counterrevolutionary policies. The May 1937 uprising of the working class in Barcelona against the Popular Front government's treacherous policies was ruthlessly suppressed. Trotsky wrote:

> One must understand exactly nothing in the sphere of the interrelationships between the class and the party, between the masses and the leaders, in order to repeat the hollow statement that the Spanish masses merely followed their leaders. The only thing that can be said is that the masses who sought at all times to blast their way to the correct road found it beyond their strength to produce in the very fire of battle a new leadership corresponding to the demands of the revolution.[120]

Trotsky recalled the overused epigram that every people gets the government it deserves. Applied to the sphere of social struggle, this argument would hold that every class gets the leadership it deserves. Thus, if the workers have bad leaders, that is what they deserve; for they are incapable of producing better ones. Trotsky responded to this formal and mechanical argument.

> In reality leadership is not at all a mere "reflection" of a class or the product of its own free creativeness. A leadership is shaped in the process of clashes between the different classes or the friction between the different layers within a given class. Having once arisen, the leadership invariably rises above its class and

---

119. Ibid., pp. 355–56.
120. Ibid., p. 357.

thereby becomes predisposed to the pressure and influence of other classes. The proletariat may "tolerate" for a long time a leadership that has already suffered a complete inner degeneration but has not as yet had the opportunity to express this degeneration amid great events.

A great historic shock is necessary to reveal sharply the contradiction between the leadership and the class. The mightiest historical shocks are wars and revolutions. Precisely for this reason the working class is often caught unawares by war and revolution. But even in cases where the old leadership has revealed its internal corruption, the class cannot immediately improvise a new leadership, especially if it has not inherited from the previous period strong revolutionary cadres capable of utilizing the collapse of the old leading party. The Marxist interpretation, that is, the dialectical and not the scholastic interpretation of the interrelationship between a class and its leadership, does not leave a single stone unturned of our author's legalistic sophistry.[121]

Bourgeois criticism of Marxism—especially as it is propagated in the academy—generally claims that deterministic philosophical materialism pays insufficient attention to the "subjective factor" in history. Marxism, preoccupied with the socioeconomic and class structure of society, does not take into account the influence of consciousness, especially in its suprahistorical and irrational manifestations, in the chaotic development of society. This criticism, which attributes to Marxism a rigid separation of objective and subjective factors, combines ignorance with distortion and outright falsification. A central theme of Trotsky's writings over a period of many years had been the crucial role of the subjective factor—assigning particular significance to the role of political leaders—in determining the outcome of revolutionary struggles. Most famously, in an entry in a diary he kept in 1935, Trotsky had emphasized the critical role that Lenin had played in the victory of the October Revolution. "Had I not been present in 1917 in Petersburg, the October Revolution would still have taken place—*on the condition that Lenin was present and in command* [emphasis in the original]."[122]

---

121. Ibid., p. 358.
122. *Trotsky's Diary in Exile 1935* (New York: Atheneum Press, 1963), p. 46.

In his refutation of *Que Faire*, Trotsky returned to the role of Lenin in the October Revolution. He dismissed the review's substitution of "mechanistic determinism for the dialectical conditioning of the historic process" and "the cheap jibes about the role of individuals, good and bad." The class struggle does not unfold as a supra-human process. Real human beings are involved, and their actions play a role—in some cases, a decisive one—in determining whether the revolutionary insurrection meets with success or failure, or even whether it occurs at all. "The arrival of Lenin in Petrograd on April 3, 1917, turned the Bolshevik Party in time and enabled the party to lead the revolution to victory."[123] Trotsky continued:

> Our sages might say that had Lenin died abroad at the beginning of 1917, the October Revolution would have taken place "just the same." But that is not so. Lenin represented one of the living elements of the historical process. He personified the experience and the perspicacity of the most active section of the proletariat. His timely appearance on the arena of the revolution was necessary in order to mobilize the vanguard and provide it with an opportunity to rally the working class and the peasant masses. Political leadership in the crucial moments of historical turns can become just as decisive a factor as is the role of the chief command during the critical moments of war. History is not an automatic process. Otherwise, why leaders? why parties? why programs? why theoretical struggles?[124]

In his pamphlet, Bortenstein noted bitterly that all the parties and individuals whose political errors and even outright treachery ensured the defeat of the Spanish Revolution claimed in its aftermath that no other outcome was possible. "If we listen to the explanations of the leaders of the Popular Front, including the Anarchists, and if we take these explanations seriously, all we can do is to despair of everything and lose hope in the revolutionary capacities of the proletariat, its future and even its historic mission."[125] There was no shortage of excuses for the defeat.

---

123. Trotsky, *The Spanish Revolution 1931–39*, p. 361.
124. Ibid., pp. 361–62.
125. *Spain Betrayed*, available: https://marxists.architexturez.net/history/etol/document/spain2/ch21.htm

> According to our petty-bourgeois Popular Front democrats, everything was inevitable. The Republicans and Socialists justified the defeat by the military superiority of the Fascists, and the Communists by the existence of a pro-Fascist bourgeoisie (a discovery, this!) which, by its policy of non-intervention, favoured Franco. They forgot to add that they supported the Blum government, which inaugurated this policy. The Anarchists justified their capitulations and repeated betrayals by the blackmail exercised by the Russians through the weapons that they were sending to the Republicans. As for the POUM, it too joined the fatalist chorus and said: "We were too weak, and we had to follow the others, and above all we could not break unity." Thus everything was inevitable. What happened had to happen, and it was written in advance in the Koran...[126]

Trotsky, in a magnificent passage, endorsed wholeheartedly Bortenstein's indictment of the self-justifying fatalism of those who led the Spanish workers to defeat:

> This impotent philosophy, which seeks to reconcile defeats as a necessary link in the chain of cosmic developments, is completely incapable of posing and refuses to pose the question of such concrete factors as programs, parties, and personalities that were the organizers of defeat. This philosophy of fatalism and prostration is diametrically opposed to Marxism as the theory of revolutionary action.[127]

* * * * *

Trotsky continued to work on his biography of Stalin. The last chapter of the uncompleted volume is titled "The Thermidorian Reaction," in which he presented a devastating portrait and appraisal of Stalin and his entourage.

> Generally, in the camp of Stalinism, you will not find a single gifted writer, historian or critic. It is a kingdom of arrogant

---

126. Ibid.
127. Trotsky, *The Spanish Revolution 1931–39*, p. 364.

mediocrities. Hence, the ease with which highly qualified Marxists began to be replaced by accidental and second-rate people who have mastered the art of bureaucratic manoeuvering. Stalin is the most outstanding mediocrity of the Soviet bureaucracy. I cannot find any other definition than this.[128]

The transformation of Stalin into a "genius" was the work of the bureaucracy, which found in him a brutal instrument of its striving for privilege. The myth of Stalin, developed out of lies, was the creation of the bureaucracy. "This massive, organic, unconquerable character of the lie," Trotsky observed, "is the undeniable evidence that it is not merely a matter of personal ambitions of an individual, but something immeasurably greater: the new caste of privileged upstarts had to have its own mythology."[129]

The entire cultural development of the Soviet Union was being suffocated by the bureaucratic regime. "The literature and art of the Stalinist epoch," Trotsky wrote, "will go down in history as examples of the most absurd and servile Byzantinism."[130] Even the genuinely gifted artists were compelled to prostitute themselves in the service of Stalin. Trotsky cited a poem by Alexis Tolstoy where Stalin is depicted as a deity: "Thou, bright sun of the nations, /The unsinking sun of our times," etc. Commenting on these lines, Trotsky wrote, "To call things by their right name, this poetry is more reminiscent of the grunting of a pig."[131]

Even Soviet architecture was distorted and degraded by Stalin. The House of Soviets, built to Stalin's specifications, was "a monstrous building that, with its imposing uselessness and crude grandiosity, provides the concrete expression of a brutal regime devoid of any ideas or perspective."[132] As for films, their directors and actors were compelled to take instructions from Stalin. Their sole purpose became the glorification of the dictator. "In this way Soviet cinematography, which made such a promising start, has been killed stone dead."[133]

As for Stalin the man, to the extent that the living person could be separated from the myth in which he was encased, his essential characteristic,

---

128. Trotsky, *Stalin*, p. 663.
129. Ibid., p. 671.
130. Ibid.
131. Ibid.
132. Ibid.
133. Ibid.

Trotsky emphasized, "is personal, physical cruelty, which is usually called sadism."[134]

> Unable to appeal to the best instincts of the masses, Stalin appeals to their basest instincts—to ignorance, intolerance, narrow-mindedness, primitiveness. He seeks contact with them through coarse expressions. But this coarseness also serves as a camouflage for his cunning. He puts all his passion into carefully-nurtured plans, to which all else is subordinate. How he detests authority! And how he loves to impose it![135]

Of his own subjective attitude toward Stalin, Trotsky wrote on the penultimate page of the biography:

> The point which I now occupy is unique. I therefore feel that I have the right to say that I have never entertained a feeling of hatred towards Stalin. There is a lot said and written about my so-called hatred for Stalin which apparently fills me with gloomy and troubled judgments. I can only shrug my shoulders in response to all this. Our ways have parted so long ago that whatever personal relationship there was between us has long ago been utterly extinguished. For my part, and to the extent that I am the tool of historical forces, which are alien and hostile to me, my personal feelings towards Stalin are indistinguishable from my feelings towards Hitler or the Japanese Mikado.[136]

* * * * *

The world of 1940 seemed to be living through a nightmare. How fragile and helpless civilization appeared in the face of advancing barbarism! Under the pressure of reaction, even the most intelligent and sensitive representatives of the European intelligentsia abandoned all hope. Walter Benjamin, living in a precarious exile, translated his personal despair into a morbidly demoralized "On the Concept of History." Hitlerism was not the negation of

---

134. Ibid., p. 667.
135. Ibid.
136. Ibid., p. 689.

civilization, but its true essence. "There is no document of culture," he opined, "which is not at the same time a document of barbarism. And just as such a document is never free of barbarism, so barbarism taints the manner in which it was transmitted from one hand to another."[137]

Benjamin called attention to the artist Paul Klee's painting *Angelus Novus*. In this work, the real nature of the historical process was depicted: "His face is turned toward the past. Where a chain of events appears before *us*, *he* sees one single catastrophe, which keeps piling wreckage upon wreckage and hurls it at his feet."[138] Benjamin's despair led him to cynicism, which he directed against the perspective of socialist revolution. "Marx's epigones," he wrote bitterly, "have derived (among other things) the notion of the 'revolutionary situation,' which, as we know, has always refused to arrive."[139]

What course of action, then, was left to Walter Benjamin but to take his own life? Fleeing Vichy France, and in sight of the Spanish border, Benjamin—convinced of the hopelessness of his situation—committed suicide on the evening of September 26, 1940. Had he waited but one more day, the writer would have passed safely across the border.

Trotsky doubtlessly would have felt great empathy for Benjamin. But feelings of despair were alien to the revolutionist. His powerful sense of history enabled him to place the bestialities of his time in their appropriate context. In a section of the Stalin biography that bears the heading "A Historical Parallel," Trotsky observed: "In this period of capitalist decline Europe's regression produces many of the traits of capitalism's infancy. Present-day Europe strongly resembles 15th century Italy."[140] Of course, that was an era in which the small states "represented the baby steps of an infantile capitalism." But the period of the Renaissance resembled the modern era in one important respect: "It was an epoch of transition from old to new norms—an amoral, and *per se*, immoral period."[141] Cardinals "wrote pornographic comedies and the Popes produced them in their courts."[142]

---

137. Walter Benjamin, *Selected Writings*, Vol. 4: 1938–1940 (Cambridge and London: Belknap Press, 2003), p. 392.
138. Ibid.
139. Ibid., pp. 402–03.
140. Trotsky, *Stalin*, p. 682.
141. Ibid.
142. Ibid., p. 683.

> Corruption was the keynote in Italian politics. The art of governing was practised in cliques and consisted in the gentle arts of lying, betrayal and crime. To fulfil a contract, to keep a promise, was considered the height of stupidity. Slyness walked hand-in-hand with violence. Superstition and lack of confidence poisoned all relations between the heads of the states. It was the period of the Sforzas, the Medici, the Borgias. But it was not only the period of treachery and forgery, of poison and craftiness. It was also the period of the Renaissance.[143]

As in the period of the Renaissance, modern man finds himself

> on the border of two worlds—the bourgeois-capitalist, which is suffering agony and that new world which is destined to replace it. Now, once again, we are living through the transition from one social system to another, in the epoch of the greatest social crisis which, as always, is accompanied by a crisis in morality. The old has been shaken to its foundation. The new has scarcely begun to emerge. Social contradictions have once more achieved exceptional sharpness.[144]

Such periods impose immense pressure on individuals.

> When the roof has collapsed and the doors and windows have fallen off their hinges, the house is bleak and hard to live in. Today, stormy winds are blowing across our entire planet.[145]

* * * * *

Trotsky viewed his survival of the May 24 assault as no more than a reprieve. He knew that the GPU would make another attempt on his life. Harold Robins, in a discussion with this writer, recalled that Trotsky requested a meeting with the guards in early August. The world news was dominated by the air attacks launched by Nazi Germany against Britain. Trotsky told

---

143. Ibid., p. 682.
144. Ibid., p. 689.
145. Ibid.

the guards that he expected that Stalin would seek to take advantage of the public's distraction by attempting as soon as possible another assassination. A well-known Mexico City journalist, Eduardo Tellez Vargas, who wrote for *El Universal*, met several times with Trotsky after the May 24 raid. In an interview conducted with the International Committee in December 1976, Tellez Vargas recalled his final meeting with Trotsky, which occurred on August 17, 1940, just three days before the assassination. Feeling sincere admiration for the great revolutionary, Tellez Vargas was deeply troubled by what Trotsky told him.

> There came a moment when Trotsky trusted absolutely nobody. He trusted in no one. He didn't specify or name names, but he did say to me: "I will be killed either by one of them in here or by one of my friends from the outside, by someone who has access to the house. Because Stalin cannot spare my life."[146]

On the day of Tellez Vargas' last interview with Trotsky, there was another visitor to the villa on the Avenida Viena. Jacques Mornard, this time without Sylvia Ageloff, was admitted to the compound. Mornard claimed that he had written an article, which he wanted Trotsky to read. Trotsky, who had several brief encounters with Mornard, had already indicated that he did not like the man. Mornard had taken to speaking in Trotsky's presence of his "boss" who had become rich through business speculations. In her autobiographical account of her life with Trotsky, Natalia Sedova recalled that he "was utterly indifferent" to Mornard's talk of his boss's exploits. "These short conversations used to irritate me," Sedova wrote, "and Leon Davidovich disliked them as well. 'Who is this fabulously rich boss?' he asked me. 'We should find out. After all, he might be some profiteer with Fascist tendencies and it might be best to stop seeing Sylvia's husband altogether....'"[147]

The meeting with Mornard on August 17 intensified Trotsky's concern. Trotsky emerged from his office after only ten minutes. He was disturbed by Mornard's behavior. Trotsky noted that Mornard had failed to take off his hat upon entering the office and then proceeded to sit on the corner of Trotsky's desk. This was strangely inappropriate behavior for a man who claimed to be

---

146. International Committee of the Fourth International, *Trotsky's Assassin At Large* (New York: Labor Publications, 1977), p. 16.
147. Victor Serge and Natalia Sedova Trotsky, *The Life and Death of Leon Trotsky* (New York: Basic Books, 1973), p. 264.

Belgian and to have been raised in France. Trotsky, after only a few minutes with Mornard, had doubts about the visitor's nationality. As recounted by Isaac Deutscher:

> Who was he [Mornard-Jacson] really? They should find this out. Natalya was taken aback; it seemed to her that Trotsky 'had perceived something new about "Jacson", but had not yet reached, or rather was in no hurry, to reach, any conclusions'. Yet the implications of what he had said was alarming: if 'Jacson' was deceiving them about his nationality, why was he doing it? And was he not deceiving them about other things as well? About what? These questions must have been on Trotsky's mind, for two days later he repeated his observations to Hansen, as if to ascertain whether similar misgivings had occurred to anyone beside himself.[148]

The fact that Trotsky, after only a few minutes alone with Mornard, developed doubts about his nationality and suspected that he might be an impostor, leads one to wonder why Alfred and Maguerite Rosmer, both French, never developed similar suspicions—even though they spent a far greater amount of time with the man who was to be Trotsky's assassin.

In the late afternoon of Tuesday August 20, Mornard, without an appointment, again came to see Trotsky. Despite the concerns conveyed to him directly by Trotsky, Joseph Hansen—whose GPU connections were to be exposed nearly forty years later—approved Mornard's entry into the compound. Although the weather was warm and the sky cloudless, Mornard was wearing a hat and carrying a raincoat. Concealed within the coat was a knife, an automatic gun, and an alpenstock. Mornard was not searched. He was allowed to accompany Trotsky into his office. He gave Trotsky what he claimed to be a redraft of the article that he had presented on August 17. As Trotsky read the article, Mornard withdrew the alpenstock from the coat and brought it crashing down on Trotsky's skull. Though mortally wounded, Trotsky rose from his chair and fought off the assailant. Harold Robins, having heard Trotsky cry out, raced into the study and subdued the assassin.

---

148. Isaac Deutscher, *The Prophet Outcast, Trotsky: 1929–1940* (London: Verso, 2003), p. 404.

While en route to the hospital in Mexico City, Trotsky lost consciousness. He died, with Natalia at his side, the following evening.

*****

Six months before his assassination, on February 27, 1940, Trotsky had written his *Testament*. He intended the statement to be published after his death. Though his capacity for work remained undiminished, Trotsky believed that he did not have long to live. In addition to the ever-present threat of assassination, he was suffering from high blood pressure, for which there was, at that time, no effective treatment. The *Testament* rejected "the stupid and vile slander of Stalin and his agents: there is not a single spot on my revolutionary honor."[149] He expressed his conviction that future revolutionary generations would rehabilitate the honor of Stalin's victims "and deal with the Kremlin executioners according to their deserts." With evident emotion, Trotsky paid tribute to Natalia Sedova: "In addition to the happiness of being a fighter for the cause of socialism, fate gave me the happiness of being her husband."[150] Trotsky then restated for posterity the purpose, principles, and philosophy that had guided his life work:

> For forty-three years of my conscious life I have remained a revolutionist; for forty-two of them I have fought under the banner of Marxism. If I had to begin all over again I would of course try to avoid this or that mistake, but the main course of my life would remain unchanged. I shall die a proletarian revolutionist, a Marxist, a dialectical materialist, and, consequently, an irreconcilable atheist. My faith in the communist future of mankind is not less ardent, indeed it is firmer today, than it was in the days of my youth.[151]

Trotsky's humanity and breadth of vision found its consummate expression in the conclusion of the *Testament*:

---

149. "Testament," *Writings of Leon Trotsky [1939–40,]* p. 208.
150. Ibid., p. 209.
151. Ibid.

> Natasha has just come up to the window from the courtyard and opened it wider so that the air may enter more freely into my room. I can see the bright strip of grass beneath the wall, and the clear blue sky above the wall, and sunlight everywhere. Life is beautiful. Let the future generations cleanse it of all evil, oppression, and violence and enjoy it to the full.[152]

* * * * *

Eighty years have passed since the assassination of Trotsky. And yet the passage of time has not diminished his stature. The shadow cast by this political giant of the twentieth century looms even larger in the twenty-first.

History has vindicated Trotsky and vanquished his enemies. The edifice of Stalinism has been smashed to bits. The name of Stalin is now and will be forever associated with criminal betrayals. The damage that his crimes did to the Soviet Union—politically, economically, and culturally—was irreparable. Stalin will be remembered only as one of the two most monstrous figures of the twentieth century, a counterrevolutionary mass murderer of socialists, surpassed in evil only by Hitler. Trotsky was right: "The vengeance of history is far more terrible than the vengeance of the most powerful General Secretary."[153]

Trotsky's place in history endures and grows ever larger because the basic tendencies and characteristics of contemporary capitalism and imperialism correspond to his analysis of the dynamic of global capitalist crisis and the logic of global class struggle. His writings—indispensable for an understanding of the contemporary world—remain as fresh as the day they were written. Trotsky's life and struggles, his unyielding devotion to the liberation of mankind, will live on in history.

The world has not passed beyond Lev Davidovich Trotsky. We still live in the epoch he defined as the death agony of capitalism. The solution that he advanced to the crisis of capitalism—the world socialist revolution—provides the only historically progressive way out of the existential crisis of the capitalist system.

---

152. Ibid.
153. Trotsky, *Stalin*, p. 689.

But this *solution* requires the *resolution* of the crisis of revolutionary leadership. This is the task to which the International Committee of the Fourth International rededicates itself as it commemorates the eightieth anniversary of Trotsky's death.

11

Trotsky and the Self-Determination of Ukraine

Eighty-two years ago today, on August 20, 1940, Leon Trotsky was assassinated by an agent of the Stalinist secret police, the GPU, in his villa in Coyoacan, Mexico, where he spent the final three years of his life as a political exile. Trotsky died of the wound inflicted by the killer, Ramon Mercader, on the following day.

This anniversary does not mark a five- or ten-year interval, which, as a matter of formal custom, imparts to the observance of historical events a special significance. However, the commemoration of Trotsky's death does not require symbolic justification. The importance of the eighty-second anniversary of Trotsky's death flows from the relevance of his life as a Marxist theoretician and strategist and leader of world socialist revolution.

The political conditions that existed in August 1940 resemble to an extraordinary degree those that exist today. In the final year of his life Trotsky's work was concentrated on the outbreak of World War II and its implications for the international working class, the world socialist movement, and the fate of humanity. Trotsky, the most realistic political thinker of his age, was not inclined to paint the world situation in rosy colors. He confronted

---

Published on the World Socialist Web Site, August 20, 2022, in commemoration of the eighty-second anniversary of the assassination of Trotsky.

with brutal frankness the catastrophe that had befallen the working class as a consequence of the betrayal of the October Revolution by the Stalinist bureaucracy that held power in the Soviet Union, and the spinelessness of the pro-capitalist social democratic-led labor organizations.

It is a measure not only of Trotsky's astonishing political farsightedness but also of the parallels between the conditions of 1940 and today, that he devoted an immense amount of attention to the place of Ukraine in the fate of the Soviet Union and all of Europe. Just four months before the outbreak of the Second World War, Trotsky warned:

> The Ukrainian question is destined in the immediate future to play an enormous role in the life of Europe. It was not for nothing that Hitler so noisily raised the question of creating a "Greater Ukraine," and likewise it was not for nothing that he dropped this question with such stealthy haste.[1]

Trotsky recognized the legitimacy of the striving of the Ukrainian masses for national self-determination. The formation of the Union of Soviet Socialist Republics by the Bolshevik government in 1922, when Lenin and Trotsky were still the dominant figures, insisted on the voluntary character of the Union and opposed all tendencies to subordinate its Ukrainian component to the pressure of Great Russian chauvinism. The Declaration of Union and Treaty of Union, dated December 30, 1922, defined the USSR as "a voluntary union of equal peoples," whose formation would prove "a decided step towards the union of the workers of all countries into a World Socialist Soviet Republic."[2]

By the late 1930s, fifteen years of escalating violations of socialist internationalism and bureaucratic terror and despotism had generated deep hostility among the Ukrainian masses toward the Soviet Union and created a constituency for the revival of the most reactionary political tendencies. Trotsky wrote:

> Not a trace remains of the former confidence and sympathy of the Western Ukrainian masses for the Kremlin. Since the latest

---

1. Leon Trotsky, "The Ukrainian Question," *Writings of Leon Trotsky [1938–39]* (New York: Pathfinder Press, 1974, second edition, ninth printing, 2023), p. 301.
2. Rex A. Wade, ed., *Documents of Soviet History*, Vol. 2 (Gulf Breeze, FL: Academic International Press, 1993), p. 445.

murderous "purge" in the Ukraine no one in the West wants to become part of the Kremlin satrapy which continues to bear the name of Soviet Ukraine. The worker and peasant masses in the Western Ukraine, in Bukovina, in the Carpatho-Ukraine are in a state of confusion: Where to turn? What to demand? This situation naturally shifts the leadership to the most reactionary Ukrainian cliques who express their "nationalism" by seeking to sell the Ukrainian people to one imperialism or another in return for a promise of fictitious independence. Upon this tragic confusion Hitler bases his policy in the Ukrainian question. At one time we said: but for Stalin (i.e., but for the fatal policy of the Comintern in Germany) there would have been no Hitler. To this can now be added: but for the rape of Soviet Ukraine by the Stalinist bureaucracy there would be no Hitlerite Ukrainian policy.[3]

Accounting for the passage of time and changing what needs to be changed, Trotsky's analysis remains an indispensable historical foundation for an understanding of the present war. The dissolution of the Soviet Union and the creation of a capitalist regime in Russia cannot attract the population of Western Ukraine. In the demoralized environment created by the restoration of capitalism, the political situation in Ukraine, in the words of Trotsky, "naturally shifts the leadership to the most reactionary Ukrainian cliques [i.e., that of Poroshenko, Zelensky, and the neo-Nazi militias] who express their 'nationalism' by seeking to sell the Ukrainian people to one imperialism or another in return for a promise of fictitious independence." And, on the basis of Putin's bankrupt and reactionary policies, the US and its NATO allies develop their policies in Ukraine.

Trotsky advocated the formation of an independent *socialist* Ukraine. He rejected with contempt all claims that Ukrainian independence, in any politically progressive sense, could be achieved on a capitalist basis.

> The Ukraine is especially rich and experienced in false paths of struggle for national emancipation. Here everything has been tried: the petty-bourgeois Rada [government], and Skoropadsky, and Petlura, and "alliance" with the Hohenzollerns, and

---

3. Trotsky, "The Ukrainian Question," *Writings of Leon Trotsky [1938-39]*, pp. 390–91.

combinations with the Entente. After all these experiments, only political cadavers can continue to place hope in any one of the factions of the Ukrainian bourgeoisie as the leader of the national struggle for emancipation. The Ukrainian proletariat alone is capable not only of solving the task—which is revolutionary in its very essence—but also of taking the initiative for its solution. The proletariat and only the proletariat can rally around itself the peasant masses and the genuinely revolutionary national intelligentsia.[4]

Today the imperialist proxy war in Ukraine is justified by propaganda in its most debased form. The hack journalists of the capitalist press, ignorant of history, function as the public stenographers of their national intelligence agencies. The vast majority of academics, even those who have studied the history of Ukraine and Russia, have fallen into line with the pro-war hysteria. These intellectual sycophants are incapable of displaying independence of thought and critical judgment. No better and probably worse are the denizens of pseudo-left organizations who posture as socialists and even Marxists as they offer deceitful and hypocritical justifications for not only the imperialist operations in Ukraine but also the preparations for war against China.

Trotsky, in his time, did not refrain from expressing his contempt for the demoralized and dishonest middle-class intellectuals who capitulated in the face of political reaction. His political intransigence was rooted in a profound grasp of historical processes and confidence in the revolutionary potential of the working class. "World reaction has unquestionably assumed monstrous proportions nowadays," he wrote on the eve of World War II. "But thereby it has prepared the soil for the greatest revolutionary crisis."[5]

These words reverberate in our own times. Eighty-two years after his assassination, Trotsky, a giant in the history of the last century, remains an immense intellectual and political presence in the revolutionary struggles of the twenty-first.

---

4. Ibid., p. 394.
5. Leon Trotsky, "Intellectual Ex-Radicals and World Reaction," *Writings of Leon Trotsky [1938-39]*, p. 254.

12

Leon Trotsky and Revolutionary Strategy in the Twentieth and Twenty-First Centuries

Exactly one hundred years ago, on October 20, 1922, Leon Trotsky delivered one of his great political speeches before the membership of the Moscow organization of the Russian Communist Party.[1] The speech was presented in anticipation of the opening of the Fourth Congress of the Communist International (the Comintern), which began two weeks later on November 5, 1922.

The Congress coincided with the fifth anniversary of the 1917 October Revolution, the conquest of power by the working class led by the Bolshevik Party, which transferred power to the workers councils (Soviets) and created the first workers state in history. The Bolshevik victory provided an immense impulse for the creation of the Communist (Third) International, which held its first Congress in March 1919. At that point the Bolshevik regime was under siege, fighting against counterrevolutionary armies backed by world imperialism to strangle the revolution. But by 1922, the counterrevolutionary forces had been defeated by the Red Army, whose principal commander was Leon Trotsky. His political authority and prestige within the Soviet Union was exceeded only by that of Lenin.

Published on the World Socialist Web Site October 21, 2022.

1. Leon Trotsky, The Fifth Anniversary of the October Revolution and the Fourth World Congress of the Communist International, October 20, 1922. Available: https://www.marxists.org/archive/trotsky/1924/ffyci-2/18b.htm

The workers state had survived, but the Bolshevik regime confronted the consequences of the economic devastation of the three years of the World War that had preceded the October Revolution and the three years of civil war that followed it. Moreover, the Soviet regime had been established, not in an advanced capitalist country—such as France, Germany, Britain, and the United States—but in economically and culturally backward Russia.

The possibility of the working class coming to power in a backward country had been foreseen by Trotsky in his elaboration of the Theory of Permanent Revolution more than a decade before the 1917 October Revolution. But neither Trotsky nor Lenin and the Bolshevik Party had believed that socialism could be constructed within the confines of a single national state, let alone one that was economically and socially backward.

Even as they organized the overthrow of capitalism in Russia, Lenin and Trotsky insisted that the fate of the socialist revolution in Russia depended on the conquest of power by the working class in one or more of the advanced capitalist countries. The centrality of world socialist revolution in the political calculations of the Bolsheviks was not an expression of utopian daydreaming. The "Great War" of 1914–1918, which had emerged out of the contradictions of capitalism as a world system, accelerated and intensified the economic crisis and social conflicts, generating a massive wave of militant and overtly revolutionary working class struggles that swept across Western and Central Europe.

But the ruling classes of Germany, Italy, and other countries fought back viciously against the revolutionary tide, and the Soviet Union remained an isolated workers state. This compelled the Bolshevik regime to adopt the New Economic Policy within the USSR, which involved accepting the limited revival of capitalist activity in order to stabilize the Soviet economy.

At the Third Congress of the Communist International in 1921, the Russian delegation—with Lenin and Trotsky playing the leading roles—had fought to redirect the newly founded European Communist parties toward a protracted struggle to establish their authority in the working class. This process of reorientation and political education was to continue at the Fourth Congress.

Trotsky's speech on October 20, 1922 was an extraordinary analysis of the challenges confronting the new Communist International. Many of the issues dealt with in this address were further developed in his monumental three-hour report delivered little more than three weeks later before the Fourth Congress. On that one day, November 14, 1922, Trotsky spoke for nine hours, delivering his report first in German, then in French, and, finally, in Russian.

Trotsky examined the contradictory development of the world socialist revolution, which had achieved its first great victory in backward Russia rather than in the advanced centers of world imperialism.

He noted a basic difference in the revolutionary process in Russia, compared to that in an advanced country such as the United States. In the former, the great problem was not in the seizure of power but in holding it after the overthrow of the capitalist state.

In the advanced countries, attaining power would be more difficult because "the bourgeoisie is far better organized and more experienced, because there the petty-bourgeoisie has graduated from the school of the big bourgeoisie and is, in consequence, also far more powerful and experienced..."[2] Prophetically, Trotsky warned that, having witnessed with horror the overthrow of the Russian ruling class, the bourgeoisie in the advanced countries were arming "counterrevolutionary gangs" to destroy the revolutionary socialist movement.

Explaining the significance of Mussolini's rise in Italy, Trotsky described fascism as "the revenge, the vengeance exacted by the bourgeoisie for the dread it had experienced during the 1920 September days,"[3] when massive strikes swept Italy.

But why did the revolutionary movement fail and lead to the upsurge of fascism? Answering the question, "What was lacking?" Trotsky stated:

> Lacking was the political premise, the subjective premise, i.e., cognizance of the situation by the proletariat.
>
> Lacking was an organization at the head of the proletariat, capable of utilizing the situation for nothing else but the direct organizational and technical preparation of an uprising, of the overturn, the seizure of power, and so forth. This is what was lacking.

Trotsky rejected mechanical formalism that insisted on the inevitable and fully predictable outcome of great socio-economic and historical processes. In the "dialectic of historical forces," the action by the working class, influenced and led by the Marxist party, is decisive.[4]

---

2. Ibid.
3. Ibid.
4. Ibid.

The Fourth Congress of the Communist International was the last attended by Lenin, who had already suffered the first of a series of strokes that were soon to bring his political activity to an end. Only one month later, in December 1922, the political conflict within the leadership of the Russian Communist Party, which was to lead to the founding of the Left Opposition in October 1923, began to emerge. The process of bureaucratization and political reaction exemplified by the rise of Stalin led to a repudiation of the strategy of permanent revolution and the perspective of world socialist revolution and to the adoption of the anti-Marxist nationalist program of "socialism in one country."

This nationalist overthrow of socialist internationalism had devastating consequences for the Communist International, the international working class, and the Soviet Union itself. The dissolution of the Soviet Union in December 1991 was the final devastating confirmation of the counterrevolutionary essence of Stalinism and all related conceptions of a nationalist path to socialism.

Nevertheless, the heritage of the great theoretical work of Trotsky was continued by the Fourth International, which he founded in 1938, and which is represented today by the International Committee of the Fourth International.

Trotsky's speech of October 20, 1922 exemplifies the outstanding relevance of his political thought. Delivered a century ago, this speech has barely aged. It is hardly even necessary to consult a glossary. Trotsky is dealing with economic, political, and social issues that are comprehensible in fully modern terms. The essential significance of revolutionary leadership, the dynamic of world capitalist crisis, the political significance of fascism, and the relation of objective and subjective factors in the revolutionary transition from capitalism to socialism are all dealt with in Trotsky's report.

And, in what might appear as a remarkable coincidence, Trotsky even calls attention to the implications of British Prime Minister David Lloyd George's sudden fall from power on October 19, 1922, exactly a century before the precipitous collapse of Liz Truss' ill-fated premiership. Of course, the six-year leadership of Lloyd George cannot be compared to the six-week farce of Liz Truss. But it is not difficult to imagine that Trotsky would have interpreted the Trussian farce as a symptom of the imminent breakdown of bourgeois rule in Britain and the development of a revolutionary crisis. Trotsky would have seen in this crisis an immense opportunity for Marxists to expand their authority within the working class and overcome the influence of the reactionary Labour Party and trade union organizations.

Trotsky remains the towering figure in the history of revolutionary socialism in the twentieth century. The careful study of his writings is essential for the elaboration of the strategy and tactics of socialist revolution in the epoch of imperialism's death agony. Trotskyism is the Marxism of the twenty-first century.

13

Greetings to the Fifth Anniversary Meeting of the Young Guard of Bolshevik-Leninists

Dear Comrades,

Permit me to extend to you the revolutionary greetings of the International Committee of the Fourth International and its sections throughout the world on the occasion of the fifth anniversary of the founding of the Young Guard of Bolshevik-Leninists.

This milestone is worthy of celebration. The history of the YGBL records the progress of the organization toward Trotskyism, which during the last year has culminated in the establishment of comradely relations and close political collaboration with the International Committee. As is to be expected, the path of the YGBL toward genuine revolutionary Marxism has been complex and contradictory. Hegel, in the Preface with which he began his monumental *Phenomenology of Spirit*, belittled the pragmatic conception that there existed a problem-free "royal road" to scientific truth. His criticism of vulgar thought, which contents itself with the superficial and commonplace, may be applied to the sphere of politics. A Marxist party—whose aim is the education of the working class and its organization as a political force capable of overthrowing the capitalist system and replacing it with socialism on a world scale—develops through

---

Published on the World Socialist Web Site February 23, 2023.

the systematic working out and clarification of the historical problems of an entire epoch.

The International Committee of the Fourth International recognizes the enormous significance of the emergence of the Trotskyist movement in Russia. Given the origins of the Trotskyist movement, what was known as the "Russian Question"—that is, the foundational issues of history and program raised by the struggle against the Stalinist perversion of Marxism and betrayal of the October Revolution—necessarily played a central role in the history of the Fourth International.

In one or another form, conflicts within the Fourth International invariably raised issues relating to the class nature of the Soviet state, the historical role of Stalinism, and the fate of the Soviet Union and its relationship to the World Socialist Revolution. The first major struggle within the Fourth International in 1939–1940 was provoked by the emergence of a faction, led by Max Shachtman and James Burnham, which rejected the defense of the Soviet Union, even in a war with Hitler's Germany. It argued that the designation of the USSR as a degenerated workers state was no longer valid, and that the Soviet Union represented a new form of exploitative "state capitalist" society unforeseen by the Marxists.

The theoretical and political essence of this theory, as its elaboration in the years that followed made clear, was that the entire historical perspective of socialism, based on the revolutionary role of the working class, was false. Virtually all those who advanced this demoralized perspective—first and foremost, Shachtman and Burnham—soon deserted to the camp of imperialist counterrevolution.

The next major form of anti-Marxist and anti-Trotskyist revision was advanced by Michel Pablo and Ernest Mandel. Between 1951 and 1953, they argued with ever greater insistence that Stalinism, contrary to the analysis advanced by Trotsky in *The Revolution Betrayed* and the program of the Fourth International, would still play a revolutionary role. Pablo and Mandel went so far as to argue that revolutions led by the Stalinist parties would result in the creation of "deformed workers states" that would last for centuries!

Though the theory of Pablo and Mandel seemed to be the polar opposite of that of Shachtman and Burnham, both conceptions attributed to the Stalinist bureaucracy and its network of political parties a decisive historical role. The Shachtmanites transformed the Stalinist bureaucracy into a new form of class society. The Pabloites glorified the bureaucracy as the decisive revolutionary force that would overthrow capitalism. Both revisionist tendencies rejected the revolutionary potential of the working class and its unique historical role.

The International Committee of the Fourth International, whose founding was initiated by the Open Letter written by Socialist Workers Party leader James P. Cannon in November 1953, exposed the Pabloite revisions of Marxism and upheld the Trotskyist analysis of Stalinism, the revolutionary role of the working class, and the decisive significance of the Fourth International in the struggle for the development of socialist consciousness in the working class and resolution of the crisis of revolutionary leadership.

In this historic document, written almost exactly seventy years ago, Cannon insisted that the "main obstacle" to the victory of the World Socialist Revolution

> ... is Stalinism, which attracts workers through exploiting the prestige of the October 1917 Revolution in Russia, only later, as it betrays their confidence, to hurl them either into the arms of the Social Democracy, into apathy, or back into illusions in capitalism. The penalty for these betrayals is paid by the working people in the form of consolidation of fascist or monarchist forces, and new outbreaks of wars fostered and prepared by capitalism. From its inception, the Fourth International set as one of its major tasks the revolutionary overthrow of Stalinism inside and outside the USSR.[1]

In the decades that followed, this analysis of the counterrevolutionary role of Stalinism was upheld by the International Committee against the Kremlin bureaucracy and the innumerable apologists for "real existing socialism," which included the Pabloites, who did all in their power to prop up the prestige of the bureaucracy and divert the struggle against it.

Even within the International Committee, there was from the mid-1970s and into the early 1980s an increasing adaptation on the part of the leadership of the Workers Revolutionary Party to Stalinism. This political retreat evoked opposition and played a major role in provoking and intensifying the conflict that led to the split in 1985–1986. It is hardly an accident that the political conflict between the Workers League (the forerunner of the Socialist Equality Party

---

1. Cited in David North, *The Heritage We Defend* (Oak Park, MI: Mehring Books, 2018), p. 230.

in the United States) and the WRP emerged into the open between 1982 and 1985, the very years during which the Soviet bureaucracy entered into its final crisis as it shifted decisively, with the accession of Gorbachev, toward a policy that would precipitate the dissolution of the USSR and the restoration of capitalism.

In the immediate aftermath of the split, the three principal leaders of the Workers Revolutionary Party repudiated Trotskyism. The WRP's general secretary, Michael Banda, denounced Trotsky and declared himself a fervent admirer of Stalin. Gerry Healy, who had broken with the British Communist Party in 1937 in response to the Moscow Trials and had been one of the original signers of the Open Letter in 1953, embraced the policies of Gorbachev as the beginning of the political revolution in the USSR. As for Cliff Slaughter, members of his faction rapidly evolved into anti-communist enemies of the October Revolution and supporters of imperialism.

The International Committee, having decisively defeated these renegade factions, upheld and developed the program and principles of the Fourth International. It is a matter of historical record that the ICFI, between the years 1986 and 1991, exposed and denounced the fool's gold of Gorbachev's *perestroika*, and repeatedly warned that it would lead to the dissolution of the USSR and restoration of capitalism.

During these critical years, the ICFI did everything in its power to alert the Soviet workers and sections of the intelligentsia who continued to profess support for socialism and the heritage of the October Revolution. I visited the Soviet Union in 1989 and 1991 and had the opportunity to speak with substantial numbers of workers, students, and intellectuals. In these discussions it became clear that the resistance to the reactionary Stalinist policy of capitalist restoration had been undermined by an almost-complete absence of knowledge of the history of the October Revolution and its aftermath. More than sixty years of the systematic falsification of Soviet history by the Stalinist regime had created an environment of political disorientation, which was exploited by the supporters of Gorbachev and Yeltsin to advance their claims that the October Revolution was a catastrophic error and that socialism was to be viewed as either a criminal enterprise or a utopian illusion.

The essential falsification upon which these denunciations of the October Revolution and socialism was based was the denial that there had existed any alternative to the policies pursued by the regime in the aftermath of the Revolution. The path from 1917 to 1991 was an inevitable and non-stop drive to catastrophe. Stalinism was not an aberration, a perversion and betrayal of October 1917, but rather its inevitable and necessary outcome.

The International Committee of the Fourth International recognized that the refutation of this false narrative was a critical task for the revival of Marxism, not only in the former USSR, but also throughout the world.

Exactly thirty years ago this month, in February 1993, I met the historian and sociologist Vadim Rogovin for the first time in Kiev. He had been reading the *Bulletin of the Fourth International*, published by the International Committee, for several years. Finally, Rogovin was able to establish contact with the ICFI, and we arranged to meet in Kiev, where I was to give lectures on the history of the International Committee. During several days of discussion, we agreed on all essential questions of history. Above all, we agreed that the greatest task of the International Committee, upon which the realization of its program depended, was the clarification of the history of the October Revolution and its aftermath. This required, above all, the refutation of all the lies directed by the bureaucracy since 1923 against Lev Davidovich Trotsky and the Left Opposition. It had to be demonstrated that Trotsky and the Left Opposition had advanced and fought for a program that represented a revolutionary socialist and internationalist alternative to Stalinism.

In the aftermath of the dissolution of the Soviet Union, historians in Russia and the West had sought to preempt a revival of interest in Trotsky and Trotskyism, not only by repeating the old lies of the Stalinist regime, but also by inventing new ones. It would be necessary to refute all the lies, both old and new. And so, in Kiev, Comrade Rogovin agreed that he would devote all his intellectual energies to fighting alongside the International Committee of the Fourth International in a worldwide campaign against the Post-Soviet School of Historical Falsification.

In the five years that followed, Comrade Vadim—despite the fatal illness that was first diagnosed in 1994 and which claimed his life in September 1998—lectured throughout the world at meetings organized by the International Committee and wrote his epochal seven-volume work on the struggle of the Left Opposition and the Fourth International against Stalinism. He decisively answered the question: "Was there an alternative to Stalinism?"

As you mark the fifth anniversary of the founding of the Young Guard of Bolshevik-Leninists, it is important that its cadre not only pay tribute to the memory of this great Trotskyist and revolutionary historian, but also recognize that the fight for historical truth remains the most critical task in the building of the Fourth International in Russia and throughout the former USSR.

The contemporary fight against the Post-Soviet School of Historical Falsification now develops under conditions of a war that is exposing the disastrous consequences of the dissolution of the USSR and the restoration of capitalism. It must be noted that political contact between the YGBL and the International Committee began in January 2022, on the very eve of the outbreak of the war in Ukraine. The extensive correspondence between the ICFI and Comrades Ritsky and Roerich began under the shadow of the approaching war and has continued throughout the year of this escalating conflict.

Great events test political tendencies, and the response of the comrades of the YGBL in both Russia and Ukraine—opposing NATO imperialism and Russian national chauvinism—testifies to your commitment to the foundational principles of Trotskyist internationalism. Your intransigent stand against the reckless and desperate policies of the Putin regime has been vindicated by events. Putin's speech of February 21, 2023 on the war is a pathetic self-exposure of not only his political miscalculations but also the bankruptcy of the historical perspective of his regime.

Employing the language of a disappointed and rejected lover, Putin now complains that his efforts to woo the imperialists have failed. He has been cruelly betrayed by his "Western partners." They did not share his desire for peace. Putin complained:

> The promises of the Western rulers, their assurances of a desire for peace in Donbass turned out, as we now see, into a forgery, a cruel lie. They simply dragged out the clock, engaged in a lot of pussyfooting, turned a blind eye to the political murders, the Kiev regime's repression of the unwanted, the bullying of believers. They increasingly encouraged Ukrainian neo-Nazis to commit terrorist acts in Donbass. The officers of nationalist battalions were trained in Western academies and colleges, and weapons were supplied.[2]

With a patience that rivals even that of Tolstoy's Alexei Karenin, the deceived husband of Anna, Putin gave his beloved Western partners every benefit of the doubt. But he was betrayed.

---

2. Translation by author. Putin's speech is available at: http://en.kremlin.ru/events/president/transcripts/70565.

It turns out that all the time when Donbass was burning, when blood was shed, when Russia sincerely—I want to stress this—sincerely sought a peaceful solution, they were playing on people's lives, playing, in fact, as they say in well-known circles, with split cards.

This disgusting method of deception has been tried many times before. They behaved in the same unscrupulous, duplicitous way when they destroyed Yugoslavia, Iraq, Libya, Syria. They will never be able to wash themselves of this shame. The concepts of honor, trust, decency are not for them.

And, in a final lament, Putin announces his shocking discovery:

During the long centuries of colonialism, dictatorship, hegemony, they got used to being allowed everything, got used to not giving a damn about the whole world. It turns out that they treat the people of their own countries with the same disdain and dignity—they have also cynically deceived them with fables about seeking peace, about adherence to UN Security Council resolutions on Donbass. Indeed, Western elites have become a symbol of total unprincipled lies.

The imperialists acted as imperialists. What a shocking surprise! Putin might have spared himself the trauma of this revelation had he studied the writings of Lenin and Trotsky on the subject of imperialism. But, as he made clear in his speech, he draws his inspiration not from the brilliant Marxist leaders of the October Revolution, but from the architect of the tsarist counterrevolution, Pyotr Stolypin. But the perspective of the ill-fated tsarist prime minister will prove no more effective in combating the forces of revolution in the twenty-first century than it was in resisting the approach of revolution more than one hundred years earlier.

The work of the Young Guard of Bolshevik-Leninists is of the greatest historical significance. In carrying forward the task of building a section of the International Committee of the Fourth International, you are resolving in theory and practice the historic "Russian question."

Your comrade,
David North

14

Forward to May Day 2023! Build a Mass Movement of Workers and Youth against War and for Socialism!

On Sunday, April 30, 2023, the International Committee of the Fourth International, the International Workers Alliance of Rank-and-File Committees, the International Youth and Students for Social Equality, and the World Socialist Web Site will hold an online global rally to celebrate May Day 2023.

Two processes dominate this year's celebration of the international unity of the working class: the war in Ukraine, which is escalating toward a global conflagration, and an international resurgence of the class struggle. These two processes are profoundly related. The same economic, geopolitical, and social contradictions that drive the imperialist ruling elites onto the path of war provide the objective impulse for the radicalization of the working class and the outbreak of revolutionary struggles.

The war in Ukraine is now in its second year. The most reliable casualty reports estimate that over 150,000 Ukrainian soldiers have been killed and that Russian deaths are between 50,000 and 100,000. Far from being horrified by this terrible toll in human life and issuing calls for a ceasefire, the United States and its NATO allies are pouring weapons into Ukraine. Having

---

Published on the World Socialist Web Site April 8, 2023.

committed the prestige of the US and NATO to victory in the proxy war, the Biden administration cannot tolerate the political consequences of a failure of its military and geopolitical objectives. The logic of its war aims leads to reckless policies.

The pro-war media cannot restrain its enthusiasm over the prospects of an imminent Ukrainian spring counteroffensive, which, if and when it occurs, will result in casualty figures that will recall the horrors of the Battles of the Somme and Verdun during World War I. Having imposed, in response to the COVID-19 pandemic, policies that resulted in the deaths of millions, capitalist governments and the media propaganda organs are inured to the fatal consequences of their war aims in the conflict with Russia. Mass death as a consequence of the subordination of social need to the imperatives of capitalist profit-making and individual enrichment has become a regular occurrence under capitalism. The earthquakes in Turkey and Syria, which are believed to have killed over 150,000 people, are among the endless series of preventable disasters that mark contemporary life.

In order to drum up support for the war, the Biden administration adheres to the absurd narrative of the "unprovoked war." The public is expected to believe that it all began when Vladimir Putin woke up one morning and declared, for no apparent reason, "Let there be war in Ukraine." But history shows that wars are the outcome of a complex interaction of economic, geopolitical, and social processes. More than one hundred years after the outbreak of World War I in 1914, historians are still trying to understand the different levels of causation that resulted in that conflict.

As the German scholar Jörn Leonhard has recently written:

> Ever since Thucydides, historians have been aware of the difference between structural and immediate causes of war; they have also understood the need to subject official justifications of war to an ideological critique. Distinctions can be made in this area, as in the search for causes of revolutions; identification of long-term, medium-term, and short-term causes involves separating out determinants, catalysts, and contingencies. Especially with regard to the outbreak of war, moreover, the question of external and internal factors continues to play a key role to this day. To what extent does the root cause of a war lie in the system of international relations, and

to what extent does it lie in the internal composition of states and societies?[1]

The narrative of the "unprovoked war" explains nothing about the historical, economic, social, and political origins of the war. It directs attention away from any examination of the connection between the US-NATO war in Ukraine and 1) the previous thirty years of virtually uninterrupted war waged by the United States in Iraq, Serbia, Afghanistan, Somalia, Libya, and Syria; 2) the relentless eastward expansion of NATO since the dissolution of the Soviet Union in 1991; 3) the escalating geopolitical conflict with China, which is viewed by American imperialism as a dangerous threat to its own dominant world position; 4) the protracted decline of the global economic position of the United States, which finds its starkest expression in the growing challenge to the supremacy of the dollar as the world reserve currency; 5) the series of economic shocks that have required desperate bailouts to forestall the complete collapse of the US financial system; 6) the evident breakdown of the American political system, exemplified in President Donald Trump's attempted overthrow, on January 6, 2021, of the result of the November 2020 national election; 7) the increasing domestic instability of a society scarred by staggering levels of inequality, intensified by the impact of the pandemic and a new inflationary spiral, which is radicalizing the American working class.

The most powerful refutation of the "unprovoked war" narrative is to be found in the innumerable statements of the International Committee of the Fourth International (ICFI), posted on the World Socialist Web Site, which has during the last quarter century analyzed the economic, political, and social contradictions that have driven the US corporate-financial elites' desperate efforts to find a way out of intractable crises through war.

Twenty years ago, just one week after the Bush administration launched the March 2003 invasion of Iraq, the Socialist Equality Party, the American section of the ICFI, explained: "The strategy of American imperialism consists of utilizing its massive military power to establish the unchallengeable global hegemony of the United States and completely subordinate to itself the resources of the world economy."[2]

---

1. Jörn Leonhard, *Pandora's Box: A History of the First World War*, translated by Patrick Camiller (Cambridge, MA: The Belknap Press of Harvard University Press, 2018), pp. 62–63.
2. David North, *A Quarter Century of War: The U.S. Drive for Global Hegemony 1990–2016* (Oak Park, MI: Mehring Books, 2016), p. 277.

Given its central role in world capitalism, the crisis of American imperialism had destabilized the entire political and economic system. Its policies, the SEP explained, were a response to what were, in essence, a global, rather than merely a national, crisis. The brutally aggressive policies of successive American governments were an

> attempt to resolve, on the basis of imperialism, the world historical problem of the contradiction between the global character of the productive forces and the archaic nation-states system.
>
> America proposes to overcome this problem by establishing itself as the super nation-state, functioning as the ultimate arbiter of the world's fate—deciding how the resources of the world economy will be allocated, after it has grabbed for itself the lion's share. But this sort of imperialist solution to the underlying contradictions of world capitalism, which was utterly reactionary in 1914, has not improved with age.
>
> Indeed, the sheer scale of world economic development in the course of the twentieth century endows such an imperialist project with an element of madness. Any attempt to establish the supremacy of a single national state is incompatible with the extraordinary level of international economic integration. The profoundly reactionary character of such a project is expressed in the barbaric methods that are required for its realization.[3]

While the European imperialist allies of the United States in the NATO alliance are compelled by the present global balance of power to follow the scenario set by Washington, they are by no means innocent bystanders in the confrontation with Russia. All the old European imperialist powers—weather-beaten veterans of two world wars in just the last century, along with savage crimes in their former colonies and experiments with fascism and genocide in their own countries—are beset with the same political and economic diseases that afflict the United States, while possessing even fewer financial resources to deal with them.

Although unable to pursue their imperialist ambitions independently, neither Britain, France, Italy, and Germany, nor "lesser powers" such as

---

3. Ibid.

Sweden, Norway, Denmark, Spain, Belgium, and Switzerland are prepared to accept their exclusion from the redistribution of territory and natural resources and access to financial advantages that they expect will follow from the military defeat of Russia and its breakup into numerous statelets.

But even amidst its proclamations of unity, the NATO alliance is itself beset by deep internal divisions, which, in the near-term future, may suddenly explode in armed conflict. Among the little-discussed consequences of the war is the reopening of territorial disputes arising from the post-World War II settlement. The German ruling class has not forgotten that the Polish city of Wrocław was once called Breslau, which was, at the turn of the twentieth century, the sixth largest city in the German Empire.

Nor has the virulently nationalistic and fascistic Polish government forgotten that the city of Lviv in western Ukraine was, prior to the outbreak of World War II, known as Lwów, the third largest city in Poland.

Between the lines of the "unprovoked war" narrative, the fact that the Ukraine war is part of a much larger global conflict, which is leading to World War III, is being ever more openly acknowledged. The question is not so much whether there will be a war between the United States and China, but rather when it will begin, where the conflict will break out, and whether it will involve the use of tactical and/or strategic nuclear weapons.

The former German foreign minister, Joschka Fischer, recently wrote that the war is "about the future world order, about its great revision in the 21st century." He denounced China and Russia for having "entered into an unformalized alliance to break the dominance of the United States and the West—the two great Eurasian powers against the transatlantic and also Pacific alliance of the West, led by the United States."[4]

Gideon Rachman, the leading foreign affairs correspondent of the *Financial Times*, wrote on March 27:

> The fact that the president of China and the prime minister of Japan paid simultaneous and competing visits to the capitals of Russia and Ukraine underlines the global significance of the Ukraine war. Japan and China are fierce rivals in east Asia. Both countries understand that their struggle will be profoundly affected by the outcome of the conflict in Europe.

---

4. Peter Schwarz, "Former German foreign minister Joschka Fischer declares Ukraine war is 'Global power struggle for future world order,'" World Socialist Web Site, April 4, 2023, available: https://www.wsws.org/en/articles/2023/04/05/ijhm-a05.html

This shadow boxing between China and Japan over Ukraine is part of a broader trend. Strategic rivalries in the Euro-Atlantic and Indo-Pacific regions are increasingly overlapping with each other. What is emerging is something that looks more and more like a single geopolitical struggle.[5]

Although Rachman remains a fervent proponent of the "unprovoked war" narrative, he concludes his self-contradicting analysis with a stark warning:

But the danger of a slide into global conflict is far from over. The outbreak of war in Europe, combined with the rise in tensions in east Asia – and the growing connection between these two theaters – still has distinct echoes of the 1930s. All sides have a responsibility to make sure that, this time, linked rivalries in Europe and Asia do not culminate in a global tragedy.[6]

When events leading up to the Russian invasion of Ukraine on February 24, 2022 are placed in the necessary historical and political context, there is no question but that the war was instigated by the United States and its NATO allies. All attempts to assess "blame" for the war by concentrating on the question of "who fired the first shot?" require an extremely limited time frame that isolates a single episode from a far longer succession of events. As Trotsky explained in 1934, "The character of war is determined not by the initial episode taken by itself ('violation of neutrality,' 'enemy invasion,' etc.) but by the main moving forces of war, by its whole development and by the consequences to which it finally leads."[7]

Contrary to the "unprovoked war" horror story, the February 2022 invasion was the outcome of a complex of events that extend back not only to the CIA-funded and orchestrated Maidan coup of 2014, which overthrew the elected pro-Russian government of Viktor Yanukovich, but to the unleashing of reactionary nationalist tendencies, both within Ukraine and Russia, as a consequence of the dissolution of the Soviet Union.

---

5. Gideon Rachman, "China, Japan and the Ukraine war," *Financial Times*, March 27, 2023, available: https://www.ft.com/content/9aa4df57-b457-4f2d-a660-1e646f96c8cb

6. Ibid.

7. Leon Trotsky, "War and the Fourth International," *Writings of Leon Trotsky, [1933–34]* (New York: Pathfinder Press, 1975), p. 308.

However, the fact that the war was instigated by the United States and NATO does not justify the Russian invasion of Ukraine, let alone diminish its reactionary character. Those who defend the invasion on the grounds that it was a legitimate response to the NATO threat to Russia's borders are simply ignoring the fact that Putin is the leader of a capitalist state, whose definition of "national security" is determined by the economic interests of the oligarchic class whose wealth is based on the dissolution and theft of the previously nationalized property of the Soviet Union.

All of Putin's miscalculations and blunders, in both the launching and prosecution of the war, reflect the class interests that he serves. The aim of the war is to counteract military pressure from the Western imperialist powers and to retain for the national capitalist class a dominant position in the exploitation of natural resources and labor within the borders of Russia and, to the greatest extent possible, in the Black Sea region and the neighboring countries of Central Asia and the Transcaucasus.

There is nothing progressive, let alone anti-imperialist, in these objectives. When Putin evokes the heritage of tsarism and denounces Lenin, Bolshevism, and the October Revolution, he is testifying to the historically reactionary and politically bankrupt character of his regime.

Regardless of their present conflict, the new post-Soviet ruling classes in Russia and Ukraine share the same criminal origin. Less than three months before the formal dissolution of the USSR, this writer, speaking on October 3, 1991, at a public meeting held at a workers' club in Kiev as a representative of the International Committee, I warned of the disastrous consequences that would flow from the nationalists' agenda:

> In the republics, all the nationalists proclaim that the solution to all problems lies in the creation of new "independent" states. Allow us to ask, independent of whom?
>
> Declaring independence from Moscow, the nationalists can do nothing more than place all the vital decisions relating to the future of their new states in the hands of Germany, Britain, France, Japan and the United States. Kravchuk [leader of the Ukrainian Communist Party and future president of post-Soviet Ukraine] goes to Washington and squirms in his seat like a schoolboy while he is lectured by President Bush. ...
>
> What path, then, should the working people of the USSR follow? What is the alternative? The only solution

that can be found is one based on the program of revolutionary internationalism. The return to capitalism, for which the chauvinist agitation of the nationalists is only one guise, can only lead to a new form of oppression. Rather than each of the Soviet nationalities approaching the imperialists separately with their heads bowed and their knees bent, begging for alms and favors, the Soviet workers of all nationalities should forge a new relationship, based on the principles of real social equality and democracy, and on this basis undertake the revolutionary defense of all that is worth preserving in the heritage of 1917. ...

At the very heart of this program is the perspective of revolutionary internationalism. ... All the problems that haunt the Soviet people today have their origins in the abandonment of the program of revolutionary internationalism.[8]

The warnings made by the International Committee nearly thirty-two years ago have been tragically vindicated. The working people of Russia and Ukraine have been drawn into a fratricidal conflict. Eighty years ago, they fought together, in defense of the October Revolution, to expel the Nazi army from the Soviet Union. Now, acting on the orders of capitalist regimes, they are shooting and killing each other.

The International Committee's call for the unification of the international working class has not only acquired greater urgency. Objective conditions are now far more favorable for its mobilization on the basis of the program of revolutionary socialist internationalism. Alongside the deepening crisis of US imperialism and the intensification of global capitalist contradictions, there has been an immense growth of the international working class. Its economic weight and potential power have been vastly augmented by the emergence of massive urban centers, populated by tens of millions of workers, in countries where the proletariat had been, until the last decade of the twentieth century, only a small fraction of the population.

During the past decade there has been a steady escalation of the class struggle. A striking characteristic of the class struggle has been its international character. The revolutionary advances in communications technology are

---

8. David North, "After the August Putsch: Soviet Union at the Crossroads," *Fourth International*, Fall-Winter 1992, Vol. 19, No. 1, pp. 110–11.

dissolving the barriers between the workers of different countries. Regardless of where it begins, the social conflict in any particular country almost immediately acquires an international audience and becomes a world event. Even the age-old barrier of language is being overcome by the application of translation and transcription programs that make documents and speeches, regardless of the languages in which they were written and spoken, easily comprehensible to a global audience.

These advances in technology facilitate a global revolutionary response to economic, social, and political problems that confront the working class of all countries. China's sudden abandonment of its Zero-COVID policy in late 2022, resulting in more than one million deaths within less than two months, has demonstrated the impossibility of devising a national solution to a global crisis. This fundamental truth is being hammered home by the reality of the deepening social crisis.

The Ukraine war and the massive growth of military budgets have assumed the form of a war against the social conditions of workers in every country. Inflation, unemployment, and the slashing of budgets for social services has provoked an upsurge in strike activity throughout the world. Major social struggles have broken out on every continent.

Notwithstanding the differences that exist between countries, certain common features manifest themselves in the political conditions confronted by the working class in all countries. Regardless of how limited the demands of workers are, they confront bitter resistance from the employers and the state.

With ever greater frequency and intensity, the capitalist state is assuming direct leadership, on behalf of the ruling class, of the war against the working class. In countries as different in their economic development as Sri Lanka and France, the working class confronts as its central enemy the leader of the state—in Sri Lanka, President Ranil Wickremesinghe; in France, President Emmanuel Macron. Despite their use of democratic phraseology whenever it is politically convenient, their decisions, relying on the police and military for their enforcement, assume a blatantly dictatorial character. The present universal breakdown of bourgeois democracy confirms the analysis of Lenin: "Political reaction *all along* the line is a characteristic feature of imperialism."[9]

---

9. V.I. Lenin, "Imperialism and the Split in Socialism," *Collected Works*, Vol. 23 (Moscow: Progress Publishers, 1964), p. 106.

For this reason, the logic of the class struggle assumes the character of a political struggle against the state and raises the necessity for the development of independent organs of workers power. The call of the Sri Lankan section of the International Committee for the convening of a Socialist and Democratic Congress of Workers and Rural Poor, and the demand raised by the French section of the ICFI for the bringing down of the Macron government, are both necessary responses to the escalating conflict between the working class and the capitalist state.

A basic lesson of the twentieth century is that the struggle against imperialist war can be waged successfully only through the political mobilization of the working class on the basis of an uncompromisingly anti-capitalist, socialist program. All proposals for opposing war that ignore and cover up for the causes of war—which are rooted in the nation state system and the capitalist profit system—are doomed to failure.

The great obstacle to the mobilization of the working class is the political influence retained by the pro-capitalist bureaucracies in the trade unions, reactionary labor and fake socialist parties, and a broad array of pseudo-left organizations of the affluent middle class. Their insidious influence must be overcome.

The International Committee has made significant advances in the development of an alternative revolutionary leadership in the working class. The International Workers Alliance of Rank-and-File Committees (IWA-RFC) is the concretization of the perspective advanced by Trotsky in the *Transitional Program* for the formation of factory committees. He called on the sections of the Fourth International "to create in all possible instances independent militant organizations corresponding more closely to the tasks of mass struggle against bourgeois society; and if necessary, not flinching even in the face of a direct break with the conservative apparatus of the trade unions."[10]

Moreover, the impulse given by the International Committee to the development of the IWA-RFC is based on Trotsky's analysis of the fate of trade unions in the epoch of imperialism. In an uncompleted manuscript found on Trotsky's desk after his assassination, he had written: "There is one common feature in the development, or more correctly the degeneration,

---

10. "Leon Trotsky, *The Death Agony of Capitalism and the Tasks of the Fourth International: The Transitional Program* (New York: Labor Publications, 1981), p. 8.

of modern trade union organizations in the entire world: it is their drawing closely to and drawing together with the state power."[11]

It was, therefore, necessary "to mobilize the masses, not only against the bourgeoisie, but also against the totalitarian regime within the trade unions themselves and against the leaders enforcing this regime."[12]

When the petty-bourgeois pseudo-left agents of the ruling class denounce the ICFI for opposing the unions, what they really are attacking is the refusal of the International Committee to accept the subordination of the working class to the dictatorship of the pro-imperialist and corporatist labor bureaucracies. Far from abstaining from the struggles of workers who remain within the prison walls manned by the police guards of the AFL-CIO in the United States, the IG Metall in Germany, the CGT in France, and their equivalents all over the world, the IWA-RFC is involved in countless struggles within the trade unions, doing all it can to encourage and strengthen the rebellion against the bureaucratic apparatus. The votes cast by 5,000 auto workers in October 2022 for Will Lehman, the socialist candidate for the presidency of the UAW, who ran on a program that called for the establishment of workers' control of the auto industry and the obliteration of the union apparatus, testifies to the growing influence and organizational and political potential of the IWA-RFC.

The International Workers Alliance of Rank-and-File Committees is creating a worldwide network to assist in the development of a global strategy and the tactical coordination of the class struggle against corporate power and capitalist rule. Its aim is not to apply pressure upon and reform the reactionary bureaucracies, but to transfer all decision-making and power to the rank and file.

The (IYSSE) is expanding its work to educate young people as Marxists, to develop their understanding of the struggle waged by Trotsky and the Fourth International against Stalinism and all forms of national opportunism, to turn to the working class, and to direct their boundless energy to the fight to build the World Party of Socialist Revolution.

The World Socialist Web Site, which is now celebrating twenty-five years of daily publication, is continuously developing the depth and scope of its political coverage and analysis of the class struggle, and on the basis of

---

11. Leon Trotsky, "Trade unions in the epoch of imperialist decay," *Marxism and the Trade Unions* (New York: Labor Publications, 1972), pp. 9–10.
12. Ibid., p. 12.

this essential theoretical work, expanding the influence of Trotskyism in the struggles of the international working class.

The May Day rally will build on these achievements and dedicate the celebration of this historic day of working-class unity to advancing the struggle against war and for the transfer of power to the working class and the building of socialism throughout the world.

Index

9/11
   War on Terror 143
1905 Russian Revolution 71, 117, 173

A

Abern, Martin 17, 85, 167
Adler, Victor 39
Adorno, Theodore 114
Ageloff, Sylvia 100, 103, 198–199, 232
Albright, Madeleine 145
Alexander, Robert J. xiv
   International Trotskyism xiii
Andropov, Yuri viii

B

Badiou, Alain 113
Banda, Mike 3, 4, 9, 254
Benjamin, Walter 61, 114, 229–230
Bernstein, Eduard 40, 72–73
Bezos, Jeff 144
Biden, Joe 78, 260
Black, Thomas L. 100
Bogdanov, Alexander 117
Bolshevik-Leninist Party of India
   (BLPI) 131

Bolshevik Party xvi, 5, 10, 12–13,
   16, 20, 42, 44, 53, 69–71, 83,
   96–97, 108, 114, 120, 125, 134,
   136, 188, 191–192, 195, 226,
   245–246
Bortenstein, Mieczyslaw [a.k.a. M.
   Casanova] 221–223, 226–227
Brezhnev, Leonid viii
British General Strike 18, 84
Browder, Earl 189, 202
Budenz, Louis 100
Bukharin, Nikolai 13, 83–84, 138
bureaucratic collectivism 167, 169
Burnham, James 167–168, 170–177,
   212, 215, 252
Bush, George W. 261

C

Campa, Valentín 189
Cannon, James P. 17, 24, 85, 90, 100,
   139, 167, 200, 207–208, 253
Cárdenas, Lazar 98, 189
Carr, E. H. 155–156
Carrillo, Rafael 189
centrism 20, 32–33, 87–89, 222

Chernenko, Konstantin viii
Chiang Kai-shek xvii, 137–138
Chinese revolution 137–138
Churchill, Winston 64
Codovilla, Vittorio 190
Communist Party of the United States (CPUSA) 189, 202
Cornell, Charles 200
COVID-19 pandemic 260

D

Dallin, Lola 97, 99–100, 102
Dalrymple, Theodore 59–64
Deutscher, Isaac 195, 233–234
Dewey, John 63, 98, 162
  Dewey Commission 98–99, 162
Dias, Wije xix
Dobbs, Farrell 200, 207–208
Dühring, Eugen 111
Duranty, Walter 97
Dzerzhinsky, Felix 11, 12

E

Engels, Frederick 27, 31, 52, 62, 71, 108–110, 114, 118, 162, 170, 172, 173, 219, 221

F

Federal Bureau of Investigation 8
Fischer, Joschka 263
Fourth International
  founding of 32, 67–80, 81, 91, 125–127, 136, 140–141, 248
France
  Vichy government 222
Franco, Francisco 141, 222, 227
Frankfurt School xviii, 114–115, 135

Franklin, Sylvia [a.k.a. Caldwell, Callen] 24, 100
Franklin, Zalmond 100
Fukuyama, Francis ix
  and "End of History" ix, 127

G

German Communist Party 22, 24–26, 70, 86, 140, 155, 157
German revolution 44–45
glasnost viii
Goldman, Albert 177
Gorbachev, Mikhail viii–ix, 254
Gordon, Sam 200
Great Depression 75, 126, 220

H

Hansen, Joseph 187
  links to FBI 8
Harte, Robert Sheldon 102, 184, 186–187
Healy, Gerry 3–4, 6, 187, 254
Hegel, Georg W.F. 14, 19, 52–53, 108–111, 118, 172, 176, 251
  Logic 118
  Phenomenology of Spirit 251
Henehan, Tom 1–4, 6, 7–10
  death of 7
Hitchens, Christopher 59–60
Hitler, Adolf xii, xvii, 22–27, 60, 70, 82, 86–87, 95, 97, 140, 155–157, 162, 166–167, 170, 177, 179, 193, 199–201, 213, 215–216, 229, 235, 240–241, 252
Hoover, J. Edgar 186
Horkheimer, Max 114

Index

I
India 131–133
  Gandhi 132
International Committee of the Fourth International
  Security and the Fourth International investigation 8
  split of 1986 6
International Left Opposition 24
International Workers Alliance of Rank-and-File Committees 269
International Youth and Students for Social Equality 269

J
James, C.L.R. 162
Joseph Hansen 8, 24, 187, 200, 233

K
Kamenev, Lev 16, 53, 54, 98
Kautsky, Karl 5, 40, 50–51, 55
Klee, Paul 230
Klement, Rudolf 67–68, 81, 82, 100
Konikow, Antoinette 200, 203, 211
Kugelmann, Ludwig 111

L
Laborde, Hernán 189
Laclau, Ernesto xviii
Landauer, Gustav 116
Lanka Sama Samaja Party (LSSP) 131–133
Left Opposition xv, 10, 12, 16–20, 24, 42, 69, 70, 83, 85, 97, 125, 151–153, 157, 196, 203, 248, 255
  founding of xv, 12, 136

Lenin, V.I. xi, xv, 5, 10–12, 14, 17, 19, 21, 27–28, 31–32, 34–36, 40–44, 50, 53, 55, 62, 70–72, 83, 85, 104, 107–108, 113–114, 118–121, 139, 152, 162–163, 170, 176, 193–194, 207, 219–220, 223, 226–227, 240, 245, 246, 248, 257, 265, 267
  April Theses 120
  Conspectus of Hegel's Science of Logic 176
  Imperialism 120
  Materialism and Empirio-Criticism 118
  and monopoly of foreign trade dispute 11
Leonhard, Jörn 260–261
Lewis, John L. 203
Lunacharsky, Anatoly 117–118

M
Maassen, Hans Georg 146
Macdonald, Dwight 215–219
Macron, Emmanuel 267
Mandel, Ernest 252
Mao Zedong 138
Marcuse, Herbert 114, 115
Marx, Karl 6, 13, 27, 28–30, 43, 49–52, 56, 71, 73–74, 108–111, 114, 116, 118, 120, 152, 162, 170, 172, 173, 219–221, 230
  Critique of Hegel's Philosophy of Law 109
  Das Kapital 110–111
  German Ideology, The 109
  Preface to a Critique of Political Economy 110
Mehring, Franz ii

Menshevism 40–41
Mercader, Ramon [a.k.a. Frank Jacson, Jacques Mornard] 100, 103, 187, 194, 198–199, 207, 232–233, 239
Mexican Communist Party 187–189, 199
Mouffe, Chantal xviii, 147–148
Mussolini, Benito 45, 126, 247

N

Naville, Pierre 67–68, 82
Nietzsche, Friedrich 116–117

O

Obama, Barack 75–76, 78
October Revolution viii, x, xvi, 5, 28, 31, 42, 47, 68, 70–71, 83, 95–96, 107, 113, 115, 161, 167, 168, 192, 220, 225–226, 240, 245–246, 252, 254, 255, 257, 265–266
Operation Barbarossa 200
Orjonikidze 12
Orlov, Alexander 102

P

Pabloism 3, 18, 90–91
Pablo, Michel 90, 252
perestroika ix, 254
Permanent Revolution 83
  theory of 13–16, 61, 71, 120
Plekhanov, Georgi 40, 51, 173
political revolution 87
Popular Front xvii, 27, 82, 141, 146–147, 167, 222–223, 224, 226, 227
POUM 88, 222, 227

Putin, Vladimir 133, 241, 256–257, 260, 265

Q

Que Faire 221, 223, 226

R

Rabinowitz, Gregory 100–101
Rachman, Gideon xiii, 263–264
Red Referendum 24
Reich, Wilhelm 114
Reiss, Ignace 68, 81, 99
Renner, Karl 52
Revolutionary Communist League (RCL) 132
Rivera, Diego 98
Robins, Harold 185–186, 200, 205–207, 231, 233
Rogovin, Vadim 255
Roosevelt, Franklin 76, 202
Rosmer, Alfred and Marguerite 199
Russian Social Democratic Labor Party 40, 72, 117

S

Second International 27–28, 32, 35–36, 39, 41–43, 45, 50–52, 72, 83, 89, 182
Sedova, Natalia 98–99, 151, 153, 184, 232, 234
Sedov, Leon 68, 81, 82, 97
  death of 99–100
Sequinot, Edwin 7–9
Serge, Victor 193
Service, Robert xiv, 158
Shachtman, Max 17–18, 85, 167–168, 170–173, 177, 212, 215, 252

Index

Siqueiros, David Alfaro 102, 103, 183, 187
Slaughter, Cliff 3–4, 6, 254
Sobolovecius brothers [Senin; Well] 97
Social Democracy, German 21–29, 116, 140, 155–156
Social Fascism, theory of 23
Socialism in one country
  theory of ix, xvi, 13–15, 83–84, 126, 136–138, 180, 197, 248
Socialist Workers Party 2, 8, 24, 31, 100–103, 167–169, 174, 176, 177, 186–187, 198–208, 211, 213, 253
  1940 minority 31
  GPU spy ring inside 24
Sosyalist Eşitlik 1, 159
Spector, Maurice 85, 139
Stalin-Hitler Non-Aggression Pact 27, 95, 166–167, 193, 202
Stalinism
  The Great Terror 18, 27, 31, 68, 95, 97–98, 126, 133, 141, 153, 161–162, 167, 240, 254
Stalin, Joseph 13, 10–15, 227–231, 235
  fear of Trotsky 96–97
  and monopoly of foreign trade dispute 10
State-ism 47–50
Swain, Geoffrey xiv, 158

T

Tellez Vargas, Eduardo 232–233
Thatcher, Ian xiv, 158
Third International (Comintern) xi, 5, 13–14, 16–21, 25–28, 32, 35–36, 42–47, 48, 49, 55, 70, 83–89, 103, 120, 136–140, 155–157, 182, 187–193, 204, 241, 245–248
  Fourth Congress 245–248
Tobin, Dan 203
Tolstoy, Alexis 228
Torres, Angelo 7–9
Trotsky, Leon
  as literary figure 60–61
  assassination of 95–99, 163, 233
  biography of Stalin 163, 193–197, 227–231
    Malamuth, Charles 194–195
  "The Comintern and the GPU" 187–188, 191
  History of the Russian Revolution 154
  Lessons of October 53–58
  Manifesto for the Emergency Conference of the Fourth International 177, 183
  My Life 154
  on the American working class 214–215
  Revolution Betrayed, The ix, 28–31, 69, 252
  "Stalin Seeks My Death" 184, 187
  Testament 234
  Theory of Permanent Revolution xiv–xv, xviii, 3, 15, 71, 120, 173, 180, 246
  The Transitional Program 33, 75, 82, 88, 92, 127, 143, 158, 212
  "Trade Unions in the Epoch of Imperialist Decay" 208–211
Truman, Harry 64
Trump, Donald ix, 128, 144–145, 261
  January 6 261

U

Ukraine 240–244
  Trotsky's conception of 241–244
  Ukraine war xiii, 242, 256, 259–270
  casualties in 259
United Front 22, 86, 155
USSR
  capitalist restoration in ix, x
  dissolution of 127, 241, 265
  New Economic Policy 196, 246
  political revolution 28, 32, 70, 141, 169

V

Vielot, Jacques 7–9
Volkogonov, Dmitri A. 68, 96–97, 190–191

W

Wall Street crash 154–155
Weil, Ruby 100
Weimar Republic 21, 25
Wickremesinghe, Ranil 267
Wilson, Woodrow xi, xii
Wohlforth, Tim 2
Wolf, Erwin 68, 81–82, 99
Workers League xviii, 1–2, 5, 6, 7–10, 30, 33, 253
  Bulletin newspaper 6
Workers Revolutionary Party 3–6, 9, 253–254
World War I xi, 35, 64, 166, 178, 193, 246, 260, 261
World War II x, xiii, xvii–xviii, 70, 76–77, 95, 114–115, 143, 146, 158, 163–164, 166–167, 170, 181–182, 193, 199, 211, 220, 239–240, 242, 263

Y

Yeltsin, Boris 254
Young Guard of Bolshevik-Leninists 251–258
Young Socialists 8

Z

Zborowski, Mark ["Etienne"] 68, 97–103
Zinoviev, Grigory 16, 53–54, 98